Praise for
A Year in the South: 1865

"Ash has drawn a vivid picture of everyday people scrambling to survive with Darwinian tenacity as their world collapses around them. Through his intelligent choice of diverse subjects . . . Ash tells a tale that reads like a novel, while illuminating important historical themes: the impact of the war on women and slaves, the powerful influence of evangelical Christianity, and most important, the nuanced political, social, and cultural landscape of a tottering Confederacy that was anything but monolithic or harmonious. This book—an original blend of social, military, and local history, crafted by an author with a muscular style, a keen eye for memorable details, and the good sense to avoid scholarly jargon and weighty theory—is refreshingly difficult to pigeonhole and will be of interest to both Civil War buffs looking for something new, and to those who simply like a good yarn well told." —*Publishers Weekly*

"Ash writes history with the vision of a scholar but with the skills of a novelist. . . . For the Civil War buff, the book is a must. For those interested in history, there is much here that illuminates a time and a place of so much importance." —*Knoxville News-Sentinel*

"*A Year in the South* is history from the bottom up, micro rather than macro. . . . The book's a good read—compelling, detailed, yet swift. . . . The book successfully blends characters, time, place, and lots of conflict." —*Nashville Scene*

"Historians tend to gloss over the dislocations experienced by Southerners as their society and government collapsed in the last months of war and the first months of peace. By tracing the lives of four such people during 1865, Ash vividly recounts the hopes, fears, and uncertainties of that year. . . . Ash's account of their actions and perspectives greatly enhances our understanding of the tenor of that time. . . . Highly recommended." —*Choice*

"In this fascinating and moving book, Stephen Ash presents an intimate look at four Southerners in 1865. Wonderfully evocative of place and time, this compelling narrative takes the reader inside the lives of four seemingly ordinary men and women whose stories nevertheless reveal much about the South at the end of the Civil War and beyond. Ash recaptures the hopes, fears, uncertainties, and despair of four people enmeshed in the clashes of armies, races, ideas, and emotions. The interplay of public events and private heartaches makes this not only a compulsively readable tale but also a fine piece of history. A gem of a book."

—George C. Rable, Charles Summersell Professor of Southern History, University of Alabama

"From the serendipitous reunion of slave siblings after decades apart to the narrow escape of a former Confederate confronting a lynch party, from a stuttering suitor's awkward romance to a widow's moving struggle to feed her children, Ash's deft and eloquent portraits are emblematic of war's chaotic thrall. Each chapter overflows with rich research, from numbers culled from the census data to sketches of combat from regimental histories, which sets the stage for the ordinary and extraordinary lives of Ash's diverse quartet. Ash's creative format and narrative skills make the Civil War come alive as he weaves together civilians and soldiers, Yankees and Confederates, blacks and whites, masters and slaves, men and women, lovers and enemies, all caught in war's untangling skein."

—Catherine Clinton, author of *Fanny Kemble's Civil Wars*

"This book enables readers to experience, through the eyes of four Southerners of disparate backgrounds and geographical locations, the transforming events of 1865. Avoiding the common device of using the death of the Confederacy as a closing point, Ash employs his witnesses to tell a gripping story that includes the fateful last months of the Civil War as well as the tumultuous early transition to a postwar world that would offer hardship and promise in full measure. Few Americans have had to wrestle with more unsettling times, as Ash's excellent narrative makes abundantly clear."

—Gary W. Gallagher, John L. Nau III Professor of History at the University of Virginia

"Stephen Ash has taken us deep into one of the most exciting times in American history. With sensitivity, imagination, and skill, Ash recreates the South of 1865, allowing us to see it from perspectives we have never seen before. This is a remarkable book."

—Edward L. Ayers, Dean of the College and Graduate School of the Arts and Sciences, University of Virginia

University of Tennessee Photographic Services

About the Author

STEPHEN V. ASH is Professor of History at the University of Tennessee. He is the author of several books on the Civil War, including *When the Yankees Came: Conflict and Chaos in the Occupied South, 1861–1865*. He lives with his wife in Tennessee.

A YEAR IN THE SOUTH: 1865

The True Story of Four Ordinary People Who Lived Through the Most Tumultuous Twelve Months in American History

STEPHEN V. ASH

Perennial
An Imprint of HarperCollins*Publishers*

For Paul H. Bergeron:
mentor, colleague, and friend

A hardcover edition of this book was published in 2002 by Palgrave Macmillan, a division of St. Martin's Press, LLC, under the title *A Year in the South*. It is here reprinted by arrangement with St. Martin's Press, LLC.

HarperCollins books may be purchased for educational, business, or sales promotional use. For information please write: Special Markets Department, HarperCollins Publishers Inc., 10 East 53rd Street, New York, NY 10022.

First Perennial edition published 2004.

Designed by Letra Libre, Inc.

Library of Congress Cataloging-in-Publication Data

Ash, Stephen V.
A year in the South: 1865: the true story of four ordinary people who lived through the most tumultuous twelve months in American history / Stephen V. Ash—1st Perennial ed.
p. cm.
Originally published: New York: Palgrave Macmillan, 2002.
Includes bibliographical references and index.
ISBN 0-06-058248-0
1. Southern States—History—1865–1877—Biography. 2. Hughes, Louis, 1832– . 3. McDonald, Cornelia Peake, 1822–1909. 4. Robertson, John Collier, b. 1846. 5. Agnew, Samuel A., b. 1833. I. Title.

F216.A85 2004
975'.014'092—dc22
[B] 2004044401

08 ❖/RRD 10 9 8 7 6

CONTENTS

PART FOUR
FALL AND ANOTHER WINTER

ACKNOWLEDGMENTS

AT EVERY STEP IN THE CREATION OF THIS BOOK I HAVE BEEN BLESSED with help from friends, acquaintances, and strangers. It is a pleasure to acknowledge their generosity.

At or near the top of every historian's list of debts are those owed to archivists. I especially want to thank Steve Cotham, director of the McClung Historical Collection in Knoxville, and his staff members Sally Polhemus and Ted Baehr; it was Steve who brought to my attention the fascinating memoir of John Robertson. I have also received assistance far beyond the call of duty from the director and staff of the Special Collections department of the University of Tennessee, Knoxville: Jim Lloyd, Nick Wyman, Bill Eigelsbach, and Aaron Purcell. When doing research at the National Archives in Washington, I have had the benefit of Mike Musick's vast knowledge of federal records. Archivists at the Southern Historical Collection of the University of North Carolina at Chapel Hill, the Tennessee State Library and Archives, the Virginia Historical Society, the Mississippi Department of Archives and History, the Alabama Department of Archives and History, the Library of Virginia, the Perkins Library of Duke University, the Illinois State Historical Library, the Rockbridge Historical Society of Lexington, and Historic Elmwood Cemetery of Memphis have been of great help, too; I wish that space permitted me to name them all.

I am also in debt to many fellow historians. Nelson Lankford, Lynda L. Crist, Robert Kenzer, John D. Fowler, Kent Dollar, and Trevor Smith are just a few of those who have generously provided information. Three of my colleagues in the History Department of the University of Tennessee, Knoxville—Kathy Brosnan, Lorri Glover, and Bruce Wheeler—deserve special thanks for their interest in and encouragement of this project, not to mention their good company at our late-afternoon "seminars" at Charlie Pepper's.

A number of people outside the archival and academic realms have also gone out of their way to help me. Walter Davis of Jackson, Alabama, took me around the site of the Clarke County saltworks and explained the process of salt making. Tommy Lee and Edwina Carpenter of the Brice's Crossroads Museum and Visitors Center in Baldwyn, Mississippi, arranged for me to see the site of the Agnew plantation and provided me with some wonderful photographs. Mr. and Mrs. Buddy Lipscomb of Como, Mississippi, introduced me to J. Paul White of Senatobia, who showed me Fredonia Methodist Church and the site of the McGehee plantation. Robert E. Gartz of Brookfield, Wisconsin, tracked down Louis Hughes's grave and date of death. David Frazier of Guntown, Mississippi, sent me information on Samuel Agnew by way of Brenda Rayman of Knoxville. A special thank you goes to Pat Tindle of Topeka, Kansas, who has provided a wealth of helpful material and assisted me in other ways too numerous to mention. I am also deeply grateful to the legions of genealogists across the country whose unsung labors have unearthed an enormous amount of historical data—much of it now online—without which this book could not have been written.

I can find no words to properly acknowledge two final debts, and so I must acknowledge them plainly and inadequately. My family has been an unfailing source of encouragement, support, and wisdom. And so too has Paul H. Bergeron of the University of Tennessee, Knoxville, who took me under his wing when I began graduate school nearly thirty years ago and has been my guide and friend ever since; to him this book is dedicated.

LIST OF ILLUSTRATIONS

PREFACE

THIS BOOK IS ABOUT FOUR ORDINARY PEOPLE IN AN EXTRAORDINARY time. Their names were Louis Hughes, Cornelia McDonald, John Robertson, and Samuel Agnew. From birth to death, they lived far apart from one another and in very different circumstances. They had little in common except this: they were Southerners who lived through the pivotal moment of Southern history.

The moment was 1865. When that year began, the Old South—incarnated forty-seven months earlier as the Confederate States of America—still stood. When that year ended, the Old South was gone and a New South was taking shape.

Surely no other sizable portion of the American people ever experienced so wrenching a year, or one so brimming with possibilities, as Southerners did in 1865. It was a year that began in war and ended in peace, a year that saw disunion give way to reconstruction, a year that marked the passage from slavery to freedom. The story of those people in that tumultuous time is not only fascinating but also instructive, for it can tell us much about how the New South came to be and about what the Old South was.

Storytellers confront the same dilemma as painters and photographers: the broader their perspective, the more comprehensive their scene, but the less distinct their subjects' features. A narrative that tries to embrace all the Southern people in 1865 risks reducing them to a faceless crowd. I have adopted a different approach that poses its own risks.

In focusing on four individuals, I have sought a balance of breadth and depth, while obviously forfeiting any claim to comprehensiveness. I have selected Hughes, McDonald, Robertson, and Agnew from among many possible subjects in the belief that their stories would reflect something of the experience of Southerners as a whole in 1865. But if these four were in some ways typical, they were also in many ways unique, and much that is recounted herein is essentially personal, illuminating no lives but their own.

This book begins with a prologue that introduces the characters and sketches their lives up to 1865. The four parts that follow move chronologically from the beginning to the end of 1865, with each part corresponding to a season of the year. The characters appear sequentially in each part, and an epilogue summarizes their lives after 1865.

Although each of the four wrote a personal account of some sort, they also left a great deal unsaid. I have examined other sources to find out more about them and about the places they lived, the people they knew, and the events they lived through. Even so, much about these three men and this one woman remains obscure. What this book offers, therefore, is not the whole story but rather a vivid part of the story of four Southerners as they stepped across the threshold between the old world and the new.

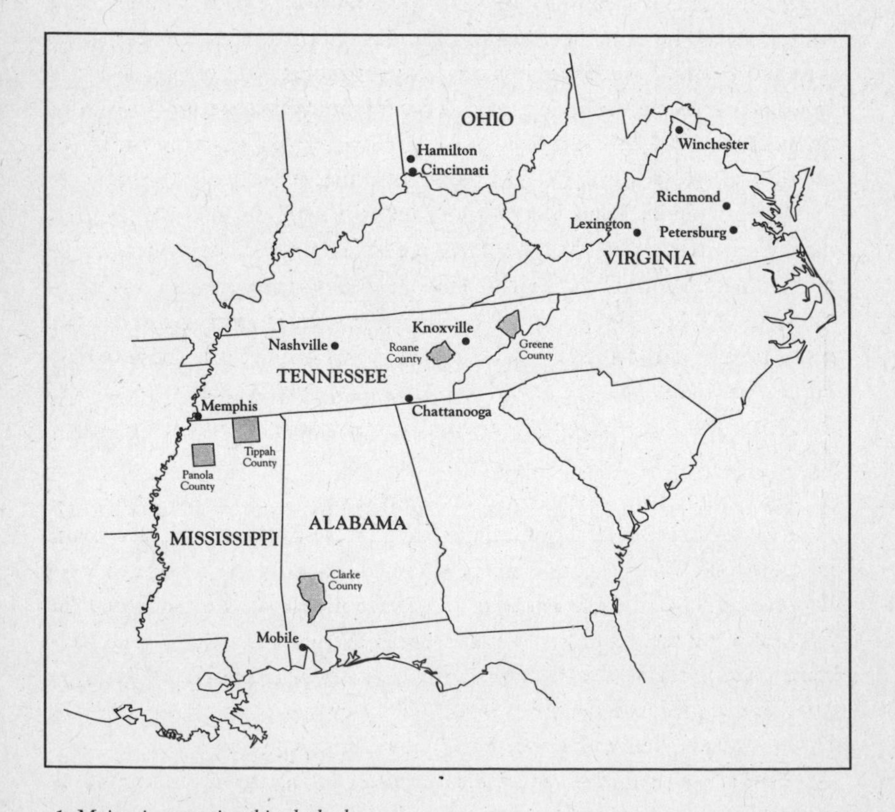

1. Major sites mentioned in the book

PROLOGUE

FOUR SOUTHERNERS

LOUIS HUGHES WAS THIRTY-TWO YEARS OLD WHEN THE YEAR 1865 began, and he was a slave—a mulatto slave, born of a black mother and a white father. The memoir he published in his old age is a vivid and in many ways frank reminiscence, but it is curiously reticent about his paternity. In it Louis mentions but does not name his father, though he certainly knew who he was. Nor does he explain his own surname, which was not that of his mother's master or any of his own subsequent masters.[1]

In his memoir, Louis Hughes does relate that he was born in Virginia, near Charlottesville, in 1832. At about age eleven he was sold away from his mother to a man who lived nearby. A few months later he was taken to Richmond and sold to another man. Louis never saw his mother again. In 1844 his owner got fed up with the boy's sickliness and decided to dispose of him. He put him on the auction block in a Richmond slave market and sold him for $380. The buyer was a Mississippi planter named Edmund McGehee, whom Louis would come to call Boss.[2]

Louis and some others bought by McGehee soon set out from Richmond, heading southward to Georgia and then westward to their new home in Mississippi. They were among the many thousands of slaves brought from the older regions of the South in the antebellum years to clear and plant the fresh lands on the expanding cotton frontier. When McGehee's newly purchased laborers arrived at his Pontotoc County plantation in late December 1844, he singled out the twelve-year-old Louis, brought him to the Big House, and gave him to his wife, Sarah, as a Christmas present.[3]

Motherless, friendless, and traumatized by his abrupt uprooting, Louis grieved for a long time but gradually adapted to his new life. Duty as a houseboy

2. Louis Hughes, ca. 1897

exempted him from much of the drudgery of plantation labor but kept him at the beck and call of Mrs. McGehee (known to the slaves as Madam), who was bad-tempered and abusive. Louis soon came to loathe her. He grew more or less fond of Boss, however, who recognized Louis's intelligence and occasionally took the boy away from housework to assist him in some task. But Boss, too, had a cruel streak.[4]

Around 1850 Louis's circumstances changed again. Boss, who had become quite wealthy, built a magnificent mansion on a fourteen-acre estate two miles outside Memphis. There he moved his family and a dozen or more of his slaves, including Louis, whom he appointed butler and manservant. At the same time, he sold his Pontotoc plantation and bought another in Bolivar County, Mississippi, on the banks of the Mississippi River below Memphis. He put this property in the charge of an overseer.[5]

By the early 1850s Louis Hughes had grown to manhood. Slight of build and standing just five and a half feet tall, he was hardly an imposing figure. But he was smart, and he was resolute: he had by then made up his mind that he was not going to live out his life as a slave if he could help it.[6]

What sparked Louis's quest for freedom was an epiphany of a kind that every enslaved man and woman eventually experienced. He was now a grown man, and yet, he came to see, slavery denied him full manhood. His master and mistress continued to scold and slap him like a child, continued to dictate his every activity from the minute he rose in the morning until he went to bed at night. That such humiliations were accompanied by a good measure of paternalistic care and indulgence made them no less demeaning.[7]

Most adult slaves thus came to hate slavery and yearn for freedom. Louis Hughes came to hate and yearn more deeply than some because of the nearly unbearable circumstances in the McGehee household. To the daily cruelties of Madam were added the not-infrequent barbarities of Boss and other white men in his employ. Most Southern slaves, after weighing the miseries of their situation against the dangers of resistance, reluctantly accommodated themselves to slavery; but Louis was impelled to challenge the institution. Twice in the 1850s he ran off by stowing away on a steamboat at the Memphis wharf. Both times he was caught and returned to his master.[8]

Louis was living at the Memphis estate when the Civil War began in the spring of 1861. By then he was about twenty-nine years old and had been married for two and a half years. His wife, Matilda, was a cook purchased by Boss in 1855.[9]

When the Union army and navy advanced down the Mississippi River in the spring of 1862 and threatened Memphis, Boss abandoned his estate and took his family and slaves to Panola County, in northern Mississippi, where his father-in-law, John "Master Jack" McGehee, lived. Soon thereafter Louis was sent to the Bolivar plantation and was kept there until early 1863. He then was sent back to Panola, where he rejoined his wife and the McGehee family.[10]

The outbreak of war and the coming of the Yankees excited Louis and others who sought freedom. Across the South, blacks whispered among themselves at rumors of Union victories and watched for a chance to flee to the invaders. At the same time, war and invasion magnified white Southerners' fear of black restlessness and their determination to stifle it. In the winter of 1862–63 Louis tried a third time to escape, setting out overland toward the rumored location of a Union army force. But he blundered into a company of Confederate troops who returned him to captivity. A couple of months later, encouraged by reports that other Panola County slaves were getting away, Louis tried again. This time he headed toward Memphis, which was now in Union hands. Matilda and three others joined him in this attempt. The five were swiftly tracked down and brought back to Master Jack's plantation.[11]

By the spring of 1863, Boss—forced by Yankee incursions to abandon his Bolivar plantation, too—had decided to move most of his slaves to a safe place deep in the Confederacy's interior. At a site on the Tombigbee River in Alabama the state government, using leased slaves, manufactured salt. Louis and Matilda Hughes were sent to the saltworks along with other McGehee slaves. They were there in early January 1864, when they learned that Boss had died unexpectedly while preparing to move his family to Alabama. They were still at the saltworks one year later, on the first day of 1865.[12]

When 1865 began, Cornelia McDonald was forty-two years old and living in a rented house in Lexington, Virginia, with her seven children. She was a widow and a war refugee. The death of her husband, a Confederate army officer, and the loss of her home had brought her to the verge of poverty and despair.

She was born in Alexandria, Virginia, in 1822, the youngest child of Humphrey and Anne Peake. Her father was a physician who, although not wealthy, was well off, and Cornelia grew up being waited on by slaves and driven about in a carriage. While she was still a girl, the family moved to rural Prince William County, where her father pursued farming along with medicine. Later they settled in the hamlet of Front Royal in the Shenandoah Valley. Cornelia thus became acquainted with farm and village as well as town life. She developed a passion for horseback riding but was also drawn to intellectual and artistic pursuits: reading, writing, drawing, and painting. She loved browsing in her father's library and wandering through the countryside with her sketchbook in hand. As one of her daughters later wrote, "Everything that happened interested her."[13]

In 1835 the family moved to Palmyra in eastern Missouri. Though no longer a true frontier area by that time, it was raw and wild by contrast to genteel Virginia. For the rest of her life Cornelia retained vivid memories of her Palmyra years, especially of riding out onto the prairie and galloping through head-high grass with her black maidservant mounted behind her, and of watching wide-eyed as thousands of Potawatomi Indians passed on the road, heading westward to a reservation. But there were painful memories of Palmyra, too. Anne Peake died there in 1837, leaving fifteen-year-old Cornelia motherless. Anne was bedridden for months before her death, and Cornelia spent long hours sitting with her. When her mother slept, Cornelia would open a volume of Byron and read until she awoke.[14]

Sometime after his wife's death, Dr. Peake moved the family to nearby Hannibal, a small town on the Mississippi River, and there Cornelia came of age. Among the inhabitants of Hannibal in those days were little Samuel Clemens and his comical friend Ruel Gridly, supposedly the model for Huckleberry Finn. Cornelia saw them often playing in the street outside her home. Dr. Peake appears as a character in one of Mark Twain's stories.[15]

Once she was grown, Cornelia regularly visited relatives in St. Louis during the winter social season. It had become a big and lively city by the 1840s and Cornelia enjoyed the round of activities there, especially the glittering dinner parties and balls. She was a favorite of the young bachelor gentlemen of St. Louis, some of whom were U.S. army officers stationed at Jefferson Barracks. Among those she dined and danced with were Lieutenant Ulysses "Sam" Grant and Lieutenant James "Pete" Longstreet.[16]

It was back in Hannibal, however, that she met her husband-to-be. He was a widower, twenty-three years her senior, named Angus McDonald. A Virginia native, he was educated at West Point but had left the army a year or two after graduation to pursue various adventures, including frontier fur

3. Cornelia McDonald, ca. 1890

trading, Indian fighting, and real estate speculation. His brother was married to one of Cornelia's sisters. Twenty-five-year-old Cornelia was awed when she first met this "tall, fine-looking," middle-aged gentleman with such a commanding presence. Angus in turn was captivated by her youthful high spirits, her talents, and her graceful bearing.[17]

The two were married in 1847 and took up residence in Virginia, where Angus had a law practice. Cornelia bore a baby within eleven months of the wedding, and eight more over the next thirteen years. The third child, a son, and the last, a daughter, died in infancy. In 1857 the couple settled in Winchester, in the northern part of the Shenandoah Valley. Their home was a beautiful estate called Hawthorn, on the edge of town.[18]

Angus was often away, seeing to his various business and legal dealings. One of his trips took him to England for nearly six months. These absences left Cornelia alone to oversee a household that included six slaves and a hired servant. She proved to be a capable manager and a woman of great strength of will; indeed, she struck some people as imperious, uncompromising, and sharp-tongued. At the same time, however, she embodied many of the qualities that defined the ideal woman in the Old South, for she was pious, nurturing, and devoted to her family.[19]

When the Civil War broke out, Angus was commissioned a colonel in the Confederate army. He commanded a cavalry regiment for several months in 1861 but his advanced age and deteriorating health rendered him unfit for field duty. Thereafter he served in various desk jobs in Richmond and elsewhere, while Cornelia remained at Hawthorn.[20]

Winchester was in the path of the invading Northern armies and the town was intermittently occupied by Union forces beginning in March 1862. Living under enemy rule with small children and no husband was an enormously trying experience for Cornelia. Troops frequently searched and pillaged her house and made a wreck of the grounds. Union army authorities quartered sick and wounded soldiers in the house and took over one room for an office. Cornelia lived in fear that they would seize the whole place and throw her and the children out onto the street.[21]

The periodic recapture of the town by Confederate forces bolstered the spirits of Cornelia and other Winchester residents, but when Robert E. Lee's army retreated south from Gettysburg in the summer of 1863 Cornelia decided that she could not endure another Yankee invasion. Loading the children and some of her belongings into two wagons, and leaving behind her remaining slaves, she set out on the road, joining the many thousands of other Southerners turned into refugees by the war.[22]

She settled in the little town of Lexington, which at 120 miles southwest of Winchester seemed safely distant from the enemy. Angus joined her there in December 1863, having secured an appointment as post commander. He was by this time close to sixty-five years old and enfeebled by rheumatism.[23]

In June 1864 a large Union raiding force penetrated all the way to Lexington and briefly occupied the town. Angus fled but was captured in the countryside by Union cavalrymen. When the raiders withdrew northward they took their prisoner with them, and he spent months in various Northern prisons under harsh conditions. By the time he was exchanged in November 1864, his health was completely destroyed.[24]

After word came of Angus's release from prison, Cornelia waited anxiously for him to rejoin her in Lexington. She was unaware that he was near death. In late November she received a letter from Richmond, dictated by Angus, telling her that he was too unwell to travel and that she should come there. Concerned about his health but still not suspecting that he was on his deathbed, she traveled to the city, arriving on December 2. It was one day too late to see him alive.[25]

She stayed in Richmond long enough to see to Angus's burial there and then returned to Lexington, still in shock. The winter that had just begun would be the bleakest she had ever faced. Since abandoning Hawthorn, along with its dairy and garden and orchard and slaves, she and the children had been heavily dependent on Angus's salary for survival. Now that was gone, and she was a widow, and she did not know what to do.[26]

The first day of 1865 was a Sunday, and on that day eighteen-year-old John Collier Robertson went to a country church not far from Knoxville, Tennessee, and prayed that Jesus Christ would come into his heart. Robertson had changed since the war began. In his own estimation, he had grown from "a rude and wicked boy" into a fairly decent young man. But he felt that his transformation was incomplete. He was struggling now to find a path to a new life of the spirit.[27]

Most of his life to that point had been spent on his parents' farm in Greene County, in upper east Tennessee, about seventy-five miles northeast of Knoxville. The county lay in the shadow of the high mountains that divide Tennessee and North Carolina and it bore little resemblance to the plantation regions that many people in those days thought of as the real South. In Greene County, as in the rest of east Tennessee, there were hardly any big planters and not many slaves. Small and middling-size yeoman farms dominated the region's landscape.[28]

The farm of John's parents, Jesse and Margaret, was typical. It consisted of 200 acres that were cleared and fenced and another hundred or so of woodland.

148

Chap 15.

Jan. 1865. New-Year's-day

One more year had passed; and was I any wiser or better? One year befor, or at the commencement of 1864, I was at the same place I now was*; I was a wild and rude boy. Easy to be drawn off by temptations, and frequently was. I was now one year older, but the question arises—was I one year better? In my own estimation I was. I was now more sober in my habits, and more calculated to resist evil temptations. A great change had come over me. If I was no better in heart, I was striving to be so. I had studied more during this year than for some previous years. Consequently I was some the wiser.

New-Year-day was very cold. As cold as it ever gets in this climate. I went to Church, at McClain's, with my cousins, and suffered no little from the cold. There was a great revival up at the place, and I had resolved to let no opportunity pass, without improving it, till I should become changed in heart; but Alas! My intentions were foiled this day, by the discourse delivered by Rev. Miller, a baptist Minister, on the subject of baptism. Up to this time I had been an approver of immersion and was yet. He spoke very roughly against the Pedo-baptists which rather wounded my feelings. I was invited, and plead at by friends to go to the anxious seat, but refused to go. Afterward I felt that I had done a great wrong by refusing to do what was for my own benefit. I also felt that Miller had done wrong, by preaching as he did, on such an occasion.

* page 85

4. *Page from the handwritten memoir of John Robertson, recounting his activities on the first day of 1865*

The Robertson family owned no slaves, but they hired enough extra labor to produce plenty for their own needs and a modest surplus to sell. They owned horses, cows, sheep, and hogs; grew a good deal of wheat, corn, and oats, a little rye, and some tobacco; raised peas and potatoes in their garden; got beeswax and honey from the bees they kept. The wool that the sheep provided was turned into cloth by John's mother and his sister, Debbie, who also churned the family's butter. The Robertsons were neither rich nor poor. The life they made for themselves was comfortable, but never easy.[29]

John turned fifteen in the spring of 1861, and by then he had mastered all the practical skills that a farmer of the Old South needed. He could plow a field, slaughter a hog, shear a sheep, mend a fence, and ride a horse. He knew when to sow and when to reap, and he could shuck corn, thresh wheat, and cure tobacco. He valued higher learning, too, and pursued it whenever he got a break from farm work. He applied himself diligently in the classroom, regularly practiced writing, and did a lot of reading—not just the Bible but works of history as well. By the standards of the Southern yeomanry, he became quite literate. But his was a narrow and unpolished sort of literacy. He read no fiction, for he had been taught that it was frivolous. He knew almost nothing of poetry, drama, art, philosophy, or science. And try as he might to appear cultivated, his speech and writing invariably betrayed his rustic origins. He said such things as "I had went" and "I disremember," and pronounced "once" as "wunst."[30]

If the Robertsons were in many respects typical east Tennesseans, in certain other respects they stood apart from the majority of their neighbors. For one thing, they were Democrats in a region where the Whigs had long predominated. For another, when the war came they supported their state's secession and pledged their loyalty to the new Confederacy.[31]

Most east Tennesseans, especially Whigs, bitterly opposed secession and remained steadfastly loyal to the United States. By late 1861 these unionists had moved beyond passive to active resistance, and the Confederate authorities cracked down. The unionists struck back, and by 1862 east Tennessee was in a virtual state of rebellion against the Confederacy. The minority who cast their lot with the rebels, including the Robertsons, found themselves in an uncomfortable position. The authorities were on their side, but most of their neighbors were enemies. Violence against secessionist families, carried out by bands of unionist guerrillas, became common.[32]

Luckily for the Robertsons, their community remained free of violence well into 1862. In March of that year John enlisted in the Confederate army.

Although not yet even sixteen years old, he had become, as he wrote in his memoir, "excited at the notion of becoming a soldier." When his parents said no, he ran away from home, made his way to Knoxville, lied about his age, and joined an infantry regiment that was stationed in the town. For the next few weeks he lived in a rough camp, sleeping on the ground, eating bad food, and getting worn out by drill and guard duty. Before long he fell very ill with pneumonia and while in the hospital he had a change of heart. He realized he was miserable in the army and too young to leave home. He got word to his family, and his father came to plead John's case before the regimental commander, who permitted John to go home.[33]

Back on the farm in Greene County, John recuperated quickly. But before long, east Tennessee's internal war spilled into the Robertsons' community. When unionist guerrillas became active in the area, John joined a secessionist home guard outfit. Periodically he would mount up with this armed company of civilians and ride out to search for guerrillas. Those apprehended were turned over to the authorities for punishment. The home guardsmen did not content themselves with such scouting: frequently they forced their way into the homes of unionist families, seizing weapons and stealing valuables. "In this manner," John recalled, "we were constantly adding enemies to those we all ready had." Some of them retaliated. Twice, while at home, John was fired on from ambush in the dark; he survived the first attack unscathed but was wounded in the second.[34]

The war in east Tennessee took a dramatic turn in August 1863 when a Northern army invaded from Kentucky and secured control of most of the region. John's home guard unit was absorbed into the Confederate army forces that had been ordered to carry out a delaying action and John fought bravely in several sharp skirmishes. Again, however, he developed pneumonia and was permitted to go home. Traveling stealthily to avoid enemy troops, he arrived at his parents' farm in early October.[35]

He found the situation in his community drastically changed. The Yankee invasion had given the local unionists the upper hand and in John's words, "when they got the power over us . . . they made us pay." Guerrillas repeatedly pillaged the Robertsons' farm, taking horses, saddles, food, and more. In late October John was kidnapped at gunpoint from his sickbed by a unionist whom the home guard had harassed. His captor turned him over to the federal army provost marshal in Greene County, who sent him to a military prison in Knoxville.[36]

Offered the opportunity to take an oath of allegiance to the Union and thereby gain his freedom, John resisted at first. But as the days went by and he sat in prison, sick, cold, and hungry, his determination wavered. When threatened with removal to a prison in Ohio, he decided that the disgrace of apostasy was preferable to "certain death" in the North. In November 1863 he took the oath.[37]

For the next nine months John moved around the Knoxville area doing a variety of things: chopping wood for the U.S. government, buying provisions in the countryside and peddling them to the Yankee garrison troops, working on the farm of an uncle who lived near town, attending school at an academy. In July 1864 he risked a visit home, although he knew that that section of east Tennessee was unpacified and extremely dangerous. He found his neighborhood ravaged, his family tormented by unionists, and many of his friends driven from their homes.[38]

After returning from Greene County, he got a job teaching at a school eight miles from his uncle's farm, but he found that his oath of allegiance was no protection against unionist vengeance. He was repeatedly harassed by unionists who had learned of his Confederate service and in October 1864 he was forced by threats of violence to give up his job. After that, he bought a pistol and moved to Roane County, southwest of Knoxville, where another of his uncles had a farm.[39]

Since a time in early 1863 when his mother had gently reproached him for his all-night carousing, John Robertson had worried about his character and his soul. He had resolved at that moment to abandon his dissolute and sinful ways and was pleased thereafter when God saw fit to help him along his new path. Now, as the year 1865 began, John wanted nothing so much as to put the war behind him and devote himself to his continuing quest for moral and spiritual perfection.[40]

In a more peaceful place he might have been able to do so. But in east Tennessee there was no refuge from the war. While he might with one hand eagerly take up his Bible, he would have to keep the other firmly on the grip of his pistol.

Samuel A. Agnew was a minister, thirty-one years old at the beginning of 1865. He lived on his father's plantation in the northeastern Mississippi county of

5. *Samuel Agnew, ca. 1880–1905*

Tippah. Every day, sometimes twice a day, he wrote in his diary, meticulously recording in precise script what he had seen, heard, and done. He surely never intended for anyone else to read the diary, for he often wrote of intimate matters—everything from his own episodes of "loose bowels" to his wife's menstrual cramps. But he also took note of all that happened in his neighborhood and the wider community. Few sections of the South were struck more fiercely by the hand of war than the Reverend Agnew's, and his diary is a vivid chronicle of the death of the Old South and the birth of the New.[41]

Sam Agnew himself was a decent man, a little stodgy, but upright and earnest. He was highly educated and intellectually curious, he read widely, and he reflected thoughtfully on affairs of the day and matters of faith. And even though his father was quite well-to-do and owned dozens of slaves, Sam kept no manservant and was pretty much unspoiled. He did most of his own errands, shaved himself, shined and mended his own shoes. At the same time, he had a rather snobbish attitude toward common folk and he shared with other Southern white men of that era the usual patronizing notions about women and blacks and the usual touchiness about his honor. As a man of God he was dutiful but uninspiring. He tended to get nervous when performing wedding ceremonies and his sermons were mostly dull.[42]

He was born in South Carolina in 1833. His father, Enoch, was a physician with deep family roots in the Palmetto State (South Carolina's nickname); his mother, Letitia, was a native of Ireland. Enoch eventually gave up the practice of medicine and in 1852 moved the family to Tippah County, Mississippi, where he had purchased a plantation. Sam graduated from Erskine College just before the family moved and later returned to South Carolina to attend Erskine Theological Seminary. In 1856 he was licensed to preach in the Associate Reformed Presbyterian Church, a denomination with which his family had long been affiliated, and three years later he was ordained. He had no pastorate, however. Beginning in 1857, he served as a "stated supply" of Hopewell Church, which was near his home in Mississippi. His job was to help govern the church, to substitute as needed for the pastors of Hopewell and other ARP churches in the area, and to preach on Sundays in any neighborhood where no church of any sort existed and where the residents requested his services. He married in 1864, at the comparatively late age of thirty. His bride, Nannie McKell, was from Starkville, south of Tippah County.[43]

Sam Agnew's education, his calling, and his family's wealth set him apart from most of his contemporaries, and there were other ways in which he was different. For one thing, he never established full independence from his parents. After embarking on his ministerial career, he continued to live with them, and he remained in their household even after marrying. He had no property of his own to speak of, a mere couple of hundred dollars' worth of books, clothes, and other personal possessions.[44]

For another thing, even though he had no personal servant, he led what most people of the time would have regarded as a life of ease. His ministerial duties were not full time and, except at a few busy points during the agricultural year, his father did not expect him to take any responsibility for the plantation. Thus, Sam had a lot of time on his hands. He spent it reading, visiting in the community, gardening, pursuing his hobby (botany), writing in his diary, and sometimes, as he put it, simply "lolling about."[45]

While the lives of many Southern men changed abruptly with the coming of war, Sam's did not. As a minister, he was exempt from military service. Early in the war he considered serving as a chaplain but rejected the idea and remained at home.[46]

From that vantage point Sam Agnew witnessed and faithfully recorded the experience of a community gradually engulfed by war. He kept informed on everything that went on around him; indeed, his hunger for news must have struck many people as obsessive. He devoured every newspaper he could get his hands on (although, as a strict Sabbatarian, he would not read them on Sundays), and he pumped all his neighbors for whatever information they had picked up. When reading or writing he habitually posted himself by a window with a view of the road that ran by his house; when people passed, whether friends or strangers, he would emerge from the house, hail them, and find out what they knew.[47]

Like the great majority of other white families in that section of the South, Sam and his kin were Confederate patriots. Among the many young men in Sam's community who enthusiastically joined the rebel army in the war's early days was his younger brother, Luther. Before ever facing the enemy on the field of battle, however, Luther fell victim to disease. In January 1862 Sam traveled three hundred miles by rail to the military hospital where Luther lay ill and brought him home to recuperate. But Luther did not recover; he died in June. To Sam it was a tragic reminder of "the shortness and uncertainty of life" and the inscrutability of divine will. He and his family grieved deeply but took comfort in their faith. As time passed, the names of many other local men were added to the list of dead.[48]

From the moment the war began, many Southerners worried about enemy invasion. Tippah County seemed safe enough at first, however, for it lay deep inside the Confederacy. Few foresaw how quickly the armies of the North would conquer west and middle Tennessee and penetrate northern Mississippi. Between early 1862 and late 1864 Tippah was raided by federal troops at least sixty times. Sam's community, in the county's southeastern corner, was spared many of these visitations but still suffered enormously: farms were stripped of provisions and livestock, bridges and fences were destroyed, government and churches and trade were disrupted, and many slaves marched away with the invaders to freedom. The Agnew plantation was hit several times, with considerable property losses.[49]

The last Yankee raid that the Agnews endured prior to 1865 was an utter nightmare. In June 1864 a passing force of 7,800 federal troops was attacked by a Confederate force only half that size, under the command of General Nathan Bedford Forrest. The final stage of the ensuing day-long battle (known as Brice's Crossroads) was fought on the Agnew plantation. When the terrifying roar of cannons and small arms finally ceased and the smoke cleared, the Agnews emerged from hiding to find the plantation sacked, its buildings riddled with bullet holes, its fields strewn with the corpses of Northern and Southern soldiers. Wounded men lay in and around the Agnew house, many screaming in pain. The dead were buried quickly and the wounded removed, but the carcasses of horses and mules took days to dispose of. For a long time the place stank of death.[50]

Forrest's stunning victory in this battle cleared Tippah of invaders for a time, and the Yankees did not seriously molest the county during the remainder of 1864. Order was gradually restored and life resumed something like its customary rhythms. But neither Sam Agnew nor anybody else knew how long this state of affairs would continue. With the Yankees in possession of Tennessee, the citizens of Tippah found themselves poised vulnerably on the Confederacy's frontier. Any day might bring another invasion, another season of chaos and ruin.[51]

Part One

WINTER

LOUIS HUGHES

SOUTH ALABAMIANS SOMETIMES CALL IT SIMPLY THE BIGBEE. IT IS A short name for a long river that rolls lazily, with many twists and turns, southward from the heart of the state to Mobile on the Gulf coast. In early 1865 the Tombigbee was high and busy with steamboats. They chugged up and down the river between Demopolis and Mobile, stopping at landings here and there to load or unload. Bales of cotton and piles of Osnaburg sacks crowded the decks of many of the boats. The sacks held the more precious cargo: they were filled with salt.[1]

Many of the sacks were marked "Alabama." These were loaded aboard at a stop on the east bank of the river in Clarke County, some sixty miles north of Mobile. A road led inland from the landing there, and a short distance up that road lay the Alabama state saltworks. It was a sprawling little settlement centered around a large wooden building with a veranda. This building was the headquarters, in which Louis Hughes lived and worked.[2]

Lou, as he was used to being called, had stepped easily into his new situation when he came to the works in 1863. A well-trained butler was a prized and useful servant, and thus Lou was immediately singled out from the other leased slaves and set to work in that role. He did a good job and became a favorite of the state salt commissioner, Benjamin Woolsey, whose office was in the headquarters. Matilda, Lou's wife, was put to work as a cook. She, too, won the commissioner's approval; her bread and rolls, he said, were as good as any he had ever tasted. Woolsey, a lawyer and planter by profession, had at one time offered to buy Lou and Matilda for three thousand dollars, but Boss had turned him down.[3]

Boss was dead now, of course. January 1, 1865, was the first anniversary of his death. His sudden passing had shocked his family and slaves but resulted in no immediate changes for Lou and Matilda. They and the other McGehee slaves stayed on at the saltworks by order of Madam, Boss's widow, who remained at her father's plantation in Mississippi.[4]

There were many slaves at the works in early 1865, perhaps 200 or more. Their muscle and sweat and skills powered an extensive manufacturing operation. It was a scene of almost constant activity, for there were all sorts of tasks to be done and the Confederacy's salt famine generated a sense of urgency. Slave men did most of the heavy labor—boring wells, tending pumps and furnaces, chopping and hauling wood, making bricks, building levees, sacking and weighing and loading the salt. The slave women cooked and did laundry and other chores with the help of the older children. Whites did the other jobs: among the two dozen or so employed at the works, besides the salt commissioner, were a superintendent, a clerk, a bookkeeper, a commissary manager, a doctor, a wagon master, two steam-engine operators, several artisans, and a number of overseers.[5]

The saltworks was not just a manufacturing operation but a community, and a largely self-sustaining one. All the people who worked there lived on the site. Most of the slaves resided in barracks or cabins that were spaced neatly along a street. The whites had separate residences or took rooms upstairs at the headquarters. Like any respectable Southern village, the works had a smithy, a cooperage, a shoemaking shop, a carpentry shop, a sawmill, a gristmill, and a cemetery. It also boasted a hospital, a commissary, a sack-making shop, a storehouse, and at least one kitchen. The works produced no grain or meat (these were purchased from outside sources), but it had a dairy and a seven-acre vegetable garden that helped feed the whole community.[6]

Like any village, too, the works had its own economy, an informal system of borrowing and bartering, swapping and selling. Slaves as well as whites engaged in this casual commerce and Lou Hughes was one of those clever enough to make money from it. The story he tells about this in his memoir illustrates one of the curious things about the Old South: how the rigid laws and protocols of slavery and race relations were sometimes ignored in the intimacy of communal life.

As Lou tells it, one day in the early part of 1865 he approached the superintendent of the works, N. S. Brooks, about getting some tobacco. He had a hundred dollars he had borrowed from three other slaves; they had earned it doing extra chores at the works in their free time. Lou wanted this tobacco not to smoke but to resell. Brooks liked Lou and was happy to do him a favor, so he took the money and dispatched an order by boat to a merchant in Mobile. Four days later a package containing thirty-six plugs of tobacco arrived. Brooks turned it over to Lou, who, after finishing his morning duties at headquarters, set out to peddle the plugs among the black laborers at the works. Within an hour he had sold every plug at five dollars apiece, for a profit of eighty dollars. Later, as Lou was serving the noon meal in the headquarters' dining room, Brooks asked him how he had done with the tobacco.

"I did very well," Lou replied. "[T]he only trouble was I did not have enough."

Brooks questioned him a little more, then drew out pencil and paper and did some figuring. His own salary was a meager $150 a month in rapidly depreciating Confederate money. After the meal, while Lou was clearing the table, Brooks came in from the veranda where he had been smoking with the clerk and made a proposition: he would order all the tobacco Lou could sell if Lou would split the profit with him fifty-fifty. Lou agreed.

Brooks ordered another shipment that day—500 plugs. When it came, Lou went into business in earnest. He recruited three other slaves as agents and gave them some plugs on consignment. The three were William, who was foreman of the wood-chopping detail; Uncle Hudson, who cared for the horses and mules; and John, who worked at the hospital. Every two or three days each would turn in his proceeds and take some more plugs. Meanwhile, whenever Lou had any free time following his afternoon chores, he would saddle up an old pony and, with Brooks's blessing, ride around through the neighborhoods surrounding the works and sell more plugs. The other slaves were curious about the source of the tobacco, but Lou kept it a secret. "In two weeks we had taken in $1,600," he recalled, "and I was happy as I could be. Brooks was a fine fellow—a northerner by birth, and did just what he said he would. I received one-half of the money. Of course this was all rebel money, but I was sharp, and bought up all the silver I could find."[7]

It must be said that few other slaves in the Old South were as successful in this respect as Lou. He held a privileged position at the works, thanks to his special skills and his close relationship with Superintendent Brooks and Commissioner Woolsey. Certainly Uncle Hudson, William, John, and even Matilda, for that matter, enjoyed no such liberties, not to mention the legions of others who did the saltworks' daily drudgery with ax and spade and hoe.

Each might carve out some personal space in the informal communal setting, but that space was very narrow. For if the saltworks embodied the casual intimacy of a Southern village, it also embodied the rigorous discipline and exacting work routines of a Southern plantation.

The slaves at the works labored six days a week. Most of them, as was customary in the South, worked from sunup to sundown; those who tended the furnaces, however, had to work in shifts both day and night, for the furnaces were kept going around the clock every day except Sunday, when all work ceased. Because most of the jobs at the saltworks required very heavy labor, Brooks and Woolsey—who shared responsibility for managing the works—preferred to lease adult male slaves. They paid the slave owners not in cash but in kind: four bushels (about 200 pounds) of salt per month for an able-bodied male hand. The payment for women and children was less, and while Brooks and Woolsey would accept any healthy slave sent to them, they encouraged owners to send only men.[8]

The two managers found it easy to hire white employees, for a job at the saltworks exempted a man from Confederate military conscription. But they could never get all the slaves they wanted. They tried to recruit a work force of 300 but found that many slave owners were reluctant to put their valuable property in somebody else's hands during such uncertain times. Both spent a good deal of time corresponding with concerned lessors or potential lessors, assuring them that the slaves at the saltworks received generous rations (at least three and a half pounds of bacon and a peck of cornmeal per week, along with milk and vegetables), got skilled medical care when they needed it, and were closely supervised.[9]

This last was a particularly touchy matter. Brooks and Woolsey did their best to keep their leased bondsmen always under the watchful eye of some white person. They employed at least eight overseers at the works, and one even slept in the same quarters with the blacks. Nevertheless, slaves at the works could, and occasionally did, slip away. Few of these runaways were seeking freedom; in most cases they were simply reacting to some treatment they regarded as unfair. Mild protests of this sort were familiar to every Southern slave master. A typical instance had occurred at the works in March 1864, when twelve slaves owned by a Mobile couple named Ketchum ran off, upset because their cornmeal ration was short that week. All but one of the twelve eventually returned voluntarily and Woolsey sent them back to work without punishment. He then sat down to write an explanation to the

Ketchums, who feared that their slaves had been mistreated or had been enticed away by "disloyal white men." The slaves were well cared for and well protected, Woolsey insisted. The cornmeal was short only because the steam engine that ran the gristmill had broken down; it was now fixed, and he would see to it that full rations were always provided in the future. Moreover, he assured the Ketchums, he had not waited for the runaways to come back on their own: on learning of their flight, he had dispatched three overseers to track them down. "I spared no trouble or expense to get them back."[10]

Few if any fugitives from the works ever made it to freedom, for—as all the slaves realized—the chances of escaping from a place so deep inside the Confederacy were slim. Even if they managed to elude the pursuing overseers, they were almost certain to fall into the clutches of local authorities somewhere. Such was the fate of three of the McGehee slaves named Sam, Devro, and Lafayette; they ran off from the works in late 1864 only to wind up in a county jail, from which Brooks and Woolsey retrieved them. Blacks traveling alone in the rural South always aroused suspicion, and they could expect to be accosted frequently and forced to explain themselves.[11]

Runaways were not the biggest problem the two managers had to deal with. But even little problems can be anguishing to those working under great pressure. Brooks and Woolsey shouldered a heavy burden in running the works. It was a task of great importance, for of all the shortages that plagued the Confederacy, none was more critical than the shortage of salt.

Few Southerners had foreseen such a shortage when the war began. They took their salt for granted, as it had always been cheap and plentiful. Most of it was imported from England and the West Indies, arriving as ballast in the ships that came to Southern ports to get cotton. So inexpensive was this foreign salt in the antebellum years that the South hardly bothered to produce its own. But as the blockading squadrons of the Union navy began sealing off the Confederate ports in 1861 and 1862, salt grew scarce.[12]

The shortage of salt was not a mere inconvenience; it was a crisis that threatened the survival of the Confederacy. Humans and livestock must have salt in their diet for good health. Moreover, in the nineteenth century meat was preserved primarily by salting, butter needed salt to stay fresh, and hides required dehydration by salt before they could be turned into leather. By a conservative estimate, the Confederacy needed 300 million pounds of salt per year—thirty-three pounds, on average, for each of its nine million inhabitants.[13]

Before the war, thirty-three pounds of salt could have been bought anywhere in the South for less than fifty cents; but by 1862 it cost over thirteen dollars and was sometimes hard to find even at that price. As citizens protested and appealed for help, Confederate authorities set about developing domestic sources. There were only a few places in the South where salt could be produced in quantity, and one was in Clarke County, Alabama. Underneath the palmetto flats that bordered the Tombigbee and its tributaries in this county the ground water was so saline that a kettle of it, boiled down, would yield at least an eighth of a kettle of salt. The state government held title to most of this salt-rich land, which stretched for miles along the river, and early in the war the governor declared the state holdings open to the public and encouraged individuals and businesses to exploit them. He also ordered that the state establish its own salt-making operation.[14]

The Alabama state saltworks opened in October 1862. Considering the general primitiveness of industry in the Old South, it was an extraordinary facility—large, technologically sophisticated, efficient. The production process began at the wells that were bored in the mucky flats to a depth of a hundred feet or so and lined with cypress wood. Steam-powered pumps, mounted on tall scaffolds erected over the wells, sucked the brine to the surface and spewed it into wooden troughs that carried it to the furnaces. There were at least four furnaces at the state works, great brick contrivances thirty or forty feet long, with towering chimneys. They were fueled by vast quantities of wood, cut in the surrounding forests. On the furnaces, large kettles and pans full of brine bubbled away until nothing was left but pure salt. Twenty-four hours a day, six days a week, the furnaces roared and the water boiled. In a good month, the state works could produce over a hundred thousand pounds of salt. After being dried and sacked, it was hauled to the river by wagon to await boats. Some of it was shipped out as payment for supplies or leased slaves, but the bulk of it was distributed among the counties of Alabama, whose citizens could purchase it at cost.[15]

The state saltworks was one of the last things still functioning well in the Confederacy by 1865. The rebel states, battered relentlessly by the Yankee army and navy and disintegrating internally, were sinking to their knees. The success of Superintendent Brooks and Commissioner Woolsey was remarkable considering the problems they faced, particularly the scarcity of black laborers. The two managers benefited in one sense from the Confederacy's military reverses, for every advance of the Yankee army drove more slave owners into the Confederate interior seeking a safe place to put their slaves to work; still, the number of slaves the saltworks gained thereby was not enough.

Aggravating the chronic labor shortage at the saltworks was the health problem. The marshy lands that yielded the valuable brine were a breeding ground for disease. Sickness and death plagued the works, keeping the doctor busy, the hospital crowded, and the cemetery growing. As the year 1865 opened, the little community was just recovering from a malaria epidemic that had almost halted operations; Brooks reported in November 1864 that he was the only person at the works, white or black, who had not yet come down with this "swamp fever." As he wrote, Woolsey lay prostrate in bed, too sick even to make out his regular report, and the bookkeeper appeared to be close to death. Among those who died that fall were three of the McGehee slaves, two of them children. Brooks ordered the carpenter to build coffins for the three, and then billed Madam for the cost.[16]

During another of the epidemics that swept the works—this one typhoid—Lou Hughes got a chance to practice another skill he had acquired: nursing. It was something he had learned years before from Boss, who had been a physician. Boss had given up his medical practice when he acquired a plantation, but he continued to treat his own slaves and he trained Lou to assist him. He prepared many of his medicines himself, using the recipes in Dr. Gunn's popular treatise. He even had a large medicine cabinet built into a wall of his Memphis house. Young Lou was entranced. To him the cabinet was a wondrous thing, and when his master was practicing his healing craft, he seemed immensely wise and gentle. Patiently Boss taught Lou how to identify all the potions by sight and smell, and how to prepare each one and measure out the proper dosage. In this way Lou mastered the mysteries of ipecac and castor oil, Cook's pills and mustard baths. He learned also about the medicinal herbs that grew plentifully in the South and before long he was going into the woods himself to gather slippery elm and the root of alum, poplar, and wild cherry. He absorbed not only his master's medicinal knowledge but also his bedside skills, for Boss brought him along to the slave cabins where he treated colicky babies and dyspeptic field hands.[17]

Nursing was only one of many skills Lou acquired in the McGehee household. He could drive a carriage, cultivate an ornamental garden, and even operate a sewing machine, not to mention serve expertly as butler and body servant. But it was nursing that he liked more than anything else. When he was called on to act as a night nurse for a sick slave at the saltworks, he did so gladly. This was the first case of typhoid he had ever seen, but he remembered what Boss had taught him about the disease, and he did what he could, drawing on whatever medicines the works' hospital could offer. The patient was too far gone to respond to Lou's tender ministration, however, and he died within a few days.[18]

Disease was not the only threat to health at the saltworks; accidents, too, took a toll. Much of the work done there was hazardous. Razor-sharp ax blades and falling trees caused casualties among the wood choppers; blazing fuel and boiling brine scorched and scalded the furnace tenders. The various steam engines in and around the works posed another sort of danger, one tragically illustrated on January 19, 1865, when the *Dick Keys* blew up on the Tombigbee. This was one of the steamboats that made regular runs up and down the river; it was at a point some miles below the works when all five of its boilers exploded with a tremendous roar, blasting the vessel to bits. More than half a dozen people were killed and many others injured.[19]

There were natural disasters, too, along the river that winter. Heavy rain in late January and early February brought dangerously high water in the creeks that fed the Tombigbee, flooding out roads. An even worse deluge at the end of February sent river water spilling over the levee that protected the saltworks, inundating the furnaces and wells and halting operations for a time. It was not only a wet winter but an extraordinarily cold one, too, by the standards of south Alabama. The last part of January saw seven consecutive days with temperatures at least eight degrees below freezing. A week later came a heavy snowfall, a rare sight so far south.[20]

Louis Hughes had many matters on his mind during those chilly, soggy days of January and February. There was almost always something demanding his attention at headquarters: fireplaces or stoves to be tended, items to be fetched or delivered for Woolsey and Brooks, meals to be served. In the little spare time that he could find, there was his tobacco venture to attend to and other personal things as well, especially one: his and Matilda's new baby.

She was born in February and they named her Lydia. She was not their first child, but she was the only one now living (twins born to them in 1859 had died in infancy). The new addition to their family made the upstairs room at headquarters, where they lodged, a little more crowded, but it probably meant also some time off from cooking for Matilda, for it was customary among slave masters to accommodate nursing mothers.[21]

Matilda was thirty-four, nearly two years older than Lou, when she brought forth this child. They had married in the Memphis mansion of Boss and Madam on November 30, 1858. It was a wedding of a sort few slaves could boast of: Boss, acting on one of his frequent paternalistic impulses, arranged a formal ceremony in the parlor, brought in a white minister to officiate, and invited not only his own slaves but those of his neighbors, too.[22]

Matilda had known Lou from the time she arrived at the mansion in 1855. Her first months there had been miserable. She had grown up with her mother and six brothers and sisters in Kentucky, but in 1855 her master had decided to sell the whole family. He hired two agents to take the eight blacks to Memphis, where they were put on the auction block in the prominent slave-trading establishment of Nathan Bedford Forrest. Matilda's mother and five of her siblings were all sold to different buyers and taken away. Matilda and her sister Mary Ellen were sold to Boss, who gave Mary Ellen to his sister-in-law as a present and kept Matilda as a cook.[23]

Torn from her family, Matilda was inconsolable for a time. To Lou she seemed "a sad picture to look at. . . . Any one could see she was almost heart-broken." Her grief eventually subsided, and her blossoming relationship with Lou no doubt brought her much joy and comfort. But with the passage of time came new miseries for her to contend with, including the death of her twin babies and the cruelty of Madam, who abused Matilda no less than she abused Lou.[24]

The marriage of Matilda and Lou was in some ways a union of opposites. They had very different temperaments, for one thing. Lou was about as bold and resourceful as a slave could get away with being; Matilda was timid and tended to go to pieces in a crisis. They had spiritual differences, too. Matilda was a devout Christian whose faith consoled her in gloomy times: "God will help us," she would tell Lou; "let us try and be patient." Lou was not exactly a skeptic, but neither was he deeply religious. And he had a couple of habits that no doubt bothered the pious Matilda: he wore a voodoo bag, a little leather pouch containing roots and pins and such that supposedly had the power to protect him from harm; and he drank whiskey, often carrying a bottle around with him. With all their differences, however, the two were deeply committed to each other.[25]

The months that Lou and Matilda spent at the saltworks were undoubtedly the happiest time either had experienced since being purchased by the McGehees. This is not to say that it was some sort of idyll; Lou may have had an agreeable job, indulgent supervisors, extraordinary privileges, a lucrative business, and a healthy new baby, but he and Matilda were never for a moment allowed to forget that they were enslaved members of a despised race. Moreover, as long as they remained at this site deep within the Confederacy, Lou's dream of escape was unattainable. Still, they would remember this as a good time in their lives.

The question was how long this happy interlude was going to last. Reports of a possible Yankee advance against Mobile had reached Clarke County in December 1864. One of the few major cities of the Confederacy still unconquered, Mobile was defended by 10,000 Southern troops, 300 cannons, and five gunboats. But no one knew how big a force the North might throw against the city. And if Mobile fell, the state saltworks would be vulnerable—it was absurd to think that the two small rebel forts perched atop bluffs overlooking the Tombigbee below the works would stop the powerful Yankee army and navy.[26]

Lou Hughes probably knew that Woolsey and Brooks had a contingency plan for such an emergency. If enemy forces threatened the works, the two managers intended to evacuate all the slaves and try to return them to their owners. As the winter of 1864–65 came to a close, there still seemed no cause for alarm. The Clarke County newspaper assured the citizens as late as March 9 that "All is quiet about Mobile." But how much longer that would be was anyone's guess.[27]

CORNELIA MCDONALD

CORNELIA MCDONALD'S HOUSE IN LEXINGTON WAS A RENTED, two-story clapboard on the west side of Main Street, just north of the two-block stretch of Main that comprised the town's business district. The house was at least seventy years old and hard to heat, for it had a lot of windows and some of the rooms had no fireplace. The rats were a problem, too. But it was spacious compared to the other places she had lived in as a refugee: there were three rooms on the first floor, three on the second, and a kitchen in the basement. The yard was big, too, except on the south side where the house abutted a side street. The front yard, which stretched forty feet between the porch and Main Street, had grass and trees and was very pretty from spring to fall. But now, in early January, the grass was yellow and the trees bare.[1]

As roomy as the house was, it was nevertheless crowded most of the time. All seven of Cornelia's children were there with her, and there was a hired cook who came during the day and visitors from morning to night. The first-floor room that served as the parlor was generally the busiest part of the house, except at mealtimes, when everybody crammed into the dining room. When she first set up housekeeping there in November 1863, Cornelia had been hard-put to furnish the parlor respectably. She had salvaged only two wagonloads of possessions from her home in Winchester, mostly clothes, mattresses, and bed frames. But she did save a nice carpet and some red curtains, and after settling in Lexington she had a cheap pine table made that she covered with a red cloth. These, along with some other odds and ends of furniture that she picked up, including an old sofa covered in flowered calico and a few chairs, made for a cozy if not elegant parlor, and Cornelia was satisfied to entertain there.[2]

6. The house in Lexington, Virginia, where Cornelia McDonald and her children resided in 1865, as it appeared in the 1920s. Shown is the left side of the house as one faced it from Main Street; the front door and porch were moved to that side sometime after the McDonalds moved away.

From her backyard she could see Washington College and the Virginia Military Institute where they stood on a low ridge overlooking the town. Next door to her was a two-story building that housed Deaver's shoemaking shop downstairs and the Odd Fellows hall above. Across the street lived a demented old man named Parks. He had lost his mind one night in 1861 when a coffin containing the corpse of his son, a Confederate soldier decapitated by a cannonball, was delivered without warning at his doorstep.[3]

Lexington was a picturesque town of about 2,500 people, nestled among hills and ridges and skirted by the winding North River. It was remarkably neat and orderly, by Southern standards; except that it lacked a square, it might have been mistaken at first glance for a New England village. Other than that, however, there was nothing Yankee about it.[4]

It may well have been the most prominent small town in Virginia in 1865. Some of its fame derived from the presence of the college and the military institute, both noted educational institutions. The town was also home to John Letcher, the recently retired governor of the state. But the real source of Lexington's glory was its association with the legendary Stonewall Jackson, martyred hero of the Confederacy. He had taught at the military institute before the war, and after his death in May 1863 he was buried in the old Presbyterian cemetery on the south side of town.[5]

The two-hundred-mile-long Shenandoah Valley had been ravaged since the war began, but mostly in the lower counties in the northern part of the state, which Union troops had marched through many times. The upper counties, including Rockbridge, of which Lexington was the seat, had not been spared altogether from the enemy's wrath, but for the most part they remained secure, quiet, and productive.[6]

Had some of Cornelia's kinfolk prevailed, she would not have stayed in Lexington. In the days following the death of her husband, Angus, in Richmond—it had occurred just a month before, on December 1, 1864—she had talked with relatives in that city about her future. They bluntly reminded her that she was now facing poverty and advised her to parcel out her children among other family members and move to Richmond, where she could get a job as a government clerk. That she was facing poverty Cornelia could not deny, but she adamantly refused to break up her family. "[M]y children were given to me to care for, and bring up" was her reply. Should she renounce that duty, she thought, she would have to answer to Him who had reproached the faithless rulers of Israel with the words, "where is the flock that was given thee, thy beautiful flock?"[7]

So she remained in Lexington in the house on Main Street with her flock gathered around her. Three of them were so young they needed pretty much constant attention. Four-year-old Hunter was the littlest. Blue-eyed Donald ("my little urchin," Cornelia called him) was two years older. Roy was a yellow-haired, dark-eyed, mischievous eight-year-old. The only girl, Nelly, was a sympathetic, sad-faced child whom Cornelia dubbed "my little shadow"; she was ten now, old enough to help with the smaller ones. Kenneth, an affectionate twelve-year-old, assisted her. The two oldest boys—Allan, fifteen, and Harry, almost seventeen—were nearing maturity, and Cornelia was relying on them more and more. Harry, in particular, was a great help, for he was as large and strong as a man, dependable, and fearless.[8]

She and the children would need all the strength they could muster in order to survive and keep the family intact, for their financial situation was little short of desperate. Before the war, the family had held substantial property. The estate in Winchester, the half-dozen slaves, and Angus's other investments were together worth almost $70,000. But all of those were now lost or

7. The McDonald family in 1870. Standing, from left, are Hunter, Donald, Kenneth, and Nelly; seated, from left, are Roy, Allan, Cornelia, and Harry.

beyond Cornelia's reach. Furthermore, during her flight from Winchester in 1863 she had sold her good jewelry and most of her fine clothes. When she and the children arrived in Lexington, they had little besides the furniture, everyday clothes, china, and silverware that were piled in the wagons; the horses and wagons themselves had been borrowed.[9]

From that point on, the family had been heavily dependent on Angus's salary. As a Confederate colonel, he made $210 per month. During the half-year that he was posted in Lexington he was also entitled to a "commutation of quarters" allowance of $175 per month because he made his office in his home. The allowance had dried up when he was captured in June 1864, but Cornelia had continued to receive his monthly pay while he was a prisoner of war. That ended with his death, however, and the Confederate government made no provision for widow's benefits.[10]

As 1865 began, Cornelia's cash holdings amounted to about $300 in Confederate currency. She was preparing to file a claim with the government for money still due Angus at his death—$427—but she knew it would take weeks for the paperwork to make its way through the bureaucracy in Richmond. Once that money was in hand it would not buy much, anyway. Butter was now selling in Lexington for twelve Confederate dollars per pound and coffee for eighteen dollars. A yard of linsey-woolsey cost twenty-five dollars, and a pair of children's shoes, forty. And besides food and clothing, she had to worry about rent and firewood.[11]

Some people in town had stopped accepting Confederate money in payment for goods, knowing that it would be worth less tomorrow than today. Barter was becoming more and more common. But Cornelia had few goods to offer in exchange for what she needed, so she had to use currency. And, like everyone else, she felt compelled to spend it fast because it was depreciating so rapidly. These days, however, there was less and less to spend it on, for the shortages that had plagued the Confederacy from its beginning had by 1865 reached critical proportions. Cornelia knew a butcher on the north end of town who accepted Confederate money, but sometimes when she visited his shop he had no meat to offer at any price.[12]

To some it seemed almost incomprehensible that there could be such scarcity of food in the midst of agricultural abundance. The farms of Rockbridge County and the rest of the upper valley still produced great quantities of wheat, corn, livestock, and other foodstuffs. Where was it all going? citizens demanded to know. There was much suspicion that "speculators" and "profiteers" were hoarding it, but the truth was otherwise.[13]

As one after another of the Confederacy's food-growing regions fell to the Northern invaders, the upper valley was increasingly called on to help feed the rest of the rebel population. Army impressment agents scoured the region, taking what they needed from the farmers and paying them in Confederate money at government-set prices far below market value. And what the farmers turned over to these agents was in addition to the annual tithe—one-tenth of all harvested crops and slaughtered livestock—that the Confederate tax collectors demanded of them.[14]

These levies created agricultural scarcity in Rockbridge County, which had never known it before the war. The skyrocketing food prices that resulted brought great distress, especially among the county's poorest families. Local government stepped in, acting under new state laws that allowed county magistrates to borrow money to buy provisions for the poor. By early 1865, some 1,400 Rockbridge citizens were on the dole. But for those not poor enough to qualify for assistance—Cornelia and her family among them—there was no relief from scarcity and high prices.[15]

What worried a lot of people in Rockbridge about the food shortage was not only the suffering it caused but also the desperation. As the winter of 1864–65 went on, there were more and more reports of food theft in the county. Among the victims was one of Lexington's prominent families, the Pendletons, who were good friends of Cornelia: on a stormy night in late February someone broke into their smokehouse by ripping away the back wall and stole thirty slabs of bacon. This wave of pilferage did not yet constitute anything like a threat to order, but as everyone in Rockbridge knew, isolated acts of desperation, if multiplied sufficiently, can achieve explosive power.[16]

Cornelia's own situation as the winter began was undeniably grim, but she did not see it as hopeless. She had her older children to lean on and she had her own considerable resources of strength and talent. Beyond that, she had a circle of friends and benefactors in Lexington who were rallying around her now in her time of need.

From the moment she arrived in Lexington in August 1863—an utter stranger, homeless, with one dollar in her purse—she had been blessed with acts of kindness. She was lucky in this regard, for in many Southern communities refugees were encountering hostility. As more and more of them crowded into the dwindling number of safe havens within the Confederacy, they strained the communities' resources of food and housing and provoked resentment among the natives.[17]

Perhaps it was not just luck in Cornelia's case. Although she could be stubborn and sharp at times, she had a generous nature and an appealing way about her; and she made friends easily, at least among people of her own social class. In any event, a good number of Lexington folk took to her and went out of their way to help her. Reverend William McElwee and his wife, Anne, were among the first. Cornelia showed up at their doorstep soon after her arrival in town, having heard they might have some spare rooms in their home to rent. Even if they did, she expected them to turn her away; one shopkeeper had already done so, not caring to have seven children running around in the rooms he let over his store. But when she made her plea, Anne McElwee replied unhesitatingly "in her sweet kind voice" that the McDonalds were welcome. Cornelia was overcome. "I could not thank her [because of] the choking sense in my throat. I could have wept. . . . I can never forget the sound of her voice when she said she could not refuse a stranger and a refugee." Cornelia and the children lived there only a month, until they found roomier accommodations, but she and the McElwees remained close.[18]

As time passed, she broadened her circle of acquaintances and cemented a number of good friendships through the ritual of visiting. Among the new friends whom Cornelia began to call on frequently, and who called at her house just as often, were the Pendletons, Ann and her daughters. Ann's husband, William, had been the rector of Lexington's Grace Episcopal Church until he resigned in 1862, and the family still lived in the rectory a few blocks from Cornelia. The Pendleton women were without their husband and father now, however, for Brigadier General Pendleton, chief of artillery in Robert E. Lee's Army of Northern Virginia, was with his troops in the fortifications protecting Richmond and Petersburg. When the Pendletons' son, Sandie, was killed in battle in the fall of 1864, Cornelia comforted her friends and brought them food. When Angus died a few weeks later, the Pendletons comforted her and sewed a mourning dress for Nelly.[19]

There were others in Lexington who were not part of Cornelia's social circle but who nevertheless came to her aid. One was Thomas Deaver, the shoemaker. In November 1863, before Angus joined her in Lexington, Cornelia had needed shoes for her boys. Angus was sending her almost all his salary, but she was spending it on other necessities as fast as it came. She approached Deaver, confessing that she could not pay him right away. He never even asked how soon she might be able to; he just said she could pay him after the war and went ahead and made the shoes. A year later, the boys were shoeless again. Winter was approaching, and Cornelia's financial plight was even gloomier than before. She agonized over whether to go to Deaver once more. At last she did, again confessing that she could not pay him. "He said he would make them," she recalled, "and [said that] I must not feel uneasy or anxious about it; that he knew I would pay when I could." She left the shop in tears. Deaver was a man of modest means, with a large family of his own, and Cornelia knew that his generosity entailed substantial sacrifice.[20]

She also knew that such kindness could not be extended to her indefinitely, by Deaver or anybody else. She had to find a source of income. As it happened, an opportunity came her way in January 1865, when an acquaintance who knew of Cornelia's skill with pencil and sketchbook told her of some young ladies in town who were willing to pay for drawing lessons.[21]

As worried as she was about money, Cornelia was nevertheless deeply reluctant to take the job. For one thing, she was emotionally frail, not yet recovered from the shock of Angus's death. "The thought of being daily obliged to meet strangers," she wrote, "of not having the privilege of retirement in my present state of distress, was dreadful to me." For another thing, she was loath to proclaim her poverty so publicly. It was a matter of pride to her that she had been able to maintain in Lexington a semblance of the refined lifestyle that women of her class were expected to cultivate: "I shrank," she said, "from seeming . . . poor."[22]

Cornelia's soul-searching was short-lived. She took the teaching job because "the alternative was starvation." So, for three or four hours in the mornings, she taught drawing in her parlor. The same acquaintance who arranged this found two other young ladies who wanted advanced French lessons, and they began coming in the afternoons to read poetry and history. The two classes together brought Cornelia fifty dollars a week.[23]

Another bit of luck took care of the problem of winter fuel. Firewood cost more than thirty dollars a cord in Lexington, and the big drafty house on Main Street demanded a lot of it now that the weather had turned cold. Somehow Cornelia learned that the army quartermaster in Rockbridge County was hiring woodcutters; they would receive as payment one cord of every three they cut, delivered to their homes by army wagon. Harry and Allan both volunteered to hire on. Cornelia needed one of them to help around the house, however, so Allan stayed home while his older brother headed off each morning to join the chopping detail in the woods outside town.[24]

Clothing the family was a more difficult problem. Cornelia was determined that she and the children would present a respectable appearance no matter how poor they were, but it became harder as time went on. Ready-made clothes, when they could be found on Lexington's store shelves, were prohibitively expensive. Cornelia could sew and knit, but store-bought cloth and yarn of any sort were beyond her means, too.[25]

Friends and family helped her out to some extent. Her good friend Mrs. John Powell, whose husband was in the army, gave her two of his old suits that, with some alterations, fit Allan and Harry. From her sister in another part of Virginia, Cornelia got fifty pounds of wool; she dyed it black, paid to have it carded, spun, and woven (tasks she had never learned to do and had no equipment for), then made it into winter clothes. She also resorted to cannibalizing fabrics she had around the house. Laboriously she unraveled a cotton mattress, wound the thread, dyed half of it with walnut hulls, and then had it woven into brown-and-white checked cloth from which she made suits for the four youngest boys. She unraveled some old knit undershirts, too, and with the yarn knitted socks for the boys. For Nelly she cut up window and bed curtains and sewed a red dress and white muslin frock and apron. But for the most part the family had to make do with the things brought from Winchester. Once she had exhausted every possible source of new clothing, Cornelia recalled, "there was nothing more to do but mend and patch."[26]

Her biggest daily challenge was feeding the family. Fortunately, she was not wholly dependent on purchased food. Since moving into the house on Main Street, she had made an effort to regain some of the self-sufficiency the family had enjoyed at Hawthorn, their Winchester estate that was a small working farm. In the lawn on the north side of the house she had the boys prepare a garden. Kenneth was mainly responsible for tending it, but Roy and even little Donald helped. From the garden they gathered peas and beans and cabbages and other vegetables, the surplus of which was stored for winter consumption. There were two apple trees in the yard, too, and the children ate roasted apples all year around.[27]

When an opportunity came in 1864, the family even expanded production beyond their yard. They worked out an arrangement with a farmer south of town who was willing to let them use an acre of his land to grow potatoes in return for a share. Harry and Allan, with some help from Kenneth, planted and worked the patch. The farmer, whose name was Ruffner, prepared the ground with his plow and hauled away the harvested potatoes in his wagon, half to his house and half to the McDonalds'. Cornelia stored some in the attic and the rest in the basement. Those in the attic were ruined by an early freeze in October, but the basement held enough for the family's winter needs.[28]

They also had a steady supply of eggs and milk, for they kept chickens behind the house and had a cow that was, in Kenneth's words, "the best milker in town." The cow was a gift from a cousin of Cornelia who had passed through Lexington with a herd he was trying to keep from the advancing Yankee army. Since the yard was too small to provide enough forage for the cow, it was Kenneth's responsibility to lead her out twice a day to any place he could find some grass growing.[29]

Still, there were a number of things the family had to buy. These included meat, flour, sugar, salt, coffee, tea, and—because they had no churn—butter. Determined to be as thrifty as possible, Cornelia did not depend wholly on the stores in town for these items. Instead, she sent Harry out regularly into the countryside on a borrowed horse to dicker with the farmers for whatever provisions they had to spare.[30]

Friends helped out the McDonalds with food, too. Colonel William Gilham, a professor at the military institute, sent over a quarter of smoked beef in December 1864 that lasted a good while. Other friends made sure the

McDonalds had a Christmas turkey. Mrs. Powell frequently brought over a portion of the coffee, sugar, and molasses that her husband sent her from Richmond, where he had a position with the army commissary department; "molasses for the children," Cornelia noted with gratitude, "was a great treat." Furthermore, as the wife, and now widow, of a soldier, Cornelia was eligible to buy bacon collected by the army impressment agent at the same low price that he paid the farmers for it. The amount she was allowed to purchase was, however, so small that it was useless to try to feed the family with it, so she gave it to the cook as part of her wages.[31]

Cornelia had to hire someone to do the cooking for the same reason she had to pay for carding, spinning, and weaving: as a well-bred woman who had always had money and slaves, she had never learned those skills because she never had to perform those chores. She was pretty much helpless in the kitchen, at least when it came to cooking meat and baking bread.[32]

The cook, a black woman named Susan, was very dependable and much loved by the children. She would often join the boys in singing patriotic songs, her deep voice complementing the boys' higher voices. She was something of an anomaly, however. When the war began, she had been a slave, the property of a family in Charles Town in northern Virginia, but she was eventually liberated by the Union army. For reasons of her own, she went south to rebel territory after her owners lost control of her, rather than stay within the Yankee lines. She was a kind of free slave now, living in a place of her own in Lexington, hiring herself to the McDonalds, and under no white person's control.[33]

The authorities in Lexington were undoubtedly aware of Susan, but they chose to disregard her curious status. Perhaps, as a woman and a sort of voluntary Confederate, she seemed unthreatening. In other respects, however, the authorities took seriously their responsibility to control the slave population. With one exception—a spasm of black mayhem during the Yankee raid in June 1864—there had been no real trouble in the town or county since the war began, but the officials had never relaxed their vigilance.[34]

The magistrates of the county court maintained a patrol system in Rockbridge. Seven companies of men were appointed in each of the county's districts, each company mounting up one night per week to "visit all negro quarters and other places suspected of having therein unlawful assemblies, or such slaves as may stroll from one plantation to another without permission." It was getting harder to man these patrols, however, because so many white men were away in the army. In the Lexington district, which comprised the town and everything within a mile of it, the patrol companies earlier in the war had consisted of a captain and six privates; now, in early 1865, the number of privates was reduced to four.[35]

The magistrates worried not only about keeping the slaves in submission but also about keeping them at work. Rockbridge was not a plantation area—fewer than thirty farms in the county could qualify as plantations—but there were a good number of slaves there (4,000 on the eve of the war, almost one-fourth of the county's population) and a good number of slave owners (about one white family of every four). The county's prosperity depended heavily on the labor extracted from its black workers. As the war went on, however, Rockbridge was stripped of that labor just as it was stripped of its wheat, corn, and livestock. Repeatedly the state and Confederate authorities called on it and other Virginia counties for able-bodied male slaves to work on the fortifications protecting the rebel capital or to do other war-related tasks. These slaves were taken from their masters under the same laws that allowed the impressment of supplies. Moreover, as many as a hundred Rockbridge slaves ran off with the Yankee raiding party in the summer of 1864; after that, some of the county's slave owners, fearing another raid, sold off their slaves or moved them farther south. Now Rockbridge faced what the county officials believed was a dire situation. Many farms and artisan shops were critically short-handed. When the Confederate authorities ordered yet another draft of slaves in late 1864, the Rockbridge magistrates appealed, citing the "great scarcity of labor" in the county. To their relief, Rockbridge was exempted. But in February 1865 another call came, and this time there was no exemption.[36]

The possibility of another visitation by the federal army was on the minds of everyone in the county during the winter of 1864–65, not just the slaveholders. Only a small Confederate military force stood between the upper Shenandoah Valley and the large Union force that occupied the lower valley. This Confederate force—the remains of the so-called Army of the Valley, now consisting of just one small infantry division and some cavalry and artillery—was commanded by General Jubal Early. Few citizens of Rockbridge had much confidence in him. He had led his troops to disaster the previous fall at the battles of Winchester, Fisher's Hill, and Cedar Creek, and the Yankees had taken advantage of these victories to strip the lower valley of crops and livestock and destroy granaries, barns, mills, and anything else that might benefit the rebel army. The lower valley was now a wasteland and the people of the upper valley had no doubt that the same fate was in store for them if the Yankees came their way.[37]

Rockbridge citizens had, in fact, had a small taste of this new hard-war policy of the Northern army in June 1864, when a raiding force of some 18,000 troops under General David Hunter marched into the county and occupied Lexington for several days. Hunter's artillery shelled the town before entering it and his troops subsequently pillaged every house and store. Cornelia, having little in the way of provisions or valuables on hand, did not lose much, but many families were left destitute. Soldiers also looted the Virginia Military Institute—with help from the town's blacks, who, Cornelia remarked, "held high carnival" during the Yankee occupation. Susan, her cook, stole a brocade curtain from the institute and took it home to use as a quilt, although she had to hide it after the Yankees departed and order was restored. Before leaving, General Hunter had the institute burned, along with ex-Governor Letcher's house. Meanwhile, some of his troops roamed the county destroying mills, warehouses, bridges, and ironworks and running off cattle and horses. They also took away with them any slaves who wanted to go.[38]

If the Yankees came again and Early's little remnant of an army failed to stop them, Rockbridge would be at their mercy. A local-defense force was now being organized in the county, but it was symbolic more than anything else: no one really believed it could stand up to a Union force of any size. There were hardly any able-bodied white men of military age left in the county now, at least any who would willingly report for local-defense duty. The ever-tightening Confederate conscription laws had laid claim to almost every man between seventeen and fifty who could walk and hold a musket. The local-defense unit consisted for the most part of a scattering of men already in the army who had been detailed for duty in Rockbridge for one reason or another: quartermaster, commissary, and Nitre and Mining Bureau employees, and conscription officers and guards.[39]

Actually, there were a number of able-bodied, military-age men in the county who were not in uniform, besides the handful exempted from the draft because they did critical war-related work. The authorities did not know exactly how many or exactly where they were, for the men were deserters or draft evaders who were hiding in the remote parts of the county. Some were being shielded and provisioned by family and friends; others, as the editor of Lexington's newspaper put it, were "prowling about . . . and living by robbing loyal citizens." In early January the 5th Virginia Cavalry Regiment rode into Rockbridge with orders to scour the county, round up these skulkers, and put them back in the ranks. But this task proved to be pretty much impossible: the men were simply too elusive. Nor did Confederate president Jefferson Davis's offer of a pardon to deserters who returned to their units by March 1 succeed in luring many from their hiding places.[40]

The problem was not unique to Rockbridge. By early 1865, what was left of the Confederacy's armed forces was melting away from desertion. Spurred by the pleas of their suffering loved ones at home or by their own sense that the cause was now hopeless, rebel soldiers in growing numbers were abandoning their comrades and heading back to their families. Civilian morale was evaporating, too, in Virginia and elsewhere in the Confederacy, as the Confederate states' plight grew more and more desperate.[41]

This crisis of spirit became especially acute in the last four months of 1864, as a succession of disasters shook the Confederacy. First, Atlanta fell to the Union army, then Early's troops were routed in the lower valley, Abraham Lincoln won reelection as U.S. president with a pledge to continue the war until the Southern "rebellion" was stamped out, General William T. Sherman's Union army marched unimpeded through Georgia, and the main Confederate army west of the Appalachians was destroyed in battle.[42]

Defeatism spread with news of these calamities. Added to the rising chorus of hopelessness that could now be heard across the land were the angry voices of those who had decided that, even if the war could still be won, the Confederacy was not worth fighting for. This sentiment was especially common among poor and yeoman families, on whom the burdens of war fell most heavily. When conscription took away many of their men, they struggled to keep their small farms and artisan shops going and they grew resentful of those who had slaves to work for them. They especially resented the big planters who were exempted from the draft in order to supervise their slaves, and others of the elite who managed to secure desk jobs far from the battlefront. Many began to wonder out loud if the Confederacy was governed in their interests or those of the wealthy. The government eventually responded to their protests, revoking many exemptions and setting up relief programs, but these efforts never wholly pacified the plain folk. The feeling persisted among many that it was "a rich man's war and a poor man's fight," and ultimately they turned against their government.[43]

Cornelia had first sensed this moral crisis of the Confederacy during her journey to Richmond to meet Angus. On the boat down the James River she noticed that "every one was sad and anxious" and that among the passengers were "groups of murmuring men." When she eavesdropped on conversations, she was disturbed by what she heard: "I . . . began to realize that the patience of the people was worn out; that their long suffering and endurance was to be depended on no longer." Along with declining faith in victory, she detected deep resentment toward the Confederate government, especially over conscription. She listened as a fellow passenger, a forty-five-year-old conscript on his way to the army, told of a neighbor "who had had two sons killed [in battle], and one a prisoner . . . the father, had been taken as a conscript, and . . . the poor old wife had been left alone in her hut to abide the winter's cold, with no one to provide for or take care of her."[44]

As the winter of 1864–65 went on, there was more bad news to depress Confederate spirits. City after city fell to the invaders: Savannah in late December, Charleston and Wilmington in February. Sherman's army rampaged through South Carolina. Increasingly Cornelia saw around her "discouragement and apprehension."[45]

Yet hope endured among the Confederate faithful. While Robert E. Lee's army was still intact, the war was not lost. Trust in Lee and the Army of Northern Virginia remained strong even as trust in the rebel government dwindled. Former governor Letcher, writing in November 1864 from the house in Lexington that he had moved into after the Yankees burned him out, spoke for many Confederate patriots: with General Lee in command, he said, "I have entire confidence in our ultimate success."[46]

Cornelia herself was, by 1865, undergoing a crisis of patriotic faith. Although she had opposed secession—unlike her husband, who became a rabid secessionist after Lincoln's election in 1860—she ardently embraced the Confederate cause once the war began. She would never forget the thrill she experienced the first time she saw a Confederate flag carried by marching troops. On New Year's Day 1863 she declared herself willing to "give all I have" in defense of the cause, "even my six boys." She chafed under the rule of the "dirty Yankees" who occupied Winchester while she lived there, and she refused to take the Union oath of allegiance they demanded. Even when the war began to turn against the Confederacy in the summer of 1863, Cornelia did not despond. Victory was certain, she believed, because the cause was just: God would not deny the South "triumph over those who would deprive us of our right to do as we pleased with our own."[47]

Her belief that the cause was righteous never wavered, but by 1865 she was distraught with doubt about ultimate victory. Cold logic told her that the Confederacy must soon collapse. But she could not bring herself to renounce the struggle, as so many other Southerners were doing, for defeat was "too horrible to think of." She trembled at the prospect of her beloved South under the heel of "our insolent enemies." With ever greater urgency she prayed for divine favor, until her prayers became "almost a frantic cry to Heaven demanding help and success." And yet she knew that if the war continued, more suffering would be demanded of the Confederate people. She herself, who had suffered so much already, might have to endure worse. Sacrificing her children was no longer just an abstract notion: Harry would turn seventeen in April and would have to go to the army.[48]

These worries were compounded by the constant strain of providing for her family. She was managing, with Susan's help, to put together three meals a day for the children, but just barely. Skimpy portions of coarse food were pretty much the rule at the McDonalds' dining table all through the winter. Cornelia herself was not getting enough to eat: many days she had nothing but bread and coffee. This was not just a matter of self-denial. She was unable to stomach some of the food she had on hand—the beans and the sorghum, for example, which the children did not seem to mind—and undoubtedly her appetite was depressed by her ceaseless anxiety. She had noticed as far back as November, when she glanced in a mirror on the boat to Richmond, how thin her face was. Now she was beginning to look haggard.[49]

The unending labor was wearing her down, too. Her morning and afternoon classes added to what was already an enormous burden of work. Although Susan relieved her of kitchen chores, Cornelia had no servants to assist with the other tasks: laundry, ironing, sewing, dusting, sweeping, mopping, making beds, fetching water, emptying chamber pots. There was no time now for the long, relaxing walks in the countryside with sketchbook in hand that she used to enjoy, and hardly any time for the reading that had always been an important part of her life.[50]

The children helped a great deal around the house, of course, but the smaller ones imposed burdens of their own: they had to be bathed, dressed, and constantly watched. Roy, who seemed always to be getting into some trouble, was especially exhausting, and Cornelia often ran out of patience with her eight-year-old "imp of mischief." Harry, however, eventually stepped in to relieve his mother of this annoyance. He began taking Roy with him to his wood-chopping job and keeping him there all day. Roy loved it, especially on days when snow lay deep on the ground: because he was too little to slog through it, Harry would carry him to work and back on his shoulders.[51]

As busy and tired as she and the children were that winter, Cornelia nevertheless insisted that the long-established rituals of the family be observed. Each morning before breakfast they gathered; kneeling on the floor with her face lifted and her eyes closed, Cornelia would lead the children in devotions from the *Book of Common Prayer.* Before climbing into bed at night, the children would say their own prayers while Cornelia watched and listened. On Sunday mornings there were Bible lessons for the little ones, after which the whole clan marched off together to church.[52]

The church services helped lift Cornelia's spirits. And there were other moments of joy in her life during that bleak winter. She especially treasured the family get-togethers at home in the evenings. The children would assemble as darkness fell, gathering around her while she sewed by candlelight. By the time Harry and Roy came in, rosy-faced and breathless, the others would all be chatting and laughing in front of the fireplace. Even on her worst days, Cornelia found the merriment contagious.[53]

Often the family was joined in the evenings by friends. Mrs. Powell called frequently, sometimes bearing little gifts of food and always ready to lend Cornelia a sympathetic ear. Another regular caller was young Lottie Myers, "a pure and lovely Christian" who comforted Cornelia by reminding her of God's promise to the widow and the orphan: "Your bread and your water shall be sure." Ann Pendleton stopped by often, too, until the end of January, when she and her oldest daughter departed for Petersburg for an extended visit with General Pendleton.[54]

There were signs of cheer not just at Cornelia's house but throughout Lexington and Rockbridge County that winter, despite the hard times and the news from the front. "Crowds of young people pass from house to house," noted the town's Presbyterian minister, "with little to eat and less to wear, and spend the entire night in dancing and revelry." Dour Calvinist that he was, he decried these and the other instances of godless gaiety he observed, some of them fueled by "intoxicating liquors." The dancing and drinking continued despite his jeremiads, however, and so did the sleighing parties that appeared spontaneously that winter whenever there was a good snowfall.[55]

In the last days of February, Rockbridge citizens spotted flocks of wild geese flying northward. "This," the editor of the *Lexington Gazette* reminded his readers, "has always been regarded as an infallible sign of the breaking up of winter." Spring would bring longer days, warmer skies, and greener woods and fields—that much was certain; what else it might bring, for good or ill, could only be guessed. It would be the fifth spring of the Confederate States of America. Cornelia McDonald and many others wondered if it would be the last.[56]

JOHN ROBERTSON

WHEN THE MORNING SUN BROKE OVER EAST TENNESSEE AT A LITTLE after seven on New Year's day 1865, it illuminated a silent, snow-blanketed landscape. It was a bitterly cold Sunday—"as cold as it ever gets in this climate," recalled John Robertson.[1]

John was staying at the farm of his uncle and aunt, Thomas and Kate Collier, nine miles west of Knoxville. He had arrived a day or two earlier in a borrowed carriage that he had driven forty miles from Roane County, where he had lived since October. He brought along a large batch of cigars he had made. Although he chewed tobacco, he did not smoke; he intended to sell the cigars in Knoxville.[2]

At this point in his life John was a seeker. But it was not riches he sought, nor was it adventure. Although he was only eighteen, he had seen, as a rebel soldier and home guardsman, all the excitement and danger he cared to see. What he thirsted for now was spiritual fulfillment. He would not rest, he vowed to himself, until he became "changed in heart."[3]

On New Year's day, John Robertson went, along with some of his cousins, to a church not far from the Colliers' farm. The icy air pierced his clothing to the skin and stung his face and lungs all the way to the church, but he nevertheless went gladly and hopefully. He came away disappointed, however. There was no inspiring sermon that day to help open his heart to Jesus. Instead, there was a contentious discourse by a Baptist preacher named Miller on the necessity of baptism and the foolishness of those who opposed it. It "rather wounded my feelings," recalled John, who held contrary views on that particular point of doctrine. When fellow worshipers urged him to go forward to the "anxious seat" with the others who were seeking salvation,

John declined, and during the remainder of the service he sat sulkily in his pew. Afterward he felt guilty for "refusing to do what was for my own ben[e]fit."[4]

The next day he had some work to do. He and his friend George Whillock, who had come up from Roane County with him, had to get the carriage fixed. It had broken down during their journey as they were climbing the steep bank of the Tennessee River, just after crossing on the ferry at Loudon. Had it not broken down there, it would undoubtedly have done so somewhere else along the Loudon-Knoxville road. In normal times this road was one of the most dependable in east Tennessee, but it had fallen into disrepair over the last few years, like so many other things in this war-ravaged region. It was washed out in some places and deeply rutted in others, a victim of the marching of armies and the disruption of local government. John and George managed to patch up the carriage sufficiently with leather straps to get to Uncle Thomas's, but they knew it would never make it back to Roane without repairs by a blacksmith.[5]

The fact that the two young men had encountered no hazards on their journey other than ruts and mud was, John knew, a lucky thing. Most of east Tennessee's roads these days were not only dilapidated but dangerous. The Yankee army had wrested control of most of the region from the rebels in the fall of 1863—to the great joy of the unionist majority, who had waited impatiently while the Yankees conquered the other sections of the state—and there were now ten thousand federal occupation troops stationed in the region, distributed among the larger towns. But the Northern occupiers could exert only limited authority outside these garrisoned posts. Much of the countryside remained unpacified, crawling with secessionist guerrillas and frequently raided by Confederate cavalry. Unionist guerrillas were likewise on the prowl, terrorizing their secessionist neighbors. Bandits roamed around, too, preying on unionist and secessionist families alike. If John Robertson—a former Confederate soldier who had taken the oath of allegiance to the United States to get out of prison—should fall into the hands of any of these armed bands, he would be in extreme danger. He knew, however, that the Loudon-Knoxville road was considerably safer than most, for it was anchored at each end by a Yankee garrison and well patrolled. Nevertheless, he had made sure to pack his pistol along with his cigars.[6]

There was a blacksmith's shop two miles from the Colliers' farm. John and George drove the carriage there on January 2 only to find that the blacksmith was not in. John, who had picked up a smattering of all sorts of skills while growing up in Greene County, was undeterred. He and George fired up the forge and then "went to work and fixed [the carriage] ourselves."[7]

George then took the carriage back to the Colliers' while John walked a bit farther to see some friends, the Browns. He had lived with this family on their little farm for a time in late 1863 and early 1864, while he was employed in supplying firewood to the Yankee troops in Knoxville. He remembered the Browns fondly, for they had been "kind and good" to him, and he did not want to leave the neighborhood without paying his respects.[8]

As he approached their house he saw John Brown, the head of the family, on the porch. Brown spotted him and said, "*Well*, if there isn't John, and I was dreaming of him last night; [I dreamed] he was here." The whole family greeted him warmly and asked many questions; they were especially curious to know if he "was still a seeker of religion." When he assured them he was, they told him there was a revival in progress at a nearby schoolhouse. John Brown, who was a minister as well as a farmer, was leading the revival. The Browns begged John Robertson to stay with them while the good work continued.[9]

"Their commencing on me so sud[d]enly, gave me a great sho[c]k," John later wrote. "I knew nothing of the [revival] till I got to Brown's." He was stunned, too, by John Brown's prescient dream. Surely there was something more at work here than mere coincidence. "It seemed that by Providence I had been thrown here."[10]

He accepted the Browns' invitation to stay and that night went to the schoolhouse. When the call came for "mourners" to come forward to the anxious seat, Parson Brown approached him. "John," he said, "no doubt you have a good Mother now at home praying for you." These words struck John with great force. His mother, whom he revered, had long worried about his soul and "had sent up to the throne of God many petitions for me." Now, as her image appeared in his mind, "I felt my sins more . . . than ever." He stood and walked forward to take his place.[11]

At this stage of his spiritual life, John was, as he and other evangelicals expressed it, "deeply convicted." He had searched his heart and seen himself for what he really was: a sinner, repugnant in the eyes of God and unworthy of salvation. He was sick with guilt and remorse. His only hope was that God would see fit to forgive his sins, change his heart, and grant the gift of eternal life.[12]

The catalogue of John's sins was not a long one, but it was sufficient to damn him if God's grace was not forthcoming. By his own reckoning, the "wickedest day" he had ever known was one in 1863 when he stole a horse from a unionist neighbor in Greene County and later got drunk and threw up. He had robbed unionists on other occasions, too, when he was in the home guard, and he had played cards. While in the Confederate army he had gotten in the habit of swearing; and he had once stolen a rifle from a fellow soldier. He had obeyed all the other commandments, however, except that he might have killed some Yankees in combat. He did not know: there was so much smoke and confusion on the battlefield that only God could tell if any of the bullets he fired had found their mark.[13]

His sinfulness now oppressed him like an enormous weight on his back. Seated prayerfully on the anxious seat, he awaited the advent of the divine hand that would lift the burden. But it did not come. "I struggled hard, but to my grief I could find no relief."[14]

He returned to the Browns' home that night disappointed but undaunted. He was certain that a sign had been given him when he arrived at the Browns', and he would not throw away this opportunity. "For several days I struggled in this way. I could neither eat nor sleep." Each morning and evening he made his way to the schoolhouse. All around him "a mighty work was being done." Many of those present were seized by the spirit and transformed on the spot. At times John would leave the crowded schoolhouse for "secret prayer," hoping to find in private what eluded him in public. But this, too, availed him nothing. "[S]till I would cling to the world with one hand and reach for mercy with the other. . . . Thus I suffered under the load of guilt and sin for sever[a]l days."[15]

On the morning of January 10 he rose, ate breakfast with the Browns, and then retired to pray until time for the meeting. More fervently than ever he offered himself. "I made a bold struggle to give myself whol[l]y up to God. I vowed to spend the remainder of my days in his cause if he would only give me evidence of my pardon."[16]

It was rainy that day, and the path to the schoolhouse was muddy. John went "with a sad and weary heart." His earnest quest had so far gained him nothing but a heavier burden of guilt. He entered the building and took his seat with the mourners. As the service got under way, he prayed.[17]

It happened about noon:

> I felt that a beam of light had entered my sad and aching heart, that my weight of guilt was removed. . . . I ventured to rise. Uncle T[homas] Collier

> was there; the first man I noticed was him drawing his overcoat; he sprang forward and gathered me. This was a time of rejoicing. I was perfectly calm, no ways excited. I was greatly rejoiced, but kept it to myself. I was not of that disposition to make a noise, though it was a bright day to me. This joy did not come in the way expected. "The fire, wind and earthquake passed but the Lord was not in them; then came a Still Small Voice."[18]

He stayed with the Browns for another two weeks and went to the schoolhouse every day and night, "not feeling willing to leave the happiest place I had ever seen." No longer chained to the mourners' bench, he joined the chorus. "All the singers was worn out by the almost constant singing. I done the best I could for one week; then I was worn out too." The revival ended twenty-two days after it began. Sixty-four conversions was the final tally, sixty-four men, women, boys, and girls who, in John's words, "had been made to rejoice by the goodness of God."[19]

In the days and weeks following his conversion, John felt nearly overwhelmed by the sense of transformation. "It was now to me, as begin[n]ing to live again. I was now entering on a new life." He knew it would not necessarily be a comfortable life: "my cross would at times be hard to bear." There was always the danger that he might "backslide." So he continued to pray hard, "asking for strength and aid to bear me on through life and to enable me to resist the many temptations I knew would beset me."[20]

Almost forgotten in the euphoria of his conversion was the errand that had brought him to Knox County: selling his cigars. George Whillock had long since returned to Roane County with the carriage; and so, after bidding the Browns farewell, John gathered up his wares and made his way alone the few miles to Knoxville. He was disappointed to find that there was a cigar-making establishment in town and all the stores were well stocked with that particular commodity. "I could not sell cigars in K[noxville] for any price." As it happened, however, Uncle Thomas maintained a little grocery store in town and was looking for someone to clerk there. John, who had no urgent need to return to Roane right away, agreed to work in the store for a while.[21]

He had spent time in Knoxville before, first as a Confederate soldier and later, after the town fell to the Yankees, as a prisoner of war and as a supplier for the garrison troops. The grim ugliness of the place was therefore no surprise to him. The town, which sat on the north bank of the Tennessee River and in normal times could boast a certain charm, had suffered badly since the war began, thanks mainly to military occupation by one side and then the other. "[A] mass of dismal, dilapidated, weather-beaten buildings," is how one visitor described Knoxville in early 1865, " . . . with narrow, muddy, filthy streets."[22]

Surrounding the town was a ring of defensive works consisting of deep trenches and stout breastworks punctuated by hilltop redoubts with cannons. In the area between the edge of town and the circle of fortifications, virtually every blade of grass and every stalk of wheat and corn had been trampled into the mud. Beyond the fortifications, for hundreds of yards, every tree had been cut down and hauled away to provide a clear field of fire. In these barren stretches could be seen the shallow graves of Confederate soldiers who had died during the rebel army's abortive attempt to recapture the town in late 1863. Even in the summer there was little greenery visible in or around Knoxville. It was a hideously scarred landscape painted in shades of gray and dull brown, and now the bleak winter weather made the scene even drearier.[23]

The town was a depressing sight, but at the same time it was bustling. The population, about 5,300 before the war, was close to 8,000 now, not counting the troops. There were thousands of blue-clad soldiers, some billeted in town, others camped around the perimeter, and their presence was pervasive. Many of the town's buildings had been seized for army use and new ones had been constructed. The Lamar House on Gay Street, once Knoxville's best hotel, was now quartering troops. The Deaf and Dumb Asylum had been turned into an army hospital. There were two military prisons and a number of warehouses and repair shops. The commander of the District of East Tennessee, Brigadier General Davis Tillson, had his headquarters in Knoxville. And the U.S. Sanitary Commission, a Northern benevolent association dedicated to the welfare of Union soldiers, had an office in town.[24]

The wartime population boom and the Yankees' appropriation of buildings conspired to create a serious shortage of living accommodations. "Every house, stable, kitchen and shanty in the town is occupied," the local newspaper reported. John Robertson was fortunate to be able to room in the store where he worked, for lodging in Knoxville was very expensive. In fact, everything in town was expensive. Because so little food or other provisions could be drawn from the ravaged country around Knoxville, the bulk of the town's supplies had to come from the North by way of Nashville and Chattanooga—a long, costly trip by rail and water. High prices were at least partly responsible for the rash of thefts in Knoxville. As the newspaper noted, thieves were "digging under smoke-houses, robbing corn-cribs, breaking into stores, and stealing clothes off of lines and fences."[25]

No one broke into John's store while he was there, but he had other annoyances to contend with. The cold, for one thing. The temperature remained unusually low and the store was poorly heated. "I suffered no little, at night," he recalled. The late hours kept by some of the townsfolk interrupted his slumber, too: "The City way of sleeping did not suit me." He was particularly disturbed by the goings-on at Reed & Riley's opera house, which was right next to the store and featured musical shows or plays every night. Not only did the place generate a lot of noise and violate the sanctity of the Sabbath, but it also put temptation in John's path. He was admittedly "fond of places of amusement," but he believed them to be, like novels, a worldly indulgence that distracted one from the course of righteousness. The opera house beckoned seductively, but John remained strong: "I found it very hard to resist it, but did."[26]

Another vexation was that Knoxville was full of people he detested. It was not the Yankee soldiers who bothered him: he had made his peace with the invaders, and after he took the oath, they let him alone. His problem was the native unionists and the blacks.

John had never given much thought to the great principles at stake in the war. His family took their stand with the Confederacy and that was enough for him. The war he had known was not so much an ideological or sectional conflict as it was a community conflict, and the real enemy to him was not the people of the North but his unionist neighbors.

Now John was forced to rub shoulders with unionists every day, for Knoxville was crowded with them. Of course, every citizen in the town was at least nominally a unionist, including John. The federal authorities allowed no one to live there who refused to take the oath. But John and others who took the oath reluctantly spurned the label of unionist—that belonged to those who took it gladly.[27]

John did not regard all unionists as enemies. There were many who tried to stay on peaceful terms with neighbors and kinsmen who opposed them politically, just as there were many secessionists who tried to do the same. Both Thomas Collier and John Brown were in fact unionists, and they had never been anything but kind to John Robertson. But many others were unforgiving. It was unionists of that sort who had tried to kill John from ambush, who had plundered his parents' farm, who had kidnapped him and turned him over to the federal army, and who had run him off from his teaching job with threats of violence. In their eyes, of course, John deserved everything he got, for he had persecuted unionists with equal zeal. They had no forgiveness in their hearts for him and others like him; and he had none for them.[28]

In the year and a half since the Yankees captured Knoxville, the town's unionist population had swelled. The new arrivals were mostly refugees from outlying areas where rebel guerrillas were active or from the northeastern corner of the state, which was still controlled by the Confederate army. More were straggling in every day and they were a pitiful sight. "It is sickening to the heart," wrote one Knoxvillian, "to stand here and look at . . . men, women, and children, coming in through the mud and rain . . . driven from their homes. . . . [T]he tales they tell [of persecution by rebels] are heart-rending." Some came with a little property they had salvaged—a wagonload of clothes and furniture, a few head of cattle—but most were destitute. Because the town could absorb no more, General Tillson had ordered the construction of a refugee shelter on the south side of the river.[29]

The plight of the refugees had stirred some fellow unionists to come to their aid. In early 1864 they organized the East Tennessee Relief Association and sent agents into the North to solicit contributions. Northerners responded generously. The relief association maintained an office in Knoxville where food and clothing shipped from the North were doled out to needy refugees. The office also operated as an employment agency, finding jobs for refugees who wanted to stay in Knoxville and work.[30]

One of the founders of the relief association was Knoxville's most prominent unionist, William G. Brownlow, known to all as Parson Brownlow. He had begun his career decades earlier as a hellfire-and-brimstone Methodist circuit preacher, but later he turned to politics and journalism and became the Democrat-bashing editor of the *Knoxville Whig*. His no-holds-barred speeches and editorial diatribes were famous even beyond east Tennessee. When the war came, he took aim at the secessionists and made himself so obnoxious to the Confederate authorities that they shut down his press, threw him in prison, threatened to hang him, and finally exiled him to the North. After Knoxville fell to the Yankee army, Brownlow returned. He resurrected his newspaper, renaming it the *Whig and Rebel Ventilator*, and set about to make life miserable for his enemies. The paper's columns blazed with anger and vengefulness. Editor Brownlow openly incited unionists to retaliate for wrongs suffered at the hands of their rebel neighbors. When criticized for his vindictiveness, he was unapologetic: "If we have been instrumental," he wrote in an editorial published shortly before John Robertson arrived in town, "in bringing to a violent death any one or more of the God-forsaken and hell-deserving persecutors of Union families in East Tennessee, we thank God most devoutly. . . . Shoot them down like dogs, is our advice."[31]

John and other rebels who had taken the oath were, in Brownlow's eyes, among the God-forsaken and hell-deserving, for the parson regarded no one as a friend who had not been a staunch unionist since the beginning of the war. His extreme views were too much for some east Tennessee unionists, but they carried great weight, for Brownlow was powerful. In addition to controlling the *Whig and Rebel Ventilator*, he was the U.S. Treasury agent for east Tennessee, with broad authority to regulate trade and confiscate rebel property. Soon he would command even greater authority. Delegates representing the state's unionists had recently gathered in Nashville for a constitutional convention that marked the first step toward restoring civil government in Tennessee and getting the state readmitted to the Union. The delegates had nominated Brownlow to be governor of the restored state. An election would be held in March, and the parson was certain to win.[32]

Had Brownlow known John Robertson and been able to read his mind, his suspicions about oath-taking rebels would only have been confirmed. In his heart, John had never renounced the Confederate cause. Although his life had taken a new course and he no longer had any desire to serve in the rebel ranks or wreak vengeance on his unionist enemies, he still hoped to see a victorious Confederate States of America. He could not say so publicly, of course. And when Yankees were around, he had to keep his mouth shut about another matter he had strong opinions on: the Emancipation Proclamation.[33]

John hated blacks. He hated them with a visceral passion that would have puzzled whites from other parts of the South where blacks were more numerous. John's family, like the vast majority of east Tennessee families, owned no slaves; and in the community where John grew up, as in most other east Tennessee communities, blacks were few. Virtually all Southern whites agreed that blacks were inferior and slavery justified. But those like John who had little day-to-day contact with blacks generally sneered at the racial paternalism manifested by many whites and instead regarded blacks with loathing.[34]

Back in December 1863, when John was living in the Knoxville area and chopping wood for the federal army, he had had an encounter with blacks that left him literally nauseated. He had been assigned to a work gang that included not only Irish and German immigrants, which was bad enough in John's view, but also several men whom he described as "the greasiest looking nig[g]ers I ever saw." Just being around them made him sick. He refused to eat or sleep with the gang, and at the first opportunity he quit the job and found another.[35]

Such intense racism was common to east Tennessee's secessionists and unionists alike. Parson Brownlow himself was, before the war, one of the most vocal negrophobes and proslavery spokesmen in the South. The parson now endorsed emancipation as a way to punish rebels, but he still had no love for blacks. John Robertson not only hated them but also wished earnestly for their continued enslavement.[36]

There were more blacks in Knoxville now than John had ever seen in his life. Hundreds had come in from the countryside, having run away from their owners. Although President Abraham Lincoln had, for political reasons, exempted Tennessee from the Emancipation Proclamation, slavery was now extinct pretty much everywhere in the state because the federal military authorities refused to act to preserve it. Even unionist masters were turned away when they appealed to the Yankees for help in disciplining their slaves or retrieving runaways.[37]

The fugitive slaves who came into Knoxville joined the small number of blacks native to the town, some of whom had been free before the war. There were a good number of other blacks to be seen on the streets of town as well: they wore blue uniforms and belonged to the 1st U.S. Colored Heavy Artillery. The regiment had been organized in Knoxville about a year earlier and served as part of the garrison force. It was one of many black units mustered into the Union army since President Lincoln authorized the recruitment of blacks in 1863.[38]

If runaway slaves and black soldiers were not enough to turn John's stomach, Knoxville also had a black school with a black teacher. His name was Alfred Anderson and he had been born free in the nearby town of Maryville in 1832. Since 1849 he had lived in Knoxville and for the last four years had served as pastor of a little congregation of black Methodists. Anderson had only "a smaul education," as he put it; he could "Read Rite And A littel mour." But he had great compassion for those of his people who had been denied even that. He established the school in August 1864 to help bring the blessing of literacy to his "down troden race." About a hundred children were now enrolled. Classes were held in a building that Anderson rented for fifty dollars a month; it also served as his church. The school was run on a shoestring, for only about half the students paid any tuition; "the uthers," Anderson explained, "aint Abel." He was hoping for financial help from one of the Northern benevolent societies that had taken up the cause of educating the South's blacks.[39]

All things considered, Knoxville was about as awful a place as John Robertson could imagine, and he did not tarry long there. He could have stayed on, had he wanted to, for Uncle Thomas needed him in the store. And there was other work available: the cigar manufacturer in town was advertising for help, and John had learned to make a pretty good cigar. But he was ready to get back to Roane County.[40]

About the last day of January, John said good-bye to Uncle Thomas and made his way to the railroad station at the north end of town. He boarded a train that took him southwest on the tracks of the East Tennessee & Georgia Railroad. From the window of his car, he saw a frozen landscape. Many ponds and streams were solid with ice, an uncommon sight in that part of the country. Some twelve miles down the line, near Concord, the train passed a spot where a terrible accident had occurred just a day or two earlier. A locomotive had thrown an axle and derailed with its cars, killing four passengers and injuring sixteen. All twenty were U.S. soldiers, members of a detachment that was being rushed from Knoxville down to Athens, Tennessee, to rescue a garrison under attack by Confederate cavalry.[41]

John's train continued on, to Lenoir's Station and then Loudon, where it crossed the river on a long trestle heavily guarded by Northern troops. When the train pulled into the village of Philadelphia, a little over thirty miles from Knoxville, he got off. From here it was a twelve-mile walk to the farm of another uncle, Allen Robertson, where John had made his home since October.[42]

There was a tavern in Philadelphia, but John did not stop there. He walked on for three miles until he came to a house that he knew to be the home of some distant relatives of his. Although he had never met them, he decided to knock on the door and introduce himself. They were hospitable and invited him to stay overnight. But John wanted to get home. After visiting a while and warming himself by the fire, he pushed on.[43]

It was around five o'clock, nearly nightfall, when he reached the Blue Springs community. Here he stopped to see some friends, who informed him that a revival was in progress at Blue Springs Church. "This was joyful news

8. This modern church stands on the site of Blue Springs Church of Roane County, Tennessee, which John Robertson attended in 1865. In the woods just behind the church, John retired for private prayer.

to me," John recalled. "[T]here was where I wanted to be." But it was getting late, and so he pressed on the short distance to Uncle Allen's.[44]

Allen Robertson, a brother of John's father, was fifty-three years old; his wife, Mary, was nineteen years younger. They had six children. Until 1862 the family had lived in Greene County. Like John's father, Uncle Allen was a man of modest means, a small farmer who never held slaves and who lived by the sweat of his own brow. One of the few luxuries he enjoyed was a carriage that he had bought just before Christmas for eighty dollars and had let John use for the trip to Knoxville. Uncle Allen and Aunt Mary had been good to John, taking him into their home after he was driven from his teaching job. Now they welcomed him back after his month-long stay in Knox County.[45]

After supper on the night following his arrival, John set out for Blue Springs Church, a mile and a half away. He found a large crowd gathered there, including many friends and acquaintances. They knew of his spiritual quest and wondered why he now declined to go forward to the mourners' bench. "They soon learned the cause," John wrote, "and came to me one by one to give me their hand in token of their love, and to welcome me into the glorious work."[46]

The revival at Blue Springs Church continued for two more weeks, and John went every day and night. Sometimes he sang with the choir; at other times he encouraged the mourners or went outside to pray in secret, "bowed on my knees, in a piece of wood just above the church, earnestly beseeching God to do a mighty work among us." When the revival ended, he met with the minister in charge and was formally accepted as a member of the Methodist church.[47]

During those weeks and for the remainder of February, John thought hard about his future. He had known for some time what he was moving away from: not only his sinful past but also the war, which he was doing everything he could to avoid. He had never been exactly sure, however, what he was moving toward—until now: "Ever since my conversion I had felt it my unavoidable duty to prepare myself for the Ministry. . . . [T]o serve God acceptab[l]y I must devote myself to his cause." He worried, however, that he was "unworthy of the position. . . . I was not well read. . . . I had read history, but not religious works." On the other hand, he felt he had a "tolerable good English education" and was young enough to have time to learn more. "[C]onsequently I resolved to commence preparation for the Ministry."[48]

Uncle Allen and Aunt Mary were willing to help. John would be welcome to stay on with them while he studied. They would make no demands on him, even during the busy spring planting season.[49]

The unanswered question was whether John would be able to pursue his calling in peace. Roane County at this time was safer than many other sections of east Tennessee, but it was by no means a haven from the war. Just days before John returned from Knoxville, there had been a fierce shoot-out between a Yankee scouting party and a squad of rebel cavalry near Kingston, the county seat. Other armed and mounted parties—guerrillas or perhaps bandits—had been spotted in the area lately, too.[50]

John borrowed some books from the Methodist preacher and began his studies. He now knew what path he would follow. He did not know what lay along that path, however; and so he kept his pistol close at hand.[51]

SAMUEL AGNEW

EARLY ON NEW YEAR'S DAY 1865, IN THE SOUTHEASTERN CORNER of Tippah County, Mississippi, word spread that the Yankees were coming. The citizens of the community had heard such rumors dozens of times over the last three years. More often than not these alarms proved false, but no one was willing to gamble on this one. Men and women scurried to hide their valuables and carry the news to their neighbors, shattering the stillness of this clear, cold Sunday morning.[1]

When the report reached the Agnew plantation, Samuel Agnew knew what to do. The thirty-one-year-old minister and his family were veterans of many Yankee alarms. With the help of their slaves, Sam and his father rounded up the mules and cattle and headed for a patch of woods a mile and a half away, beyond the fields that lay waiting for the plows and harrows of spring. The woods of Tippah County were dense with pine and oak; in many places there was a thick undergrowth of blackjack, too. Even in the leafless winter, men and livestock could safely hide from Yankee scouts.[2]

Sam had an appointment to preach that day at the home of a family named Corder, but now he wondered if he should risk going. It was dangerous for a man to be accosted by the Yankees, even a noncombatant like Sam. Federal raiding parties sometimes took men away as prisoners on suspicion of being guerrillas or simply to keep them out of the hands of the rebel army's conscription agents. Sam and his father, Enoch, always camped out in the woods with their animals during Yankee alarms, taking shelter in a tent made of quilts. Because the enemy soldiers did not, as a rule, bother women and children, the rest of the Agnew family—Sam's mother, his teenage siblings, and his wife—would usually stay at home and summon Sam and Enoch when the scare was over.[3]

Anno Domini 1865

January 1 New Years day - Sabbath. In the good Providence of God
I am allowed to enter another year
May God guide and bless me and mine
this year - The day has been clear and
cool. To-night or rather late this evening
it has clouded - Mr Holland came over
early on his way to Corden. He brings news
of the approach of the Yankees from towards
Ripley. They are reported to have been
at Fryars (5 miles this side of Ripley) yesterday at one o'clock. We took our stock
to the woods - Holland & I rode over to
Corden and I found a respectable congregation there being no rumors of Yankees
on that side. Preached from Phil 2:23
Came on back. dine at Uncle Jos then to
camps in the woods, where we remained
till late in the evening - when we returned
home, having concluded that the alarm
was false because no Yankees have yet appeared in the neighborhood. To-day
we hear that Hoods army is not so much
demoralised as we hear. John Crockett
and Col Tison is at home. They report
that Thomas pursued Hood no farther than
to Columbia. Some think Hood will remain
at Corinth. others that he will retreat to Tupelo

9. Sam Agnew's diary entry for January 1, 1865

That morning's report put the Yankees just this side of Ripley, the county seat, which was about fifteen miles northwest of the Agnew plantation. The Corder home was in the opposite direction, so Sam decided to take a chance and go. There he found "a respectable congregation," as he later noted in his diary, meaning a good-sized one. The rumor of a Yankee raid had not, he learned, reached that neighborhood. Of course, a respectable congregation those days was considerably smaller than what he had been used to before the war, what with so many men away in the army or dead.[4]

Sam preached from Philippians 2:23, where Paul speaks of his faithful assistant Timotheus: "Him therefore I hope to send presently, as soon as I shall see how it will go with me." Afterward, he mounted up and headed back toward the plantation. On the way, he stopped at the home of his aunt and uncle, Mary and Joseph Agnew, and ate dinner with them. Then he made his way to the campsite in the woods and joined his father. Shortly after dusk the two men doused their fire, broke camp, and led the animals back home, "having concluded," Sam explained, "that the alarm was false because no Yankees have yet appeared."[5]

Sam wrote in his diary that night, as usual, just before going to bed. He began with a prayer: "January 1, New Year's day Sabbath. In the good Providence of God I am allowed to enter another year. May God guide and bless me and mine this year."[6]

In the weeks that followed there were signs that God had indeed blessed Sam and his family, at least in one respect. Unlike a lot of other Tippah countians, the Agnews were able to procure enough food to get them through the winter. Although the devastating Yankee raid in June 1864 had stripped them of every ounce of stored provisions, it had not left them destitute. They had managed to hide their beef cattle and work animals before the Yankees arrived (the hogs were already safe in the woods, for they roamed free until fattening time in the fall). The growing crops—corn, wheat, cotton—had suffered some damage in the battle that raged across the plantation, but were mostly unharmed; and the same was true of the garden vegetables. A good deal of fencing had been torn down, but Sam's father immediately put the slaves to work rebuilding it so that livestock and wildlife could not invade the fields and garden. The harvest that fall was not bountiful, but it was sufficient.[7]

Once the harvesting was finished, all hands worked to convert the crops and livestock into food for the table. The corn was shucked and, along with the threshed wheat, hauled to a miller for grinding. The cotton was ginned and baled, then stored until it could be sold or traded for food and other necessities. Because beef was hard to preserve, the Agnews generally slaughtered steers individually as needed. Pork was another matter, however. They were accustomed to laying in a year's supply after rounding up and fattening the hogs, but that required two things: cold weather and salt.[8]

The Confederacy's salt shortage had plagued farmers in Tippah since the war began, but this winter there was some relief. Mississippi state authorities had procured a large supply from the saltworks in south Alabama and made it available for purchase or trade at various depots. On December 15 Enoch dispatched a wagon to Guntown, a station on the Mobile & Ohio Railroad nine miles away. The wagon carried 404 pounds of flour; it returned with 195 pounds of salt. Five days later, after a cold snap set in, Enoch and the blacks began the process of slaughtering, butchering, salting, and packing. Sam joined in, this being one of the few plantation tasks for which he was needed. They killed fifteen hogs that day, hurrying to preserve the meat before the temperature rose. More cool weather on January 5 brought an opportunity to kill another seven.[9]

The Agnews were among the fortunate, for many in Tippah had been hit harder than they by the Yankees and now faced a winter of hunger. The county government was doing what it could to help them, but it was not enough. The local authorities levied a tax-in-kind and distributed whatever provisions they collected to the needy. The problem was that there was so little to go around; few families had much of a surplus. Certainly the Agnews did not. When the tax collector came to their home in early February and demanded his tithe, they grew concerned: "This tax in kind bears hard on us," Sam wrote. "We have no corn or wheat to spare."[10]

Tax collectors and Yankee raiders were not the only ones scouring the area for provisions. The rebel army's impressment officers were also active. Farmers dreaded seeing them coming almost as much as they dreaded the Yankees. Even when they operated strictly according to army regulations—which limited the amount they could seize and mandated compensation—their visitations could be ruinous. Unfortunately for Tippah County residents, northern Mississippi was "defended" by a number of ill-disciplined rebel cavalry outfits that habitually took what they pleased with no regard for regulations. "I call this an outrage," Sam had fumed on one occasion when rebel troopers rode off with a neighbor's mule, "not an impressment but a robbery." Even as the citizens prayed to be spared any more Yankee incursions, they prayed for deliverance from their own troops.[11]

As the winter of 1864–65 progressed, the food shortage in the county became acute. In mid-February Sam learned from his Uncle Joseph, one of the officials responsible for provisioning the poor, that the tax-in-kind receipts would fall far short of what was needed to prevent starvation. "The prospect," said Sam, "is gloomy now." There was talk of sending county agents south to try to purchase provisions in the less-ravaged sections of the state. No one knew what else could be done. It was possible to smuggle goods in from Yankee-occupied Tennessee in exchange for cotton, but only in limited amounts and at great expense and risk.[12]

Hauling provisions into the county from whatever direction was very difficult now, thanks to deteriorating roads and demolished bridges. Even in the best of times, Tippah was a rough place for a loaded wagon. Most of the roads were nothing more than narrow paths cut through the dense woods that dominated the landscape. Mud collected at every low spot along the way whenever it rained, and where streams crossed, the roads often washed out altogether. The county government had built bridges across the major streams, but many of these were now just piles of charred or chopped lumber, destroyed by Yankee raiders as they withdrew or by rebel troops trying to obstruct the raiders. No road maintenance or bridge repair had been done for years, so disrupted was the county by repeated enemy invasions.[13]

The wretched roads of Tippah were unusually crowded in the weeks following New Year's day 1865. There were a lot of rebel army supply wagons to be seen, mostly moving south, and Rebel infantrymen passing in every direction, many alone or in small groups. Sam questioned everyone he met about this and finally pieced together what was going on. It was bad news. Confederate general John B. Hood's Army of Tennessee had suffered disaster in a battle at Nashville in December and was now in headlong retreat. The army was not just defeated, it seemed, but wrecked. Hood had ordered what was left of it to concentrate at Tupelo, twenty miles south of the Agnew plantation.[14]

What Sam heard and saw of the condition of Hood's troops was particularly disturbing. They were scattered, demoralized, famished, and "in a bad fix, without shoes or clothes. . . . The men that I have seen are lean, ragged and jaded." He felt sorry for these "Poor fellows," but at the same time they made him uneasy. Hungry men were liable to do anything if they were not strictly disciplined, and many of those Sam saw were under no officer's control. He feared especially the coarse, lower-class men so numerous among the army's rank and file. As he had remarked on another occasion, after Confederate troops had marched past his plantation and looted one of the slave cabins, "Some of them are rough cases. We have in our army some [men] as vile . . . as the Yankees."[15]

It was certain that many of the starving ragamuffins now tramping through the countryside had no intention of rejoining their units, at least not any time soon. Whether they could stay out of the clutches of the rebel authorities would remain to be seen. The cavalry that patrolled northern Mississippi kept a sharp lookout for stragglers, deserters, and draft-evaders. And men of military age were conspicuous these days, for there were few left on the home front.

Although notoriously inefficient in many ways, the Confederate government rigorously enforced the draft. Sam had seen firsthand the thoroughness of rebel conscription. He could not count the number of times he had looked up from his reading or writing to see a squad of cavalry passing by on a man-hunting expedition. And the conscriptors were as pitiless as they were diligent. In November 1863, two men whom Sam knew were apprehended and marched off as draftees despite the fact—as Sam noted indignantly in his diary—that one was nearly blind and the other was a dwarf. Sam himself had been accosted, too. On one occasion, his protestations that he was a minister and thus exempt were dismissed by a skeptical officer until Sam pulled manuscripts of his sermons from his pocket and offered them as proof.[16]

Between the conscripts and the many volunteers, Sam's community had been bled nearly dry of men aged seventeen to fifty. Only a handful were exempted or detailed to civilian jobs, by reason of occupation or disability. Sam knew precisely how heavy a toll the war had levied on his community, for he had recently helped Uncle Joseph prepare a report on their precinct for the county government. Since the war began, exactly 200 men of the precinct had entered military service. Of these, eight had been discharged as unfit, eight were prisoners of war, thirty were deserters, and forty-three were dead. One of the dead was Sam's brother, Luther.[17]

The Confederate authorities knew full well by the winter of 1864–65 that they were scraping the bottom of the conscript barrel. There were simply no more reserves of manpower to draw on. There were tens of thousands of deserters throughout the Confederacy, of course, but getting them back into the ranks in any great number was impossible, for they were as elusive as wild game. Meanwhile, the South's armies were wasting away while the North's grew stronger.

By late winter many in the Confederacy were ready to take drastic steps to try to fill the depleted ranks. In Richmond, Congress was debating a bill to enlist slave men as combat soldiers. Sam followed the debate with interest whenever he could get his hands on a current newspaper. The great question, of course, was whether slaves would willingly fight for the South.[18]

Curious about what the slaves themselves thought, Sam spoke with some of his father's men. None would go into the ranks voluntarily, he learned. "Our negroes do not fancy the business and I believe will take [to] the woods before they would be conscripted."[19]

Enoch Agnew owned forty-five slaves on the eve of the Civil War, and since then he had lost only a few. He was luckier than many other planters in Tippah County. Since the Yankee raids had begun in 1862, large numbers of slaves had run off with the invaders. Because the Agnews' district had been plundered less often than most others in the county, the slaves there had had fewer opportunities to escape. The big raid in June 1864 had offered no chance, for the Yankees had fled back to Tennessee in panic after being whipped by Forrest, abandoning their wagons and everything else. For now, slavery was intact on the Agnew plantation and in Tippah as a whole. The county officials were maintaining slave patrols (as best they could, anyway, given the scarcity of white men), and the rebel cavalry troopers who roamed the area were keeping an eye out for black runaways. But everyone in Tippah knew that the "peculiar institution" stood close to the brink of disintegration. Another big enemy raid through the county could mean the end.[20]

Many planters in these circumstances fretted ceaselessly about their slaves and watched warily for signs of unrest. Some in Tippah had even moved their slaves, or a portion of them, to safer parts of the South. But the Agnews saw no cause for anxiety. Sam noted on the day after Christmas 1864 that the family's blacks were celebrating the holidays as they always had and "seem to be enjoying themselves." As the winter went on, there was no trouble with the Agnew slaves, no hint of restlessness or defiance. But then a shocking incident on January 27 raised questions that the Agnews were reluctant to confront.[21]

It happened in the early afternoon, just after dinner. Sam and his father were at the picket fence in front of the house, talking to a soldier who was passing by on the road. Suddenly, from the direction of the slave quarters, came the sound of an enormous explosion. Sam and Enoch rushed to the spot and joined the crowd of blacks that had already gathered. "[A] most horrible sight met my gaze," Sam wrote. Nineteen-year-old Neely, one of the family's slaves, "was lying on the ground . . . with his legs both terribly mangled, up to near his loins. One knee had the flesh entirely stripped from the bones, and the projecting naked bones and mixed mass of flesh and clothing was a harrowing spectacle."[22]

Hurriedly questioning the other blacks, Sam and Enoch discovered that the explosion was caused by an artillery shell. There were a lot of these around the plantation, live rounds left behind in June 1864 by the fleeing Yankees. Enoch had cautioned the slaves time and again not to go near them, but Neely had ignored the warning. He had taken a hammer and chisel and tried to open a shell to get out the gunpowder. Two slave children standing near when the round exploded suffered facial burns. Had they not been bundled up in winter clothing on this cold afternoon, their burns would have been more extensive. One of the two was also hit by a shell fragment, breaking his left arm just above the wrist; the other child was miraculously not hit by the several fragments that ripped his pants and one earflap of his cap. Another piece of the shell punctured Neely's abdomen and coursed upward through his body.[23]

Neely was carried into one of the eight cabins that comprised the Agnew slave quarters. Enoch and Sam immediately went to work, one ministering to the body and the other to the soul. Enoch had been a physician before taking up planting, and he still treated patients when no other doctor could be found. For Neely he could do little, however; the young man's injuries were obviously mortal. Sam conversed earnestly with him as he lay dying. "He was perfectly rational but I do not think he fully realized his danger—the transition was so sudden from perfect health to the jaws of death. . . . [H]e did not know whether he was willing to die or not. He said he trusted in Christ. He rather discouraged my proposal to pray with him." He died as the sun was setting.[24]

Sam attended Neely's burial the next day. "It was [an] affecting sight to see the sorrow of his Mother and sister. Like Rachel's daughters they refused to be comforted. The body was carried by hand to the grave. A good many neighbor negroes were present and as the procession slowly proceeded to the graveyard they sang the 103d. Psalm." A few weeks later Sam made a headboard for the grave, carefully inscribing Neely's name in black paint.[25]

To the Agnews this incident was not only tragic but also disturbing. As Sam noted, Neely had "wanted to get the powder out but he never told what he wanted to do with it." Sam did not dwell on the troubling implications, however. Neely was "a steady, quiet, industrious boy," and a church member.

Surely his intentions were innocent. And perhaps some blessings would come out of this, blessings both temporal and spiritual: "The negroes seem much affected by this terrible visitation. I hope it will be sanctified to their good."[26]

Neely's death disrupted the plantation routine only briefly. After he was laid to rest the slaves resumed their sunup-to-sundown duties. Winter was not a busy time, of course, but there were always chores to do: livestock to be tended, equipment and buildings to be repaired, fences to be mended, firewood to be chopped, cooking and laundry to be done. This winter ended early for the Agnew slaves, for during a warm spell in mid-February Enoch decided to get a head start on spring plowing. On February 17 the field hands hitched the mules to the plows and went to work breaking up the hard, weedy ground.[27]

The plantation demanded a great deal of Enoch's attention, for it was large—372 cleared acres and over 1,400 of woodland—and he had no overseer. Sam, however, was little involved once hog-killing was finished. The only other time he was summoned to help that winter was a few days after plowing began, when a wind-whipped fire that had started somehow in the woods ignited a section of fence. He assisted in tearing down unburned fencing to halt the fire's spread.[28]

Sam spent most of his time that winter indoors with his family. The house was big but unpretentious, a comfortable, two-story white frame structure with lots of rooms and fireplaces and a veranda in the rear. His waking hours were mostly occupied with reading and writing, but he also spent time tutoring his sixteen-year-old sister, Margaret, whose schooling had been cut short by the war. He gave her lessons in physiology, botany, and mathematics, while Enoch tutored the youngest child, thirteen-year-old Erskine. The older daughter, Mary, was eighteen and had finished school. The other occupants of the house were Letitia, Sam's mother, and Nannie, his wife. Nannie never left the house these days, for she was pregnant. The baby was due in early March.[29]

Sam also devoted time that winter to gardening, but not for food or recreation. He was trying to raise opium poppies. Narcotics, like all other medicines, were critically scarce, and the Confederate government was urging citizens to grow poppies. Sam obtained some seeds and in January selected a plot of ground not far from the house. After preparing it for cultivation with the help of a slave boy, he spent all of one day and part of the next planting the seeds one by one in long, straight rows. In the weeks that followed he tended his poppy patch diligently but met with frustration after frustration: cows and hogs got into the patch and trampled it, heavy rains washed away many of the sprouts. Still, he was confident he could raise several hundred flowers to maturity, "If the sheep do not eat them up."[30]

On most Sundays, and some Saturdays, Sam was called away from home by ministerial duties. He usually had a preaching appointment, either at one of the local Associate Reformed Presbyterian churches whose pastor happened to be absent or at one of the "preaching stations" (mostly private homes) where he had been summoned by the faithful. When his appointment was at Hopewell Church, fifteen miles distant, he would usually set out Saturday afternoon and spend the night at a friend's house on the way, so as to arrive in time for the eleven o'clock Sabbath service. When he preached elsewhere, there was enough time on Sunday morning to get where he was going if he kept his mount moving at a steady gait. He rode a mule these days, for there was only one horse left on the plantation and it was too decrepit to be mounted.[31]

The hazards Sam faced on his Sabbath rounds were not limited to possible encounters with Yankee raiders. Bad weather was an even bigger threat to his ministry. Even if he persevered through the rain, snow, or cold to keep his appointment, he could not be sure that the congregation would do so. On January 8, "A raw, unpleasant day," he rode to the Mt. Zion community to preach in the home of a family named Anderson, but besides the Andersons only seven people showed up. Four weeks later he made his way to the Corder home through rain and sleet, getting his feet wet crossing the swollen streams, but found not a soul there to greet him besides the Corders. On Sundays when the weather was so miserable that there was no hope of a "respectable congregation," he simply stayed home.[32]

When he had no Sabbath appointment and the weather was tolerable, he usually attended services at Bethany, an ARP church located at Brice's Crossroads, three miles away. This was the pastorate of his beloved "Uncle Young"—the Reverend James L. Young, a fifty-six-year-old widower and Sam's ecclesiastical mentor. Sam occasionally preached at Bethany himself, at Uncle Young's invitation. It was something of a miracle that the church still stood, for it had been at the vortex of the battle in June 1864. It was left riddled by bullets and shells, its floor and pews sticky with the blood of wounded soldiers. Members of the congregation cleaned up the building and grounds and repaired most of the damage in a matter of weeks, but reminders of that dreadful day remained: a bullet hole in the pulpit, and dozens of soldiers' graves in the little cemetery beside the church.[33]

All winter long, whether he was at home or traveling about, Sam continued his assiduous news-gathering. He talked to almost everyone he saw and devoured every newspaper he could get. Much of what he picked up was rumor, a lot of it absurdly improbable, but he carefully evaluated everything and generally had a pretty good idea of what was going on. The war news was very discouraging. By late January Sam knew that a large portion of what remained of Hood's army was being sent east to try to block Sherman's advance through the Carolinas. "This leaves Mississippi without the shadow of defense," he noted glumly, "and the Yankees are expected soon to occupy the whole country." When torrential rains in late February turned Tippah County's roads into quagmires, Sam and others were actually thankful, for the only thing that could stop the enemy now was mud.[34]

Almost every day he heard rumors of peace, but he had long ago learned to discount them. Great Britain and France were going to intervene, it was said, and guarantee Confederate independence; the British were massing an army and a fleet of ironclad ships in Canada and intended to attack the United States; French warships had broken the Yankee blockade of Mobile and French troops were coming to the South's aid; Lee and Grant had signed a truce. Others might credit such stories, Sam sniffed, but "I simply believe not one word. . . . Drowning men catch at straws and our people swallow with avidity everything that promises peace."[35]

One of the peace rumors that winter turned out to be factual, however, and as the story unfolded even skeptical Sam paid heed. President Lincoln, it seemed, had agreed to meet face-to-face with Confederate commissioners to discuss ending the war. The meeting took place in early February on a ship anchored in Chesapeake Bay. It ended in failure, however. Lincoln made it clear that he would cease hostilities only if the Confederates abolished slavery and returned to the Union. This was essentially a demand for Confederate surrender, and the Southern commissioners rejected it out of hand.[36]

There were those who refused to be disheartened by this news, insisting that peace might yet be negotiated. But Sam thought otherwise. There would be no armistice, he prophesied in the waning days of winter, but instead "war to the bitter end."[37]

PART TWO

SPRING

SAMUEL AGNEW

When Sam Agnew arose on the first day of March, he looked for signs of spring but saw none. The early morning sky was overcast, and he noticed no blossoms on the peach trees that grew near the house. But late in the morning the sun came out, and during the day his father spotted a blossom. "March came in like a lamb," Sam reported in his diary. "[T]he sun shone brightly" and the day was "quiet and calm."[1]

All that day Sam kept one eye on the road that ran past the house, as was his habit. At some point an ox-drawn wagon came by, heading north, and Sam hailed the driver to see if he could pick up any news. The driver was a neighbor, Miss Williams. Women driving wagons had been an uncommon sight before the war, but everyone was used to it now. Also in the wagon was a man, a wounded Confederate soldier on his way home. Alex Merrell was his name, Sam learned, and he belonged to the 51st Tennessee Infantry. Sam offered to let him stay until someone could be found to take him further along his way, and Merrell accepted the invitation.[2]

Sam had seen a good deal of the war's human wreckage, but poor Merrell was one of the more poignant examples. He had been wounded in the thigh at the battle of Atlanta in July 1864. The surgeons managed to save his leg, but only by cutting away a lot of gangrenous flesh. Later he made his way to North Carolina, where relatives took him in, and now he was trying to get to his home in west Tennessee. Walking was hard for him, and he could not sit on a horse at all. It had taken him thirty days to get from North Carolina to Guntown, located nine miles southeast of the Agnew plantation. Miss Williams found him there and offered him a ride. Merrell knew, of course, that west Tennessee was in Yankee hands, but it did not matter to him: his war was over.[3]

That evening the sky clouded up again, and by the time Sam retired for the night a heavy rain was coming down. Over the next two days it continued, "pattering on the housetop and gurgling through the gutters," in Sam's words. His poppy patch was inundated and the nearby creeks rose threateningly. "[F]rom the back piazza I can see a silver sheet of water covering the entire branch bottom." There was nothing to do but stay indoors. He talked with Merrell for hours, reread old newspapers, and watched the road. Few people passed by, however. It was still raining on the evening of the third, when Merrell left in a cotton-laden wagon driven by a friend of Sam who was going to try to get to Tennessee to trade for provisions.[4]

The weather cleared up the next day, and on Sunday morning, March 5, Sam rode to the Corder home to preach. Usually he prepared a new sermon for each Sabbath appointment, but for this occasion he dusted off an old one. His text was John 10:9, "I am the door: by me if any man enter in, he shall be saved, and shall go in and out, and find pasture." The ride over was enjoyable, for it was a lovely day, but the Corders had some unpleasant news: someone had dug into their storage shed and stolen the pork they had recently butchered and salted. They had lost the meat of a whole hog. Sam was distressed but hardly surprised, for as food got scarce in the community there were more and more such incidents. "Thieving," he remarked, "has become common."[5]

He heard more bad news the next day: Yankee raiders were headed for Tippah County. It was a thirdhand report, however, and he did not get really concerned until the following morning, when he learned from "reliable sources" that Yankees were already in the county and had skirmished with rebel troops near Ripley, fifteen miles away. "I . . . regard it as certain," Sam affirmed in a diary entry that morning, " . . . and now the question is will they come [by] this road." He was willing to wait a little longer to find out, but his father was not. Around noon they rounded up the livestock and went to the woods.[6]

No enemy soldiers appeared, however, and after nightfall Sam and Enoch returned home. But they did not rest easily, for a wagoner who camped for the night near their house informed them that he had just come from the vicinity of Ripley and knew for a fact that "there are plenty of Yankees there."[7]

No one slept well in the Agnew home that night, but the Yankees were not solely to blame. Sometime before midnight, Sam's wife, Nannie, went into labor. Sam was banished from their upstairs bedroom to the downstairs sitting room while Enoch took charge of the delivery, assisted by Letitia. "Pa and Ma were up all night," Sam reported the next day. "Nannie had a right hard labor but was happily delivered of a fine large son between 4 and 5 o'-clock. . . . This has rendered the day famous in our annals." They named the little one Enoch, after his grandfather.[8]

All that day and the next the household bustled with activity. Sam's sisters, Mary and Margaret, were "busy attending their little nephew." Kinfolk came by to see the newborn, and "The little negroes also have been curious to see him." Sam hovered around solicitously, anxious about the health of mother and child. Fatherhood was a new experience for him, and he was moved to ponder his responsibilities and the future of the human being he and Nannie had brought into the world: "May God spare his life and make him a good and useful man."[9]

The Agnews scarcely had time to enjoy this happy event before the war again intruded. Just twelve hours or so after Nannie's delivery, Sam learned from a passer-by that "The Yankees are still at and about Ripley, devastating the country, robbing the citizens of their provisions." The next day, March 9, as he was riding over to Uncle Young's place to return a borrowed book and get some castor oil for Nannie, he ran into a friend who reported that the enemy was even closer now. Back at the house, he met two cavalry scouts who insisted that a Yankee force was now this side of the Stubbs plantation, which was less than six miles to the northwest on the same road that ran by the Agnew place. "This news," Sam wrote, "impelled us to be off to the woods."[10]

They spent a miserable night. In their rush to gather up the livestock and get to their hiding place, he and Enoch failed to bring along quilts to make a tent, although they did take some blankets. It began snowing in the evening, and before long the ground was white. "It was very cold and unpleasant to be out in the woods without house or shelter. We however had a large fire and sat around it." A few kinfolk who lived nearby joined them. The sky cleared overnight, and by morning it was bitterly cold. Sam got hardly any sleep, partly because of the cold but also because "I was [so] apprehensive that our bed clothing would be set on fire by sparks that I deemed it best to sit up while the rest were snoozing."[11]

Late in the morning Enoch returned to the house, satisfied himself that there was no immediate danger, and sent word to Sam to round up the livestock and come home. It turned out that the report that had sent them to the woods was false. The two cavalry scouts, Sam learned, had not been anywhere close to the enemy yesterday and had simply made up the story that a force was near. Sam was furious. "They certainly merit severe rebuke. They are I am told poor soldiers, members of Loughridge's Reserve company, shirking all the duties of their position they possibly can. . . . I call them great liars."[12]

Later that day and the next he picked up enough reliable information to persuade him that the Yankees were headed back to Tennessee. Once again, his district had been spared. He was greatly relieved, for from all reports this was a particularly voracious party of raiders. "They have been very destructive on the scant supplies of the citizens." One man whom Sam knew lost all his mules. Another, Colonel Berry, was stripped of his stored provisions and his horses. Berry's case was particularly disturbing, for, as Sam noted, "One of his negroes went to [the Yankees], and it is thought piloted them to where his horses were conce[ale]d."[13]

Once the excitement subsided, Sam turned his attention back to Nannie and the baby, whom they had nicknamed Buddy. Mother and child were doing well for the most part, but Nannie was complaining of soreness in her left breast. An application of warm vinegar helped, but when swelling developed, Enoch had to perform some minor surgery, lancing the breast to let fluid escape. It was not serious, Sam was pleased to learn, and Nannie quickly recovered.[14]

By mid-March, spring was well advanced and the Agnew plantation was busy. On the thirteenth, Sam saw his first martin of the season, which spurred him and Enoch to repair the birdhouse that had fallen down over the winter—the more martins around, the fewer insects. The next day Letitia began sowing her vegetable garden. As the weather warmed, Sam spent a lot of time in his poppy patch, battling the invading weeds and livestock. The field hands, who had been plowing since February, started planting corn on March 24, which kept them occupied well into April.[15]

The corn was a matter of special concern. The Agnews, like everyone else in Tippah, were praying for a good crop, for the county's supply was nearly depleted. The Yankee raiders exacerbated the crisis, and so did the notorious rebel cavalry units in the area, whose ruthless impressment continued unabated. "Huff's company was up in the hills last night and 'tore up Wash Chisholm,'" Sam learned on March 12. "Their thieving propensities are much complained of." The next day he met a man from the northern part of the county who had come down in his wagon seeking corn. The man had cotton cards to trade, and was willing to give one pair for ten bushels of corn. Cards were scarce, and many people in Sam's community would have been glad to get a pair, but there was simply no corn to spare. "Everybody needs corn," Sam wrote. "Uncle Jo is entirely out. Several bags were stolen last night from Thompson's Mill. . . . It does look as if there was some danger of a famine of bread."[16]

The only place where large quantities of corn might be obtained was farther south, in the less ravaged counties of the state. During the first part of March the Agnews and some of their neighbors agreed on a plan. Two men from the area would collect money, take a train south, and see what they could buy. They had some luck. On April 1, a train pulled into the Guntown depot with a load of corn for the group. Enoch dispatched a wagon to retrieve the Agnews' share, which amounted to thirty and a half bushels. He had wanted more, but did not have enough cash.[17]

At about the same time, county officials sent an agent south to buy corn to feed the poor. He managed to get 400 bushels. Nobody believed that this would keep all the county's poor from going hungry, but it was better than nothing.[18]

As the days grew warmer and the roads dried, Sam's ministerial rounds became less onerous and the congregations got larger. He kept his appointments dutifully, faltering only twice all spring. The first time was during the Yankee raid, which forced him to miss an appointment at the Corders. The second time was a very warm Sunday later in March, when he got sick while delivering a sermon at Hopewell Church and had to stop. "I think it was caused by an overheat," he wrote. "I regretted the occurrence very much but could not help it."[19]

Two weeks later, in early April, he was at the Corders' home preaching from the book of Proverbs when he was interrupted by the appearance of some cavalry who were hunting conscripts and deserters. This business, Sam had noticed, was getting increasingly ugly. The rebel army was hungrier than ever for manpower, while a growing number of men were doing all they could to stay out of the army's clutches. Conscriptors had recently caught and dragged away a man in Sam's district, "a desperate character" who had escaped from army custody before and, in Sam's opinion, would surely do so this time, too. Near Baldwyn, a village just a few miles from the Agnews' plantation, cavalrymen tried to arrest a man named Jack Davis who was reportedly "encourag[ing] soldiers to remain away from the army," but Davis refused to be taken and "escaped under fire." Man-hunting cavalry now made it a practice to descend on churches and preaching stations on Sunday mornings, hoping to bag their quarry at worship.[20]

The hunters and the hunted would soon end their desperate game. On April 16 Sam preached at Hopewell and learned that a cavalry detachment was nearby chasing deserters and seizing horses. This was the last time he ever heard of such an outfit in his vicinity. On May 3, he visited Baldwyn and spoke with an army officer posted there. This was the last evidence of Confederate authority he ever saw. Well before spring turned to summer, the war ended and the Confederate States of America ceased to exist.[21]

Sam chronicled the death of the Confederacy meticulously. On April 11 he talked to a man who had just returned from a trading trip to Tennessee. The man swore he had seen a Northern newspaper, dated the sixth, that told of "the evacuation of Richmond by Lee and its occupation by the Yankees." His story was so convincing that Sam was not inclined to dismiss it as he did most rumors. Two days passed before Sam heard anything more. "The fall of Richmond is confirmed," he wrote. There was also a report that Lee had moved his army south "and torn Sherman all to pieces," but this he thought dubious. "When disasters come there must be some good news to be manufactured to solace the people. Bitter pills are considerably improved by sweetening."[22]

As the warm days of mid-April succeeded one another and the woods turned a deep green, Sam interrogated everyone he met more intently than ever, but news was agonizingly slow to come. Not until the seventeenth, when he spoke with a passer-by on the road near his house, did he learn more. The man had heard that Northern papers were reporting "the surrender of Lee with 25,000 men on the 9th." The papers apparently gave "minute details of the affair," Sam noted, "and from this I fear that it is all too true." By the nineteenth he had heard enough to convince him that Lee's army was gone. "This is the severest blow the Confederacy has received yet. . . . What our leaders will do remains to be seen."[23]

He was more skeptical when he heard a rumor on April 21 that President Lincoln had been assassinated. By the twenty-fourth he was pretty much persuaded, but conflicting stories about that and everything else continued to circulate. Many people he talked to refused to believe that Lee had capitulated. "Things are in a mighty 'jumble' at this time."[24]

By the end of the first week of May the truth could no longer be denied. It was certain that not only Lee's army but all Confederate forces east of the Mississippi had surrendered. The Confederate government was defunct, and Jefferson Davis and other officials were on the run. "[T]he Confederacy,"

Sam declared, "is dead. . . . Confed. currency is now worthless. Thus ends a war in which the South has gained nothing and lost millions of property and thousands of precious lives."[25]

By the second week of May returning rebel soldiers could be seen trudging along Tippah County's roads. Through the remainder of the spring hardly a day passed that Sam did not encounter one or more. The first he met were men of the commands that surrendered in Mississippi and Alabama, but before long they were joined by survivors of the final campaigns in Virginia and North Carolina. Among the returnees were many friends and loved ones of the Agnews. Uncle Young's son, James, was home by May 11. Two days later Nannie's brother, James McKell, appeared at the Agnews' door—"Nannie is rejoiced," wrote Sam. But there were others in the community who waited in vain during May for the return of their sons and brothers. One was an acquaintance of Sam's named Gambrell, who only now learned that his son Robert had been killed near Richmond just before the city fell. "Gambrell has now lost 4 sons in the war," Sam wrote, "and has not a living son in the world."[26]

Given the abrupt collapse of Confederate authority and the sudden appearance of large numbers of men loosed from restraint, no one in Tippah should have been surprised at the wave of disorder that shook the county in May. On the fifth, Sam's friend Squire Nutt suffered "an outrage" at the hands of three soldiers who, according to Sam, "were deserting in order to avoid a surrender." The three had stopped at Nutt's home and asked if they might get feed for their horses. The squire invited them in. "After sitting a while Nutt went out with them to attend to their horses. When they got out one said We have carried this far enough. We understand, Sir, that you have money and we want it. Nutt denied the fact. They hung him twice and otherwise badly injured him. They got only $4.00 from him."[27]

"Hear of more robberies," Sam wrote on May 12. "Five men, soldiers, robbed an old man near Orizaba recently. They hung him twice and burned his body severely with powder before they did accomplish their design. . . . Mrs. Duke had all her horses stolen last night. . . . The robbing parties are getting bold. . . . Lawlessness seems to be the order of the day."[28]

If the specters of famine, defeat, and anarchy were not enough to frighten Tippah residents, the citizens also confronted the prospect of an unleashed slave population. All sorts of stories were circulating about what the Yankees intended to do about the blacks. Lincoln's Emancipation Proclamation had declared them free, but Lincoln was dead now and Andrew Johnson, a Tennessee unionist, was president. "People are still ignorant of the terms of the surrender," Sam wrote on May 8. "What will be done with the negroes is still unknown." The next day, however, he got hold of a recent Memphis newspaper that indicated that the victors considered slavery "dead now immediately and forever." Reports confirming this drifted in over the next few days, and on the fifteenth Sam wrote that "The general opinion now is that slavery is dead." But, he added, "some still are incredulous because they do not want to believe it. Just like Lee's surrender it is an unpalatable truth." Only in the fourth week of May, after news came of a statement by President Johnson confirming the abolition of slavery, was all doubt removed.[29]

Nor was there any doubt by late May that the federal authorities would be able to enforce the decree of emancipation, at least in Sam's vicinity. As early as May 6 a force of one hundred Union troops had arrived in Baldwyn. They did not stay long, but another detachment passed through the village a week later, and yet another on the twenty-fifth. By the end of the month, Yankee garrison forces were posted at a number of points along the Mobile & Ohio Railroad, which ran through Baldwyn and Guntown. Their presence was sufficient to deter any slaveholder in the area who might be considering trying to hold his people in bondage.[30]

The unanswered question was what the blacks would do. Sam kept a close eye on the Agnew slaves all spring, especially after reports of the Confederacy's collapse began coming in—reports that invariably reached the slave quarters soon after they reached the Big House. As the weeks passed, the blacks grew unruly. On April 11, the day he learned from a passing trader about the fall of Richmond, Sam discovered that some of the slaves had bought liquor from the trader and were carousing in the quarters. "They had better been at work," he grumbled. "The negroes now are so indolent and disobedient that it is better to be without them than with them." There was even bigger trouble elsewhere in the district that month. "Singleton Hughes lost all of his most valuable slaves Saturday night [April 28]. They have gone to the Yankees."[31]

Slavery disintegrated on the Agnew plantation in May. On the eighth, when Sam was still trying to sort out conflicting reports about the Yankees' intentions, he noted that "The negroes themselves evidently think they are free." None left the plantation, and none threatened the Agnews in any way; they simply quit working except as it suited them. The Agnews were exasperated.

10. This double cabin, built in 1852, once stood on the Agnew plantation in Tippah County, Mississippi. It was probably used to house slaves, one of eight such cabins on the plantation. It was moved in the 1960s to a site two or three miles away.

"Got some tobacco plants . . . and planted 60 hills in the old cow lot," Sam wrote on May 25. "Would have planted more but the negroes have got so 'high' that they would not obey my orders."[32]

Neither the Agnews nor anybody else knew what to do. Crops and livestock had to be tended, but any attempt to coerce the blacks might provoke Yankee intervention. It was known that in the regions long occupied by the Yankees, former masters were paying wages to their former slaves, and by the end of spring some in Sam's community were experimenting with that system. But everything was so unsettled that little could be accomplished. One of Sam's neighbors met with his field hands to discuss hiring them, Sam learned, but they "declined contracting with him. He then drove them off from the place and has not a negroe now." Rumor had it that federal agents would soon be on hand to supervise the signing of labor contracts, and Sam and Enoch thought it best not to negotiate with their blacks until an agent arrived. Meanwhile, work on the Agnew plantation proceeded fitfully.[33]

Sam and many others were certain that emancipation would prove disastrous, not just for whites but also for the freed people. It was an article of faith among planters that blacks were incapable of caring for themselves and would not work except under threat of the lash. "The status of the negroe is changed from a slave to a hireling," Sam wrote, "and the most reflecting [persons] think that the change is fraught with sore evils to the poor negroe." It appeared to him that the blacks' idea of freedom was to "live off their masters and do nothing. . . . [T]hey will find it very different from what they suppose." He was pleased when he read President Johnson's admonition to the freed people: "liberty is freedom to work."[34]

The political situation in the last days of spring was no less confused than the labor situation. A thousand rumors circulated about the U.S. government's intentions with regard to reconstruction, but Sam could learn nothing reliable. The only formal authority now functioning in Mississippi was the army of occupation. In the latter part of May, Union troops marched into Jackson, seized the state offices and records, dissolved the legislature, and deposed the governor. County governments thereupon suspended operation. Tippah's officials held one last meeting in May—in a hotel in Ripley, for the courthouse had been burned down by Yankees in 1864—and then went home to await word of their status.[35]

The dissolution of state and local government aggravated the crises of labor, order, and food. This last was on the minds of the Agnews more than any other as spring ended. On May 27 Sam recorded a disturbing incident. He set out for Hopewell early that morning on a mule named Peter, but on the way the mule "gave out" and "fell down with me, broke my saddle girth, throwing me over his head." Neither was hurt, but Peter could no longer carry Sam and had to be led the rest of the way. "Weakness was the cause," Sam decided. Peter was "weak from heavy work and light feed."[36]

Corn for the Agnews and their neighbors continued to trickle in on the railroad, thanks to the exertions of the two men who had gone south to buy it, but it was never enough. And there was a new problem: the railroad now refused to accept Confederate money. Only specie or Yankee greenbacks could be used to pay shipping charges, and both were scarce. Greenbacks had been circulating in Tippah for some time, as a result of the clandestine trade with Tennessee, but never in large amounts. The Agnews had none at this time, so Enoch was forced to spend a couple of days going from house to house in the area trying to borrow some. He managed to get enough to pay his share of the freight but then suffered another setback: a gang of surrendered rebel cavalrymen raided a boxcar at the Guntown depot and made off with 150 bushels set aside for him and Uncle Joseph.[37]

There were other matters, too, on the Agnews' minds in late spring. Little Buddy was sick on and off, and they worried about him. Some of the poppies bloomed, but Sam was not sure they would yield opium. Everything seemed uncertain. Sam watched and prayed, but saw no sure signs: whatever God had in store for the Agnews, and for the South, He had not yet seen fit to reveal. Sam tried to imagine the world to come.[38]

JOHN ROBERTSON

THERE WERE DAYS IN THE EARLY PART OF THE SPRING WHEN JOHN Robertson was able to put the war completely out of his mind. Uncle Allen's farm was not exactly off the beaten path, but it was tucked into a corner of east Tennessee that saw few passers-by. The railroad was eight miles away and the nearest town of any size was thirteen. The view from the window of John's room, where he spent most of his time, reinforced the sense of isolation. In whatever direction he looked, tall oak trees or a rise of land loomed up to block his gaze. Like most other farms in Roane County, Uncle Allen's lay on rolling bottom land flanked by densely forested ridges, high and steep. Thick woods surrounded the fields where corn and wheat and grass grew. It was a rare farmer in that section of the country who could stand in his own yard and see a neighbor's house or barn.[1]

Friends called at Uncle Allen's farm now and then, and John left the house frequently to visit in the community or attend church or meet with the Reverend Payne, the Methodist preacher who was helping him prepare for the ministry. But unless someone brought up the subject of the war, John gave it little thought. Since experiencing conversion and deciding to devote his life to the Lord, he had put aside most worldly matters. Uncle Allen and Aunt Mary kindly provided for him and made no demands on his time. He was free to concentrate on matters of the spirit.[2]

He spent the better part of most days in his upstairs bedroom reading. "I was not satisfied," he recalled in his memoir, " . . . unless I had a book in my hand." His reading was rigidly circumscribed, however. He vowed he would open no book that did not promise in some way to make him a better servant of God. "Novels were offered me, but I refused to read them. . . . Well did I know that I might read those books of fiction till my looks were grey and I would never be wiser than when I commenced." Instead, he waded through a six-volume set of Biblical commentary that the Reverend Payne loaned him and found it very edifying.[3]

Few who had known him only in his earlier days would have recognized him now. Just three years ago, this serious young man had been a hell-raiser of a boy, rowdy, eager for military adventure, and burning with vengefulness toward his unionist enemies. All that was behind him now. Even his physical appearance had changed strikingly since then, transfigured by the hardships of camp life, combat, hospital, and prison. When he last visited his home in Greene County, his parents had barely recognized him.[4]

So sober and earnest and weathered was he now that it was easy to forget how young he was. As spring began, he was not yet nineteen. But he himself was painfully aware of his age, and sometimes he felt inadequate for the work he was undertaking. One evening, as the family gathered for their daily worship, Uncle Allen asked him to read the Bible passage. John, who had never been called on before, flushed with embarrassment and proceeded to read with trembling lips: "I could scar[c]ely utter a word distinctly," he recalled. This awkward moment was nothing, however, compared to the near-panic he experienced when the Reverend Payne singled him out to lead a prayer in church one Sunday. That he was able on this occasion to do his duty—albeit with a good deal of stumbling—he ascribed to divine intervention.[5]

As painful as these and other such incidents were, John was "determined not to falter in anything required of me," and he never declined a request. "Thus by degrees, battling against my embarrassment, I overcame my timidity."[6]

While John prepared, Uncle Allen plowed and planted. His son Jacob, who was nearly seventeen, labored alongside him in the fields. With only the two of them working it, the little farm would not produce much, but what it yielded sufficed for the family, which numbered nine including John. Uncle Allen's household had never known affluence; he and Mary and the children lived plainly and were content to do so.[7]

The other farmers in the community likewise busied themselves in the fields as the spring planting season began. Roane County was one of the quieter places in east Tennessee at this time, for which the inhabitants were profoundly grateful. Some other parts of the region were so ravaged by destruction and violence that normal life was impossible: farmers had given up trying to plants crops, churches and schools and courthouses were closed, and people were afraid to leave their homes.[8]

Roane was not wholly insulated from danger, however. The small garrisons of Yankee troops stationed at a few points in and around the county were hardly enough to secure order at all times in every community. Now and then the quiet was shattered by a rebel cavalry raid, a guerrilla ambush, or some other frightening reminder that this region was still at war—and still at war with itself.[9]

In the early days of March the county was buzzing with news of a bizarre Confederate operation that had come to an abrupt end on the bank of the Tennessee River not many miles from Uncle Allen's farm. A small band of rebel soldiers and sailors had been captured, along with their thirty-foot boat, as they were secretly making their way downriver. The boat was loaded with hand grenades, underwater mines, and incendiary devices made with turpentine-soaked cotton.[10]

A diary found on one of the men revealed some of their plan and Union army authorities learned more from interrogating the prisoners. The story that emerged was astonishing and, to many, alarming. The operation had begun weeks earlier in Richmond, Virginia, where Confederate military officials assembled a clandestine strike force of a dozen officers and men from both the army and the navy. They were supplied with provisions, munitions, and a boat, and then transported by rail and wagon to the southwest corner of Virginia. On February 4 they loaded the boat and set out down the Holston River, which flows southwest and eventually joins another river to form the Tennessee. When they passed beyond the picket lines of the Confederate army in northeastern Tennessee and into Union-held territory, they muffled their oars and began traveling at night only, hiding during the day in brush along the banks. Narrowly avoiding detection as they floated past the large Yankee garrison at Knoxville, they reached Loudon on February 24. Here their luck began to run out. A black man spotted them while they were ashore during daylight and led Yankee troops to their location. Two of the raiders were taken prisoner. The rest got away in the boat, only to be sighted two days later near Kingston and subsequently captured by a hastily assembled posse of unionist citizens, who turned them over to the federal army.[11]

The purpose of this operation, it was revealed, was disruption and sabotage. The raiders' orders were to begin destroying steamboats once they were past Kingston, and to continue doing so all the way down to Chattanooga, where they were then to set fire to the large complex of Union army depots, boatyards, warehouses, and sawmills that lay along the river.[12]

That the mission failed was a relief to the federal authorities, but they remained uneasy about its implications. By itself, it could not have amounted to anything more than an annoyance to the Union occupation forces in east Tennessee, in no way threatening their control of the region. It seemed likely, therefore, that it was part of some larger plan.[13]

One possibility—hinted at by the prisoners under questioning—was that the raid was intended to prepare the way for Robert E. Lee's army. Lee was under heavy pressure from Ulysses S. Grant's forces, and there was speculation that Lee might abandon Richmond and Petersburg, retreat into the Appalachian mountains, and head south, perhaps to Georgia. There he might fight on indefinitely.[14]

Newspapers in Knoxville and Chattanooga published detailed reports about the captured river raiders, sparking consternation among unionists. If Lee's army marched into east Tennessee and drove the Yankees out, the region's secessionists might be inspired to rise up against the unionist majority. Many were undoubtedly thirsting for vengeance, for in the year and a half that they had now spent under Yankee rule, they had experienced increasingly harsh treatment. Federal commanders in the region who endorsed the hard-war policy toward rebel civilians advocated by General William T. Sherman had joined hands with unionists who had suffered under Confederate rule and now demanded an eye for an eye; together they were making life miserable for secessionists. Those who flaunted their Confederate patriotism were imprisoned or banished to rebel-held territory, their homes and other property confiscated or destroyed. Even those who resisted only passively, by refusing to take the U.S. oath of allegiance, suffered penalties: they were forbidden to enter a garrisoned town or buy goods from a merchant, and their farms were routinely stripped by Yankee foragers. The secessionists' retaliatory guerrilla warfare only provoked the Yankees and unionists to come down harder, further embittering the secessionists. Suspected guerrillas were summarily shot or hanged. Where the guerrillas proved elusive, citizens believed to have aided them were arrested and held as hostages.[15]

John Robertson had managed to stay clear of this spiraling cycle of retribution ever since the Yankees invaded east Tennessee. He had done so by taking the U.S. oath and thereafter keeping quiet about his political sentiments, which remained secessionist, and by declining to retaliate when unionists harassed him about his Confederate army service and drove him from his teaching job, and also by exiling himself from Greene County, where as a rebel home guardsman he had made many enemies. He was not one of those who now yearned for revenge. He wanted only to be left alone to follow his chosen path.[16]

That he wanted to be left alone by those contending for control of this troubled region did not mean that he desired to follow his path alone. More and more these days, he was thinking of taking a partner. Like any other young man, he expected to marry and raise a family, and during the past few years he had flirted with many young women and called on a few. But none had seemed the perfect romantic and spiritual mate he believed a man must seek; and besides, until he found his true course in life, he had deemed himself too callow for marriage. Now, however, he thought he might be worthy enough to be some good woman's husband. He thought, too, that he had found the one God intended for him.[17]

Her name was Margaret Tennessee Robertson—Tennie, he called her, although to everyone else she was Maggie. She was a distant cousin of his and the same age as he, and she lived on her mother's farm not far from Uncle Allen's. John had met her the very day he arrived in Roane County back in October, and within weeks he had fallen deeply in love with her.[18]

She was riding alone on horseback the first time he saw her, as he was walking along the road trying to find his way to Uncle Allen's. She was neatly dressed, wore a bonnet, and had strikingly blue eyes. He asked for directions, and as she spoke he found himself drawn to her. "[T]here was something there not common in the fairer sex." He wanted to know her name but thought it would seem presumptuous to ask. She surprised him by asking if he was John Robertson—she had learned from neighborhood gossip that he was coming to live with Uncle Allen. She introduced herself and told him they were kin.[19]

He saw her again not long after that, on a Sunday morning at Blue Springs Church, and they talked again. Soon he began calling on her. They found that they had much in common besides their age and family connection. Politics for one thing: her family were secessionists, and her older brother was a lieutenant in the Confederate army. This was welcome news to John, for he would never court a "Lincolnite." Their backgrounds were similar, too. Although her father, who had died some years earlier, was a physician, the family had always lived in modest circumstances. They had a small farm, which her mother now operated with hired labor, and they owned just one horse and had never held slaves. Tennie was, moreover, a devout Christian who sought and found salvation at the same time as John. He was present when she experienced conversion at a revival meeting one night in February. When he told her of his decision to become a minister, she praised and encouraged him.[20]

For some reason Uncle Allen and his family disliked her, and they tried to dissuade John from seeing her. Perhaps it was related to some old family feud. In any event, John ignored their comments and began spending a lot of time at Tennie's house. Her mother made him welcome and graciously gave them time alone. As the weather warmed, they spent many hours sitting on the front porch, in the shade of the small grove of cedars where the house stood. Sometimes they gathered bouquets in the garden or walked together through the wooded countryside. Their favorite path was one that ran between an old, abandoned log cabin and a spring.[21]

There were never any awkward silences between them, for both were the talkative, sociable sort and they enjoyed each other's company. John was impressed by her intelligence—she was "more than my equal" in that regard, he thought—but it was her "mild and gentle manner" and "true warm heart" that touched him most. "As for beauty," he decided, "she had enough, and of course I thought her han[d]some."[22]

She had another regular caller, but gave him no encouragement and made it clear as politely as she could that she preferred John; one time the poor man was left standing forlornly in her parlor while she and John went off to church together. And in other ways, from the "bright smile" with which she always greeted him to the earnest prayers she said for him and the funny made-up games she played with him, she seemed to be trying to make John understand that she cared for him. But she never told him so, and he was so afraid of being rejected that he could not bring himself to declare his love. "Many times I resolved to do so, but when I came in her presence, my heart would fail me."[23]

Between his infatuation with Tennie and the pursuit of his calling, John was preoccupied all spring. News of the war's end caused hardly a ripple in the insular little world he now inhabited. Certainly he understood that Lee's surrender in Virginia on April 9 and the subsequent collapse of the Confederacy secured the triumph of the unionists in east Tennessee and ended the secessionists' dream of deliverance and revenge. If he read any newspapers or talked to anyone who had, he probably knew that all the organized Confederate forces in and around the region, along with nearly all the rebel guerrilla bands, laid down their arms by early May.[24]

At some point in the late spring, however, he must have become aware that the prospect of peace in east Tennessee was not so certain after all. If he talked with any of the surrendered Confederate soldiers, he surely heard stories of the harassment many experienced as they made their way home through the region. Unionists taunted them, threatened them, and even robbed them. Some of the soldiers, fearful of being bushwhacked, returned home by back roads, traveling stealthily and only at night.[25]

As the defeated rebels returned to their families, so did many of the east Tennesseans who had fought in the Union ranks, and their arrival stoked the region's already heated atmosphere. There were tens of thousands of these men: Roane County alone contributed no fewer than seven companies of infantry and cavalry to the federal army. Some had joined up after the Yankees occupied east Tennessee, but many had done so earlier, following a long and dangerous flight through rebel-patrolled mountains to the Union lines in Kentucky. They had fought the Confederates on the battlefields, and now many of them were coming back determined to exact a price for the persecution they and their families had endured at home under the secessionist regime.[26]

The vengeful mood of many east Tennessee unionists was sanctioned—and inflamed—by the state's new governor. William G. Brownlow, the Knoxville newspaper editor and die-hard loyalist who had been imprisoned and exiled by the Confederates, was sworn into office in Nashville in April. Although U.S. troops continued to occupy the state, the new civil government of Tennessee, with Brownlow at its head, was recognized by the federal authorities as the legitimate successor to the military government that had ruled since the Yankees conquered middle and west Tennessee in 1862. None but thoroughgoing unionists had been permitted to vote in the elections of February and March 1865 that created this state government, and thus Brownlow had behind him a solidly unionist legislature and judiciary. He had also at his disposal his newspaper, the *Whig and Rebel Ventilator*.[27]

The death of the Confederacy did nothing to soften Brownlow's feelings toward those who had supported it. From his desk in Nashville and from his editorial office in Knoxville, there now issued a fiery stream of pronouncements intended to let the rebels know that there would be no forgiveness for their sins. Among his first official acts was to put a price on the head of former governor Isham G. Harris, who had led the state out of the Union in 1861 and later served in the Confederate army. Five thousand dollars, proclaimed Brownlow, would be the reward for apprehending "this Arch-traitor." Brownlow furthermore announced that anyone who had taken a stand with the rebels had "forfeited all rights to citizenship, and to life itself. Every field of carnage, every rebel prison, every Union man's grave unite with a violated law and demand the penalty, and if the courts do not administer it, an outraged people will."[28]

The governor was no doubt pleased by some of the news that reached him from east Tennessee in April and May. Whether impelled by his rhetoric or by their own hunger for revenge, many of the region's unionists were assailing their defeated enemies. Some were doing so through the courts. Hundreds, even thousands, of damage suits were being brought by aggrieved unionists against their former persecutors, especially the rich and prominent and those who had enforced Confederate martial law and conscription. Criminal charges also were being levied, including many for treason. Brownlow, who himself filed suit against the officials who had imprisoned him, enthusiastically endorsed such retribution: "let justice be done. These traitors have had their day; now let us have ours."[29]

Outside the courtrooms, too, there was retribution. Some of the region's churches were taking action against their rebel members. One of these was the Cedar Fork Baptist Church in the village of Philadelphia, a dozen miles from Uncle Allen's farm, whose ruling elders formally declared "a non fellowship against all aiders and abetters of the rebel[l]ion, until satisfaction be made by them to the church in the letter and spirit of the Gosp[e]l." The secessionists of Cedar Fork and other such congregations were given two choices: humble themselves and publicly repent their sin, or be expelled from the church.[30]

Increasingly, there were reports of violence in the region: threats, beatings, even killings. Men who had served in the Confederate ranks were the most frequent targets of such vengeance. In some counties—including Greene, where John Robertson's family still resided—it seemed that hardly a day went by that some rebel was not waylaid by a band of unionists, flogged on his bare back with switches or cowhides, and ordered to leave the area. Not a few were shot from ambush on country roads or in open confrontations on town streets. To the former Confederates, this all seemed an orchestrated campaign—a reign of terror, some called it—designed to drive them from the region. If so, there were signs that it was accomplishing its purpose. Rebel east Tennesseans in considerable numbers were fleeing to more hospitable parts of the South or electing not to return from their places of wartime exile.[31]

John Robertson's little corner of the region remained mercifully peaceful through the spring. In the town of Athens, thirteen miles south, former federal soldiers were openly threatening rebels on the streets; and near Loudon, fifteen miles east, a secessionist was killed. But John heard of no trouble any closer to home, except for some rumors of robber gangs in the vicinity. Still, he rarely left the house without his pistol.[32]

It was quiet enough in those first weeks after the war's end that the Reverend Payne, with help from John, was able to accomplish one of his longtime goals at Blue Springs Church: establishing a Sunday school. He began by calling a meeting of the congregants, who warmly approved the idea and elected him superintendent of the school. At the same time, they elected John librarian and first teacher of the boys' class, and Tennie first teacher of the girls' class. The school got under way in May and was a great success; together, John and Tennie and the other teachers had nearly a hundred students. During the reverend's frequent absences, John acted as superintendent, which meant opening and closing school each Sunday by leading the students in song and prayer. "I was determined the school should not [falter], by my tardiness," John wrote, "and was always in my place."[33]

After school on Sundays, as he and Tennie walked home together over the ridge between the church and their farms, John would talk of his calling. His progress in that regard was a good deal slower lately, he was sorry to say, for he no longer had the luxury of spending all day studying. Cousin Jacob had had a bad accident in April, when a cart loaded with rails overturned on him, leaving him with a broken thigh that would take a long time to heal. At about the same time, Uncle Allen got sick and since then had been unable to do much work. This double misfortune "throwed the tending of the crop mostly on me," as John put it.[34]

Hoeing and plowing took him away from his books in the last weeks of spring, but not away from Tennie. Uncle Allen complained that he was spending all his time with her, which was untrue, but John could not deny that he was with her a good part of the time. Any other sort of self-indulgence would have burdened him with guilt, but this did not. Tennie seemed more important than anything else right now, at least more important than studying Bible commentaries.[35]

Summer was at hand. Spring had come and gone, and John had not confessed his love to Tennie. He promised himself that he would summon the courage to do so in the season ahead. If she answered as he prayed she would, and if the troubles besetting the world outside were kept at bay, it would be a summer of great joy.[36]

CORNELIA MCDONALD

AS SOON AS THE WEATHER WAS WARM ENOUGH AND THE SOIL good and dry, Cornelia McDonald put some of her boys to work in the garden that she had staked out the year before in the yard beside the house. Kenneth, who was twelve, was the principal gardener. He did not mind this duty, except for having to cut beanpoles and pea sticks from the nearby cedar thicket. He tried to convince his mother that the task was impossibly difficult, but she was adamant. His younger brother Roy also went to work in the garden, assisted sometimes by little Donald. Now and then Donald would doze off while standing up, leaning on his hoe, whereupon Roy—who was never lacking in energy—would wake him up by throwing dirt clods at him.[1]

The garden would be more important than ever this year, for the family was desperately short of food. By March, they were down to two meals a day. Breakfast was usually just bread and milk, along with some eggs if the hens were cooperating. Dinner was generally bread, sorghum, and beans or potatoes. Supper they skipped, and went to bed hungry. Sometimes when Cornelia was out in the evening and glanced through the windows of other houses where the tables were being set for supper, she felt almost resentful.[2]

She worried incessantly about food and money. What she earned from giving drawing and French lessons was barely enough to buy flour and beans and pay the cook. She was still waiting for the $427 due her from the Confederate government on her deceased husband's account. The longer she waited, the less it would buy, for prices were still spiraling upward.[3]

One day in March she received a note from her stepson Edward, a cavalry officer in Lee's army, telling her that his outfit had captured some beef cattle from the Yankees and that he was allowed to keep one. He was going to try to send it to her, he said. Sometime later she got word that the animal was in Staunton, thirty-five miles down the valley. Immediately she dispatched Harry, her eldest, to retrieve it.[4]

For three days she waited, anxious and excited. She knew exactly what she would do when the beef arrived. She would take it to the tannery down the street, where, in exchange for the hide and a bit of the meat, she could get it slaughtered and butchered. One roast she would give to Mrs. Powell, who had generously shared her own food with the McDonalds, and another she would give to some other friends. Then, after procuring salt, she would preserve the remainder. This would keep the family supplied with meat for a good while.[5]

That was not all she anticipated. The animal would also provide tallow. "[O]h what a treasure the tallow would be," she thought. "If there were even six pounds, that would make thirty-six candles, and that would give us light for seventy-two nights." Good candles were now so expensive—six dollars apiece—that she, like most other people, had to rely on "Confederate candles," crude beeswax contrivances that burned fast and required constant attention. With the tallow she could make some real candles. She had an old set of candle molds, left behind by one of the previous occupants of the house. While waiting for Harry to return, she cleaned up the molds and prepared wicks as she had seen the family servants do when she was a girl.[6]

At last Harry arrived. But, as Cornelia recalled, when she saw him approaching with the beef in tow she "did not know whether to laugh or cry." The poor animal had fared badly on its long journey from the Yankee army to Lexington: "It was so thin that the sides were transparent between the ribs, not a particle of fat on any part of it, and a teaspoon would have held all the tallow." In the end, it yielded some lean meat, but not a single candle.[7]

There were many families in and around Lexington whose plight was as desperate as the McDonalds', and a great number worse off. Even those who were doing better could hardly have been said to be living in comfort, at least not many of them. Shortages and inflation touched everyone, and the government had siphoned off much of the community's wealth through taxes and impressment. Few citizens had any surplus of provisions or money. And yet they were constantly being called on to give up more for the Confederate cause. Because the government had taken everything it could under the law, it now issued a plea for voluntary contributions of food and clothing for Lee's army. A committee was formed in Lexington in March to collect whatever the people of Rockbridge County offered and to send it to the front. Blankets, shoes, meat, meal, and anything else the citizens could spare would be gladly accepted. If they were unwilling to donate these items, the government was willing to accept them as a loan, with a promise to repay.[8]

An assortment of supplies trickled in to the committee in response to this pathetic appeal. Cornelia's neighbor Mr. Deaver, the shoemaker, hard-pressed though he was, contributed a barrel of flour and some bacon. Others did likewise, or sacrificed a precious bushel of beans, a pair of socks, or an overcoat. Cornelia herself could give nothing.[9]

She would have done so if she could. She knew that Lee's soldiers—the last hope of the Confederacy—were suffering terribly in the trenches around Richmond and Petersburg. Her friend Ann Pendleton had recently returned to Lexington from an extended visit with her husband, General William Pendleton, who was at Petersburg. What she saw and heard there was enough to depress even the most optimistic Confederate patriot. The once-mighty Army of Northern Virginia was barely clinging to life. So thin was it stretched to cover the miles and miles of defensive works that one big push by Grant's enormous army might well crush it. The troops were all underfed and most were ill clad: an army of raggedy scarecrows was what it seemed like to many who saw it. Worse yet, morale was crumbling. In the most recent engagements with the enemy it had been obvious that the fighting spirit of the men was dwindling, for they did not attack or defend with anything like their old élan. Many were now giving up altogether, crawling out of their trenches and across no-man's-land in the dead of night to surrender to the Yankees, or sneaking away in the opposite direction in the hope of getting home—sometimes in groups of ten, twenty, or more. At least 3,000 men deserted between mid-February and mid-March, of the fewer than 50,000 present for duty. The army was melting away and neither General Lee nor anybody else could stop it.[10]

Still, there were a good number of soldiers who were determined to stay at their posts to the end. How many civilians would remain steadfast was another question. Morale was collapsing on the home front as inexorably as in the army. More and more citizens were concluding that the war was lost and further sacrifice senseless. Many were conveying these sentiments in letters to their husbands and fathers and brothers in the army and pleading with them to come home. To Cornelia these first weeks of spring seemed a "gloomy and melancholy" time, for it was hardly possible now to deny the "dreadful certainty of disaster and defeat."[11]

Even so, she made no protest when Harry announced near the end of March that he was leaving to join the army. He intended to go to Petersburg and find his stepbrother Edward, who had told him he could enlist in his unit, the 11th Virginia Cavalry. If he stayed at home the conscription agents would take him in April, when he turned seventeen, and then he might be sent anywhere.[12]

If Harry must go to the army, Cornelia decided, she would see to it that he was uniformed like a proper soldier. She dug out one of her last remaining pieces of fine clothing, a crepe shawl, and talked a shopkeeper into taking it as payment for a few yards of gray cloth. The cloth was very coarse, the kind used for slave clothing before the war; but these days, as Cornelia knew, "no gentleman thought himself above wearing it." She took it home, busied herself cutting and stitching, and before long had a serviceable jacket and trousers ready for her soldier-to-be. One of her neighbors contributed a newly knitted pair of socks; a flannel shirt and a hat completed the outfit. "[H]e was soon equipped," Cornelia wrote, "and my boy was gone."[13]

Harry set out on foot, making his way eastward across the Blue Ridge Mountains. Despite the Confederacy's bleak prospects, he was eager to join the army. He had burned with a desire to fight the enemy ever since the war began, just as he turned thirteen. At the family's home back in Winchester, he and the younger boys had fashioned a battery of toy cannons that mowed down imaginary Yankee soldiers by the hundreds.[14]

As he followed the road that led to Petersburg, Harry stayed alert for any sign of the Yankee cavalry rumored to be in the area. He knew he had a journey of several days ahead of him, perhaps a week or more, for the city was a good 125 miles from Lexington. He did not know exactly where he would find Edward and his regiment, for Lee's cavalry often operated far from the siege lines.[15]

He never got to Petersburg or anywhere near it. Many miles west of the city he encountered the Army of Northern Virginia in headlong retreat. Lee had abruptly abandoned his lines on the night of April 2, after Grant launched an all-out assault. Richmond and Petersburg were now in enemy hands and Lee's troops were moving west as fast as they could, barely a step ahead of their pursuers. Their only hope was to try to reach the mountains and make a stand there, or turn south and try to link up with the small rebel army facing Sherman in North Carolina.[16]

Somehow, amid all the confusion, Harry found Edward's regiment. On April 6 he formally enlisted in Company D and was given a horse and gun and assigned to help guard the supply train. As he rode westward with the long line of wagons, the army disintegrated around him. Exhausted men dropped out of the ranks by the thousands, collapsing on the roadside amid the litter of abandoned equipment and dead horses and mules. More men were lost when the pursuing Yankees overwhelmed the army's rear guard, killing or capturing thousands.[17]

For three hellish days and nights, Harry soldiered on. The ordeal ended on Sunday, April 9, when General Lee found his retreat route blocked by fast-moving Yankee divisions. That afternoon, in the parlor of a home in the village of Appomattox Court House, Lee met with Grant and surrendered his army. At that point, Harry was one of only 28,000 men still in the ranks. They were not taken prisoner but were instead paroled and allowed to go home.[18]

News of the fall of Richmond and Petersburg and the retreat of the army reached Lexington not long after Harry left, followed soon by news of the surrender. During this time Cornelia waited anxiously for word of her son. Some of the Lexington men in the army got home as early as April 12, having tramped the fifty miles from Appomattox, but Harry was not among them.[19]

At last he appeared, haggard and bone-weary. Upon entering the house he put his hands to his face and cried. It was some time before he could speak. "To think it is all over," he sobbed, "and I did not strike a blow."[20]

He had little time to rest before he had to take on another mission. When the family received word that Edward was lying wounded in a Confederate military hospital in Charlottesville, sixty miles away, Cornelia immediately sent Harry to his aid. Edward and Harry had become separated during the chaotic retreat, and until now no one knew what had become of Edward. On arriving in Charlottesville, Harry learned the full story. Edward had been with a detachment that repulsed an assault by Yankee infantry and cavalry on April 6 at a place called High Bridge, one of a number of flank attacks that Lee's troops had had to fend off in those desperate final days as they were strung out along the road in flight. In this engagement, one of the army's very last, Edward—who had served for four years without a scratch—was shot in the face. A Minié ball smashed into his lower jaw, sliced through his tongue, and lodged near his windpipe. Knowing he could get no medical treatment in his own army and unwilling to fall into enemy hands, he stayed on his horse and headed for Charlottesville, where he eventually arrived bleeding, weak, and unable to speak. For days he lay prostrate in the hospital, taking liquid nourishment only, while the doctors debated his case. The bullet was in a dangerous spot and had to come out, but his condition made the use of chloroform risky. When at last he was informed of this predicament, Edward did not hesitate. Taking pencil and paper, he wrote: "Leave off the chloroform; cut it out; I can stand it." And so the operation was performed.[21]

Finding that Edward was recovering and that another stepbrother was already at the hospital caring for him, Harry returned to Lexington. He found the townsfolk in a state of great uncertainty. With Lee's army gone and the leading officials of the Confederate and state government on the run, many people considered the war over. But no federal occupation force had yet appeared anywhere near Lexington, and there were rebel armies still in the field elsewhere in the South. Some people were willing to continue the struggle; there was even talk of waging guerrilla war to keep the Yankees at bay.[22]

The immediate danger, however, was anarchy. There were a lot of footloose rebel soldiers roaming about, many of them not parolees but stragglers or deserters, some of them armed. There were the slaves to consider, too: although still obedient to their masters for the most part, they were well aware of Lee's surrender and might decide to try to emancipate themselves without waiting for Yankee troops to arrive. Whether the local authorities—the only authorities now functioning—could deal effectively with these threats was questionable.[23]

Some Rockbridge County citizens had taken matters into their own hands as soon as they learned of Lee's surrender. Assembling at the courthouse in Lexington on April 11, they formed a volunteer police force. Worried that this might cause trouble in the future, however, they issued a public disclaimer: "It is to be distinctly understood that this is only a temporary expedient, and that the organization is to be disbanded in the event of the county being occupied by the military authorities of the United States."[24]

These citizens acted none too soon, for in the succeeding days incidents of robbery, theft, and disorder multiplied. The police managed to keep Lexington fairly safe and quiet, although there was an incident on April 29 in which three armed and mounted men in Confederate uniform rode into town and, as the newspaper reported, "caused a ruckus." Out in the county, there was a good deal more trouble, most of it ascribed to the "vile deserters," "lawless desperadoes," and "bands of renegades" who had infested the mountainous districts for some time.[25]

11. Main Street, Lexington, Virginia, ca. 1867–70. On the ridge in the far distance stands the Virginia Military Institute.

There was little trouble from the blacks. In the opinion of most citizens and officials, until someone with formal authority and the force to back it up appeared and ordered them to obey the Emancipation Proclamation, they should keep the blacks under tight control, and they took steps to do so. On May 1, the magistrates of the county court convened in Lexington and reorganized the slave patrol system. With so many soldiers now home there was no longer a shortage of men to ride patrol, and the magistrates therefore increased the strength of each company from five to twenty-one. The patrollers were instructed "to visit all suspected places . . . disperse unlawful and disorderly assemblages, quell disturbances, and assist the Civil Authority in the preservation of the peace."[26]

There was, to be sure, a degree of doubt and hesitancy regarding the continued enforcement of slavery. As with the formation of the volunteer police, people feared there might be unpleasant repercussions when and if the Yankees arrived. Just to be on the safe side, the county magistrates made no mention of blacks or slaves in their revised patrol ordinance, disguising it as a general law-enforcement measure. For the same reason, the slave-auction house of Myler & Williams on Bridge Street in Lexington quietly withdrew its regular advertisement from the newspaper beginning with the April 13 issue. Nor were there any notices about slave-hiring or runaways to be seen in the paper from that date on. Nevertheless, slavery persisted in the town and county through the spring. "There are as yet *no* 'Freedmen' here," a Lexington resident boasted on May 26, "and our 'servants' are still *in statu quo*. . . . We have an armed patrol which keeps perfect order and makes them stand in some fear."[27]

By that date, the Yankees had made one appearance, but it was of no consequence for the black population. Before dawn on May 20, a force of 300 cavalrymen rode into Lexington to arrest former governor Letcher, whom the federal authorities deemed a public enemy. The troopers stayed only long enough to locate his home and take him into custody. They ignored the blacks.[28]

While slavery survived through the spring, the spirit of resistance did not. As news filtered in of the surrender of the remaining Confederate armies and the capture of Jefferson Davis, the last die-hard rebel patriots bowed to the reality of defeat. Even the editor of the Lexington newspaper, who had been an unwavering voice of Confederate nationalism throughout the war, now advised his readers to accept their fate and cease talk of continuing the struggle through partisan warfare: "At present it could avail nothing, and would only bring ruin upon neighborhoods in which it is carried on. . . . [T]here is no sacrifice of honor or dignity in quietly desisting from a contest that can no longer be maintained with any hopes of success. All that we can now do is to remain quietly at home, endeavor to preserve order around us, make such efforts as we can to procure what is necessary for ourselves and our families, and thus await the developments of the future."[29]

By late spring the only manifestations of rebel defiance in Lexington and Rockbridge County were the sullen avowals of a few that they would not live under Yankee rule—they would leave the country, they said, and go to Mexico or Brazil. Among the others who had once pledged their loyalty to the Confederacy, two sentiments now prevailed. Those who had given up hope before Appomattox felt enormous relief at the coming of peace. Those who had remained hopeful to the end mourned the loss of their patriotic dream.[30]

Cornelia herself felt both relief and sorrow, for in the war's last months she had been torn between head and heart: the one told her sternly that the cause was lost, the other whispered encouragement. That Southern men, including her own first-born, would no longer have to face death on the battlefield was deeply gratifying to her. But at the same time, the extinction of the Confederacy overwhelmed her with "Grief and despair . . . [and] a sense of humiliation that till then I did not know I could feel."[31]

Although she accepted defeat, she refused to embrace her former enemies as friends. She could not readily forgive the Yankees' heinous sins. They had invaded and subjugated a people who wanted only to be left alone; they had killed many thousands of men, her husband among them; they had seized and destroyed Southern property, including her own home; they had declared war on slavery and were now about to unleash an entire race fit only for servitude. When news of Lincoln's assassination came, her first impulse was to cheer: "I thought it was just what he deserved."[32]

She had little time to indulge in bitter reflections, however, for the family's plight demanded her attention. "Our condition had been desolate before," she wrote, "but now was forlorn to the last degree." The money owed her by the Confederate government had never come. Her stock of food was dwindling, and the garden would yield nothing for weeks. On the other hand, she continued to give lessons in her home and thus still had a little income. And in early May a small windfall came her way when the local agent of the Confederate War Department decided to unlock the commissary warehouse he was still dutifully guarding and distribute its contents to the citizens, or at least those he deemed worthy. Cornelia, as a soldier's widow, got some bacon and beans.[33]

Every day she was reminded that there were many whose circumstances were as dire as hers or worse. Rebel soldiers frequently came through Lexington on their way home, and some knocked on her door to see if they might get a bite to eat. As she shared with them whatever food and coffee she had, she listened to their horrible tales of combat, their sad recollections of dead comrades, and their anxious musings on their prospects for the future. Some had nothing now but the tattered uniforms they wore. Others who passed through Lexington were more pitiful still. One of Cornelia's friends reported that while walking downtown one day she saw six one-legged veterans sitting together on a stack of lumber. They were trying to get to their families in Tennessee and North Carolina, limping along on their crutches and hitching rides when they could.[34]

Even those of high rank now faced an uncertain future. General Pendleton had returned home to Lexington a few days after Appomattox to find his family's food supply reduced to one small ham, some bread and milk, and a little lettuce. He was pleased to learn that he would be able to resume his former position as rector of the Episcopal church; however, given the difficult circumstances of the church just now, the vestrymen could promise him no regular salary. But the general did have a horse, a garden beside his house, and some vacant lots on the edge of town. And, although fifty-five years old, he was blessed with strength and health. He therefore went to work as a farmer, plowing and planting and cultivating. Many days he labored in his little fields from dawn to dusk. Now and then, passing soldiers would stop to ask him where they might get something to eat, never suspecting that this dirty, sweat-streaked, gray-bearded man had been one of Lee's chief lieutenants.[35]

And then there were the civilian refugees. Many of these also trudged through Lexington in the last weeks of spring, traveling northward from their places of wartime exile to return to the homes they had abandoned when the Yankees invaded northern Virginia. Most were unsure of what they would find when they reached home and many had no idea how they would make a living thereafter. One day there appeared at Cornelia's door an old friend from Winchester, an elderly man named Joseph Sherrard, a refugee who was now heading home. He had been one of Winchester's prominent citizens before the war, a well-to-do banker and businessman. He was penniless, he told Cornelia, having put all his money into his now-defunct bank and Confederate bonds. His "hair was whiter than ever," Cornelia noticed upon greeting him, and his "aged, withered face" was "hopeless and sad." Still, he had blessings to count. His son Joseph Jr., who had served in the 11th Virginia Cavalry with Edward, had survived the war in good health, although wounded five times.[36]

Cornelia herself was a refugee from Winchester, and she too thought of going home. But before spring ended she received a discouraging report from a relative who had just been there. Hawthorn, the family's sixty-acre estate on the outskirts of the town, was an uninhabitable ruin; the destruction begun by the Yankee occupiers while Cornelia and her children were living there was now complete. Although the house still stood, everything else was gone. The barn, stable, granary, smokehouse, henhouse, and every other outbuilding had been torn down and carried away for firewood; even the privy had disappeared. The wooden fences had suffered the same fate, while the stone fences had been carted off to bolster military fortifications. The orchard had fallen to the ax, along with the stately cedar trees that had flanked the driveway. The lawn and garden had been trampled into oblivion by horses's hooves and wagon wheels. To get the place back into condition to support the family would require capital and labor far beyond anything Cornelia could muster. And besides, she could not even afford to rent the wagon and team they would need to move back.[37]

Assuming the victorious Yankees did not undertake the wholesale confiscation of rebel property—a punitive measure that some Northern leaders were urging—Cornelia would be able to sell Hawthorn and her late husband's other land holdings, and thus regain some economic security. But, given the confusion and uncertainty now gripping the South, it would likely take years to adjudicate the estate and secure a title. Nor could Cornelia count on any immediate financial help from kinfolk; from what she could learn, no one in her extended family was any better off than she.[38]

She saw no alternative: she and the children would have to stay put for now and get along the best they could. "So therefore I remained in Lexington," she wrote, "seeing no prospect of relief, and having no hope of assistance."[39]

LOUIS HUGHES

IN THE LATTER PART OF MARCH, UNION FORCES MOVED AGAINST Mobile—45,000 troops, in two great columns, approaching the city from the south and east. Word of the invasion came by steamboat sixty miles up the Tombigbee to the state saltworks, where Superintendent Brooks and Commissioner Woolsey received the news anxiously. By the end of the month the invaders were pounding the city's defensive works with siege artillery. On April 11 the battered rebels abandoned their fortifications and retreated northward; the triumphant Yankees marched into Mobile the next day. As soon as they learned of the city's capture, Brooks and Woolsey put into action their contingency plan.[1]

Lou Hughes had not yet sold all 500 of his tobacco plugs when Brooks informed him that the saltworks was being evacuated and the slaves were all being sent back to their owners. The superintendent wrote out a letter of explanation to Madam, gave it to Lou, and then set about shutting down the works. Lou and Matilda gathered up the things they intended to take along—including several hundred dollars, much of it now safely converted into silver coins, that Lou's tobacco venture had brought him—and joined the rest of the slaves as they were furnished with provisions and then led down to the river.[2]

At the river the slaves found a scene of confusion. Hundreds of local citizens, many driving wagons piled high with their possessions, jammed the area around the landing, desperate to get away before the Yankees appeared. But there was nothing anyone there could do for now but mill around nervously until a boat came by. At seven o'clock the next morning, one was spotted in the far distance, chugging upstream from the direction of Mobile.

Some of the citizens, unable to make out its markings, panicked: "It is a gun boat," they shouted. "The Yankees are coming!" However, it proved to be one of the river packets, and as it put into the landing the citizens stifled their terror and began jostling for a place in line to board. Taking passage upriver would have been the fastest way to flee, but the boat could not accommodate such a crowd. The captain did agree, however, to ferry people, wagons, and teams across the river.[3]

It took a long time for the saltworks slaves to get across, for the frightened locals insisted on going first. Once they were on the west bank, Lou, Matilda, and the rest set out northward on foot, escorted probably by some of the overseers from the works. They headed for Demopolis, about seventy-five miles away.[4]

When the little column trudged into Demopolis, after a journey of several days, Lou and Matilda and their newborn were sent to the train station. Brooks had arranged for the three to go the rest of the way home by rail. Lou was to inform Madam that the saltworks had been abandoned and that the rest of her slaves were on the way to her.[5]

The train that Lou and Matilda boarded took them westward across the state line to Meridian, where they boarded another that continued west to Jackson. There they changed to a northbound train that carried them along the tracks of the Mississippi Central to Grenada. In Grenada they transferred to the Mississippi & Tennessee line, which ran north to Panola County.[6]

Delays were inevitable on the deteriorating rail lines of the Confederacy, and it was probably well past the middle of April when Lou and Matilda stepped off the train at the depot in Panola County. Spring was well advanced by then and, although the weather had not yet turned hot, the air was humid and the foliage dense. As they walked the several miles to their destination, they passed woods of oak and hickory and pine that alternated with plowed fields. Panola was cotton country—the name in fact was derived from an Indian word for cotton—and it was now planting time.[7]

Ahead of them a lane intersected the road they were following. A large gate straddled the lane where it met the road. This was the entrance to the plantation of Master Jack McGehee, Madam's father. It was a familiar sight to Lou and Matilda, for both had lived here for a time after leaving Memphis. Passing through the gate, they followed the lane through a grove and across the yard to the Big House. There they presented themselves to Madam and delivered their news along with Brooks's letter.[8]

Madam immediately dispatched some wagons to rendezvous with the slaves coming on foot from Demopolis; the wagons would take them the rest of the way to Mississippi. They were not to be brought to Master Jack's plantation, however, for he did not need them. Instead, Madam arranged for them to be rented out in various towns along the way: some in Jackson, some in Grenada, some in the county seat. Of all the McGehee slaves who had labored at the works, only Lou and Matilda would be kept at home with Madam and her family.[9]

Matilda was sent to the kitchen and put to work. There would be plenty of cooking for her to do, for the Big House was crowded: Master Jack had taken in not only Madam and her children but also another of his widowed daughters, Mary Farrington, and her son, along with the local Methodist circuit rider and his wife. Lou, however, would not be waiting on them, for Master Jack put him to work in the fields. He and Matilda were assigned to live in one of the slave cabins, which they would share with another couple named George and Kitty.[10]

There were ten such cabins on this plantation, which before the war had been home to fifty-seven slaves. Master Jack was not the biggest slaveholder in Panola County, but he had by far the biggest plantation—4,500 acres, over seven square miles. A good part of that acreage was devoted to cotton, and the plantation also embraced fields sown with corn and wheat, pastures where cattle and sheep grazed, and 2,000 acres of woodland where hogs rooted. The estate boasted as well a large orchard and garden, a stable that could accommodate fifteen horses and forty mules, and a dairy big enough for twenty cows.[11]

As Lou looked around the plantation that spring, however, he could see that it was not what it had once been. While Panola County had never suffered the kind of massive Yankee invasion that had brought utter ruin to many other Confederate regions, it had not altogether escaped punishment. Union raiding parties had swept through the area a number of times and had pillaged Master Jack's plantation at least once. Nervously anticipating another raid, the McGehees had taken steps to preserve what was left of their valuables. They had boxed up all the silverware in the house—$250 worth of knives, forks, spoons, trays, and cake baskets—and buried it under the henhouse. Barrels and boxes of other things went down into a pit dug under the Big House. The family's finest clothes were wrapped up and stashed in the house; certain slaves were designated to come running at the first report of a raid and carry the clothing to their cabins, which the Yankees would presumably not bother to loot.[12]

The rebel army had been as destructive as the Yankees. In one corner of the plantation there lay a heap of charred wood, all that remained of a shelter that Master Jack had built in 1862 to protect his cotton. Like other planters in that section of the country, he had had to store his crop after the capture of Memphis, which cut him off from his customary market. And, like others, he then had to watch helplessly while Confederate soldiers put every bale to the torch to keep it out of the hands of the advancing army of General Ulysses S. Grant—which never reached Panola.[13]

When the county tax assessor came around in 1864, Master Jack reported some of the losses he had suffered since the war began. The 120 taxable cattle he had had in 1861 had been reduced to 70. Three of his best horses were gone, and so were his piano, his clock, and two of his three carriages. Nor were his smokehouse and grain bins as full as they once had been, for the Confederate government had seized its share of produce through the tax-in-kind: by 1864 Master Jack had surrendered 1,650 bushels of corn, 130 bushels of wheat, and 2,406 pounds of bacon to feed the rebel army.[14]

These material losses weighed heavily on Master Jack, but not so heavily as the personal losses he had endured since the war broke out. Malinda, his wife of more than fifty years and the mother of his thirteen children, had died in the spring of 1864, leaving him deeply depressed. Her death had come soon after that of their oldest son, Miles. Two of their sons-in-law, one of them Boss, had died not long before that; and a grandson had been killed at the battle of Shiloh in 1862. And now this grieving widower had responsibility for two widowed daughters and their families, and the management of a plantation with no overseer.[15]

He knew that he would not have to bear these burdens much longer. He was seventy-six years old and in bad health; his hand shook so badly he could no longer sign his name legibly. His mortality was much on his mind. In the carriage house of his plantation was stored a coffin that he intended for himself. It had been built two years earlier when his son-in-law Charles Dandridge died, having accidentally shot himself while practicing with a pistol at a neighboring plantation. Fine caskets being nearly impossible to procure in the Confederacy by that time, Master Jack had made do by ordering two of his slaves to cobble together a plain coffin using some lumber on hand. They covered it with black fabric from one of Malinda McGehee's dresses and

12. *John S. "Master Jack" McGehee*

lined the inside with the opera cloak of Charles's widow, Tabitha Ann. But when Charles's corpse was lifted up to be placed inside, it proved to be too bloated to fit. Master Jack then ordered a larger coffin prepared and put away the smaller for himself.[16]

It may be that death held no terror for him. He was a devout Christian, a pillar of the local Methodist church. And he could die with the assurance that he had a reputation as a generous man and a good neighbor. Local people remembered especially an episode in 1851, when typhoid struck among the slaves of a family whose farm adjoined Master Jack's. It was cotton-picking time, and the family stood to lose their whole crop for lack of hands to gather it. Without a word to his neighbors, Master Jack sent his own hands over to do the job.[17]

He was not so esteemed among the blacks, however. Lou, for one, was secretly contemptuous of the old man. He mocked Master Jack's peculiar way of speaking, his habit of repeating a word or part of a word ("I don't know what Edmund is thinking about-out," Lou heard him say upon first seeing Boss's mansion, "to build such a house-house"). Lou sneered, too, at the old man's bluster. He talked big, Lou recalled in his memoir, but "was the verriest coward when danger was present." Lou had been at the plantation during the Yankee raid and had seen Master Jack cringing in bed with a pretended stomach ache to avoid facing the enemy pillagers, all the while whining, "Where are they? Are they gone?" and calling for a slave to come nurse him: "Tell Kitty-itty-itty to get me a mush poultice-oltice." Lou also regarded Master Jack as a harsh slave owner. He had often heard the old man chide Boss for his paternalism, saying it only spoiled the servants. "It will ruin them," he had muttered while observing Lou and Matilda's marriage ceremony, "givin wedins-wedins."[18]

Master Jack considered Lou not only spoiled but also unreliable. Even before his first escape attempt, Master Jack had warned Boss about him: "Keep you[r] eye on that boy . . . he is slippery-slippery, too smart-art." The old man's suspicions were aggravated when, on one of his frequent visits to the Memphis estate, he discovered chalk marks on the side of the barn and correctly surmised that Lou was trying to learn to write.[19]

It may have been because Master Jack disliked Lou that he did not put him to work in the Big House when he arrived from the saltworks. Or perhaps he was needed more in the fields. Whatever the reason, Lou now found himself with a hoe in his hand. It was not unfamiliar work. Though he had been primarily a house servant, he had occasionally been sent to the fields by Boss during busy seasons on the Pontotoc plantation, and he had learned how to plow and plant and hoe and pick. Still, it was a great change for him, exchanging his nice suit and shoes and white linen apron for the rough brogans and homespun shirt and pants of a field hand, and leaving behind the polishing and dusting and serving to sweat amid the furrows. Now, too, he had to live in a crowded, dirt-floor cabin with rude wooden furniture and a primitive grease lamp for lighting. (At least his mattress was comfortable: the McGehees had hidden some of their ginned cotton from the Yankees by having the slaves stuff it into their bedticks.) And unless Matilda managed to bring some of the white folks' food back to their cabin, Lou had to eat the common fare of the field hands. This meant a lot of bacon and corn bread. The latter was nicknamed "Johnny Constant" by the slaves; they were treated to wheat bread so rarely that they called it "Billy Seldom."[20]

Of the fifty or so slaves then on the plantation, about half were "full hands," that is, fully grown but not elderly. Each had his or her assigned task. Most, like Lou, labored in the fields in a work gang supervised by the black foreman, Uncle Peter. One slave, whose name was John Smith, cared for the livestock. Of the women who did not work in the fields, some, including Matilda, spent their days cooking; others did laundry or weaving, worked in the garden, or served as maids in the Big House. The black children on the plantation, including thirteen-year-old Hannah and eleven-year-old Clarke, helped out with various tasks to the extent of their ability. Only the smaller children and babies were exempt from work. They were tended during the day in the plantation nursery by an older slave woman.[21]

Six days a week, the slaves labored from dawn to dusk. For Lou and the other field hands this meant rising before daylight and heading for the fields without breakfast. They took along a "morning bite" left over from the previous night's supper and downed it during a brief break. Around noon they halted for dinner, which was usually brought to them in the fields. After eating and resting a while, all hands went back to work until sundown.[22]

By arriving late in the season, Lou had missed some of the heaviest field work: pulling the old stalks in the cotton fields and corn fields, deep plowing with a shovel plow to break up the compacted soil, and more plowing with a turning plow to line the fields with furrows and ridges in preparation for planting. He had also missed corn-planting, which was done before cotton-planting. Most of Master Jack's cotton seed was probably already in the ground before Lou got there, too, though there was still time to plant more. This was done by running a scratch plow along each ridge to create what was called a drill, then dropping seeds into the drills and covering the seeds with soil using a hoe. As soon as the corn and cotton plants began to poke above the surface, cultivation began. For Lou and the others in the work gang, this meant long days spent with hoe in hand, bent over and moving slowly through the fields, carefully chopping away weeds and thinning out the

13. Fredonia Methodist Church still stands in Panola County, Mississippi, virtually unchanged since the days when Louis Hughes and the McGehee family attended services there.

sprouting plants. Now and then as the season progressed the hands also had to hitch a bull-tongue plow to a mule and run it down the furrows to destroy weeds and loosen up the soil for better drainage, taking care not to run over the growing plants or cut their roots. On rainy days there were indoor chores to do, including carding and spinning wool and making the oak baskets in which the ripe cotton would be collected in the fall.[23]

Daylight stretched for well over thirteen hours on these spring days in northern Mississippi. After the sun set, the bone-weary slaves generally just ate their supper and relaxed a bit before turning in. All looked forward to their weekly day of rest. But for Lou it was not altogether restful.[24]

On Sunday mornings Master Jack and his family went to church. It took two carriages to accommodate them all—Madam or Mary Farrington must have provided one, since Master Jack had just one of his own now. Lou and George were detailed as drivers, which meant they had to rise early, hitch up the horses, and have the carriages waiting in the yard of the Big House when the McGehees emerged in their Sunday clothes.[25]

The family's usual destination was the nearby Fredonia Methodist Church. The McGehees had been associated with this church for decades. Master Jack himself had designed the building back in 1842, and his wife was buried there in the little graveyard; there was a plot next to hers where one day his own remains would be laid.[26]

The church sat on a low hill surrounded by cedars. It was a white wooden building with a portico, suggestive of the Greek Revival style but very plain. Arriving at the church, the McGehees would go up the steps and through the double doors. Inside they divided to pews on either side, for here the old tradition of separate seating for the sexes was still observed. Lou and George, after securing the carriages, could also enter the church—not through the main entrance, however, but through a side door. This gave access to a stairway that led to a gallery where the slaves were seated opposite the pulpit.[27]

The gallery was not large, for few slaves in that community accompanied their masters to church. The custom was to hold services for the blacks on each plantation on Sunday afternoons. These were sometimes conducted by a local minister who rode a circuit of plantations after his morning church service, visiting each perhaps one Sunday a month. Along with the good news of salvation, this white preacher invariably delivered a message of obedience, reminding the assembled blacks that God had ordained slavery and expected servants to submit to their masters. More gratifying to the black faithful were the words of the slave preachers, or exhorters, who led the Sunday afternoon services in the absence of the white circuit rider. The fervent sermons of these unlettered men of God, so different from the preaching of the white minister, touched the black congregations profoundly. Lou attended many such black-led services on Boss's and Master Jack's plantations and he was always moved by the words of the exhorters, which were at once stirring and consoling. He recalled these times warmly in his memoir: "Many tears were shed, and many glad shouts of praise would burst forth during the sermon. A hymn usually followed the sermon, then all retired. Their faces seemed to shine with a happy light—their very countenance showed that their souls had been refreshed. . . . These meetings were the joy and comfort of the slaves, and even those who did not profess Christianity were calm and thoughtful while in attendance."[28]

These Sunday afternoon gatherings were generally held out of doors in all seasons except winter, but it was unusually cool in Panola that spring. There was a warm spell in mid-May, but otherwise it stayed cold from the time Lou came until summer arrived with June, cold enough for the slaves to wear their woolen winter clothes and keep the fires going in their cabins all night. It was dry, too—not enough rain to please the planters. The county also endured a plague of sorts that spring: gnats. The creatures were everywhere, pestering and biting people and livestock and poultry alike.[29]

While Lou swatted gnats and chopped weeds, Matilda toiled in the kitchen behind the Big House. She was no doubt grateful for the cool weather, for the kitchen was always warm. She was working hard: getting up each day with Lou, carrying her baby in its cradle to the nursery, and cooking breakfast, dinner, and supper for the McGehees while periodically returning to the nursery to breast-feed her baby. But the worst part of her daily routine was having to endure the presence of Madam.[30]

Madam and her sister Mary were in charge of household matters on the plantation now that their mother was dead. This meant overseeing the blacks who cooked, cleaned, washed, wove, waited table, and tended the garden and the nursery. Madam's daughter, who was twenty-three, and Mary's son, who was almost fifteen, were old enough to help with these responsibilities and with the care of Madam's younger children, boys ages three and six.[31]

Madam was forty-five years old at this time. She had married Boss, who was her first cousin, when she was twenty-one. Three years later, when Lou first laid eyes on her, she struck him as "a handsome, stately lady . . . brunette in complexion, faultless in figure and imperious in manner." But the family tragedies of the war years had taken a toll. Her husband's sudden death, in particular, had devastated her; and the abandonment of their Memphis and Bolivar properties had left her without a home of her own. What Lou saw now, in the spring of 1865, was a woman "sadly changed—[she] did not appear like the same person. Her troubles and sorrows had crushed her former cruel and haughty spirit."[32]

Perhaps Matilda, good Christian that she was, had by now forgiven Madam for her cruelties. Lou could not. He remembered how she had terrorized him as a boy, slapping his jaw or pinching his ear for the slightest mistake, or for no reason at all. He remembered the tantrums that belied her image of stateliness, her screaming at him or some other servant, red-faced, stamping her foot, sometimes reaching out to slap a passing servant even as she sat at the dinner table. He remembered the almost daily beatings she inflicted on the black women as she made her rounds about the Memphis estate, all the while railing about the laziness and incompetence she had to put up with. He remembered how he came to dread hearing the words that heralded an especially brutal punishment at her hands: "Ah! You put up at the wrong hotel." But, more than anything else, he remembered how she had caused the death of his twin babies.[33]

Her real aim had been to punish Matilda, whom she particularly hated. When the twins were born, late in 1859 at the Memphis property, Boss had tried to lighten Matilda's burden by giving Lou time off to help her in the kitchen. But Madam would not hear of it. She made excuses to keep Lou occupied with errands and watched closely to see that Matilda did not slack off on her duties, which included washing and ironing the McGehees' clothes as well as preparing their meals and doing the dishes. It was all Matilda could do to slip away and nurse the babies at intervals during the day. "My heart was sore and heavy," Lou recalled, "for my wife was almost run to death with work. The children grew puny and sickly for want of proper care." A doctor confirmed this diagnosis and recommended that Matilda be allowed some rest, but Madam was relentless. Exhausted and desperate, Matilda finally packed up the babies, fled the mansion, made her way to a Memphis slave market, and told the proprietor she wanted to be sold. When Boss was notified, he came in his carriage to fetch her home. As they drove up to the mansion, Madam came running out, shouting at Matilda, "Ah! . . . you put up at the wrong hotel." She then took Matilda to the barn, tied her to a joist, and beat her. Afterward, she sent her back to work. The babies died six months later.[34]

Lou had hated Madam for a long time before this episode, and he continued to do so after. But he could never bring himself to hate Boss in the same way. In his younger days he had been quite in awe of Boss and had done all he could to please him. He thought him brilliant and distinguished, a man of patience, generosity, and humanity. He loved the way Boss would take him in hand and carefully instruct him in medicine and other skills. He saw what joy Boss took in giving little gifts to his "people," like the red-and-yellow checked gingham he brought back from a business trip for the slave women, who cried with delight and fashioned the cloth into fancy turbans. He was touched when he learned that Boss wrote occasional letters to the mother of a slave boy he had bought in Virginia, addressed to her owner, so that she might have news of the son she had been separated from.[35]

But there were times when Boss revealed his ignoble side. He was, for one thing, appallingly hot-headed. On one occasion at the Pontotoc place, Lou had watched in horror as Boss armed himself with a double-barreled shotgun and prepared to kill one of his neighbors over a silly property dispute. And, for all Boss's paternalism and kindness, he often unleashed his fury on his slaves. "[A]lways there was slashing and whipping" going on at Boss's place, Lou remembered. Generally the overseer dealt out the prescribed punishments, but if Boss lost his temper or felt especially aggrieved, he wielded the whip himself. Lou saw him do so many times. One of his victims was Matilda. He assisted in Madam's thrashing of her in the barn; and on another occasion, after Madam complained about her, he became so enraged that he grabbed Matilda and choked her.[36]

Lou was not exempt from such treatment. He learned early on how quickly Boss could turn from patient mentor to brutal disciplinarian. His memory of one occasion in the 1850s, after his second escape attempt, was still vivid four decades later:

> I was taken to the barn where stocks had been prepared, beside which were a cowhide and a pail of salt water, all prepared for me. . . . I was fastened in the stocks, my clothing removed, and the whipping began. Boss whipped me a while, then he sat down and read his paper, after which the whipping was resumed. This continued for two hours. Fastened as I was in the stocks, I could only stand and take lash after lash, as long as he desired, the terrible rawhide cutting into my flesh at every stroke. Then he used peach tree switches, which cracked the flesh so the blood oozed out. After this came the paddle, two and a half feet long and three inches wide. Salt and water was at once applied to wash the wounds, and the smarting was maddening. . . . I could hardly move after the terrible ordeal was finished, and could scarcely bear my clothes to touch me at first, so sore was my whole body.[37]

Punishments such as this whetted Lou's desire for freedom. So did the outbreak of war, the Yankee invasion, and the Emancipation Proclamation. Reports of these events circulated among the Confederacy's slaves despite the efforts of Southern whites to keep the slaves uninformed. Lou himself picked up a lot of news by eavesdropping on the McGehee family's conversations, and he shared it eagerly with his fellow servants. He remembered listening on one occasion while Master Jack cursed the Confederate president for bungling the war effort: "What is Jeff Davis doin'-doin'? . . . [He] is a grand rascal-rascal." Among themselves, the slaves whispered about such stories, and as Confederate defeat became more certain, they made up songs to celebrate their coming freedom. Lou recalled one that Kitty sang:

There'll be no more talk about Monday, by and by,
But every day will be Sunday, by and by.

Always, however, the slaves had to take care to hide their feelings from the whites. One time Kitty was careless: Malinda McGehee overheard her singing in the kitchen and interrupted her sharply: "Don't think you are going to be free; you darkies were made by God and ordained to wait upon us."[38]

Even as the war raised hopes and opened new opportunities for seekers of freedom, however, it posed new dangers. Lou had learned of these dangers firsthand during his two wartime escape attempts. For one thing, Confederate army patrols were about, and they had orders to keep an eye not only on the Yankees but also on the slaves. Lou had blundered into one of these as he fled Master Jack's plantation just after Christmas of 1862, heading for a rumored Union army force at Holly Springs. The rebel soldiers held him long enough to ascertain from where he had escaped, then whipped him with dogwood switches, dragged him back to Master Jack's, and whipped him again in the presence of Madam.[39]

His next attempt, a few weeks later, had pointed up another danger: the increased vigilance of the white citizenry. On this occasion, Lou, Matilda, and three others set out from Master Jack's with the hope of reaching Memphis. They took every precaution, traveling at night only, staying off the roads, carefully skirting farmhouses. After two nights of stumbling through fields and woods and thickets and swamps, they had made about fifteen miles and were congratulating themselves on their success when they heard bloodhounds yelping and men shouting. The five scattered, but it was no use. The party of pursuers—which consisted of two McGehee relatives, a hired tracker known as "Williams the nigger-catcher," and his fourteen dogs—rounded up all the fugitives. When Lou descended from the persimmon tree in which he had taken refuge, the dogs ripped his flesh, Williams urging them on. The five were marched back to Panola by their captors, stopping overnight at a farmhouse where an old white woman taunted them: "You niggers going to the Yankees? You all ought to be killed." Once they were back at Master Jack's, Lou recalled, "All of us were whipped. All the members of the family were very angry. Old Lady Jack McG[eh]ee was so enraged that she said to my wife: 'I thought you were a Christian. You'll never see your God.'"[40]

Panola County had never been an easy place for slaves to escape from. In the Old South, the racial fears of whites were greatest where slaves were most numerous, and in Panola County there were many slaves: they constituted six-tenths of the county's population in 1860. As a result, whites in Panola strove to maintain the mechanisms of control that in many other Southern communities had been relaxed. Patrols rode regularly at night to watch for suspicious activity; slaves were required to have a written pass to travel beyond their home. Whites were especially watchful in the district around the village of Como, where Master Jack's plantation was located. In this district the county's biggest plantations were concentrated, and whites were outnumbered by blacks five to one.[41]

With the war came not only increased vigilance on the part of whites in Panola, but also increased brutality. Lou knew of three slaves who were killed while trying to escape. One was a slave of Boss who was being held at Master Jack's after Boss evacuated the Bolivar plantation. He slipped away and got a few miles from the plantation before being overtaken by Master Jack's son William, a Confederate soldier who happened to be home at the time. Instead of bringing the man back, William shot him dead.[42]

Lou got that story secondhand, but he was an eyewitness to another episode. Two slaves belonging to a neighbor of Master Jack, a man named Wallace, were caught running away and were returned to their master. Wallace decided to do the community a favor by making an example of them. He had the two hanged and notified his neighbors. Lou tells the rest of the story: "All of our servants were called up, told every detail . . . and then compelled to go and see them where they hung. I never shall forget the horror of the scene—it was sickening. The bodies hung at the roadside . . . until the blue flies literally swarmed around them, and the stench was fearful."[43]

Escape was not impossible. A number of Panola County slaves made it to freedom during the war, either by managing to elude their pursuers all the way to the Union lines or by going off with one of the Yankee raiding parties that periodically came through the county. But, as Lou had learned, evading determined pursuers for any great distance was very difficult; and, as he learned on another occasion, Yankee raids did not always offer an opportunity to escape.[44]

Lou had come face to face with Union troops at Master Jack's plantation in early 1863. One night he was awakened by a rumbling sound coming from the road, like the noise of heavy wagons. Cautiously he crept from his cabin and saw federal artillery passing and some soldiers at the creek. He remained hidden, however, fearing that if he approached the soldiers, they might get startled and open fire. After the troops moved on, Lou returned to the quarters, told Matilda and George what he had seen, and suggested that this might be a good time to flee. But George, who was older than Lou, advised him not to be hasty; they needed time to prepare.[45]

Early the next morning Lou set out on an errand, mounted on one of Master Jack's good horses. He was carrying a package and some letters that he was to mail at the Como post office. As he dismounted to open the gate, he was accosted by a Union officer on horseback leading a column of soldiers down the road. If Lou had ever fantasized about a warm reception and instant freedom upon meeting the Yankee invaders, that fantasy was now dashed. The officer seemed interested only in Lou's horse. He forced Lou to exchange mounts, leaving Lou with a very sorry nag, and then confiscated the package and letters and rode away with his men behind him.[46]

Lou returned to his cabin, sick with anticipation of the punishment he was sure to get for losing the horse and mail. Perhaps he might have gone off with these Yankees. But they had in no way encouraged him; and what if he had tried and they had rejected him, or had taken him along but then abandoned him, and the McGehees found out about it? And even if he got away, what about Matilda? A half hour later, another detachment of Yankees appeared and entered the grounds of the plantation. One old slave shouted, "My Lord! de year of jubilee am come." But Lou did not even think about escape. He just went to the Big House, reported that Yankees were pillaging the dairy, and broke the bad news about the horse and mail.[47]

It would have been different had there been a permanent Union occupation force in or near Panola. Wherever such garrisons were posted in the South, slavery disintegrated. Yankee raiding parties might be reluctant to burden themselves with black runaways, but the army post commanders were under orders to take in all who came and to see to it that the Emancipation Proclamation was enforced as far as their authority could reach.[48]

Federal authority did not reach Panola County, even as late as the spring of 1865. There were not even any raids through the county that spring. Thus the mechanisms of racial control could remain in force. As long as there were men around who had guns and were committed to preserving slavery, it would endure—until the arrival of other men with guns who were committed to ending it.

There were not as many men with guns in Panola in the spring of 1865 as there once had been, for the demands of war had taken many away. Still, there were enough. Master Jack may have been too feeble to wield a weapon, but he knew that all he had to do in an emergency was raise the alarm and armed white men would be at his side, their bloodhounds yelping. And the blacks on his plantation knew it, too.[49]

By the early part of May enough news had reached Panola to make it clear that the Confederacy had collapsed and the war was over. Federal occupation forces began to move into the interior of Mississippi. By May 13 there was a garrison at Grenada, about fifty miles south of Master Jack's. Army authorities issued proclamations warning the citizens of the state that resistance must cease and slaves must be freed. As word of these orders filtered into Panola County, some slave owners released their hold.[50]

Others did not, especially in the Como district. Master Jack, for one, was determined to preserve his little world as long as he could. He decreed that none of his blacks would be allowed off the plantation for any reason, except Lou and George on the Sunday morning church excursions. His word still carried authority. In addition to whatever neighbors he could call on, he now had the assistance of his son William, recently returned from the Confederate army and as ready as ever to gun down any black fugitive he caught.[51]

Lou, George, and Kitty spoke to one another often in those last days of May about the possibility of escape. They did not do so in the presence of Matilda, who had been so traumatized by her failed attempt in 1863 that she would not consent to another. The three knew that the war was over but had no idea when Union troops might actually be on hand to enforce their freedom. The garrison at Grenada was too distant to be of help. The nearest Yankee force, as far as they knew, was at Memphis, forty miles away.[52]

They agreed that the safest thing to do for now was to obey Master Jack and stay alert for an opportunity. And so they labored on, slaves still, amid the ruins of the Old South.[53]

Part Three

SUMMER

LOUIS HUGHES

WARM WEATHER RETURNED TO PANOLA COUNTY WITH THE ARRIVAL of June, and along with the summery heat came much-needed rain. The corn and cotton crops, which had struggled through the spring, now began to look quite promising. June brought another blessing as well: early in the month, to everyone's relief, the gnats disappeared.[1]

The question uppermost in Lou Hughes's mind was whether June would also bring his freedom. As the first week of the month gave way to the second, and then to the third and fourth, the answer seemed to be no. Though all of Mississippi was now formally under Union army rule and the state and county governments were dissolved, there were still no federal troops anywhere near the McGehee plantation. The commander of the garrison at Grenada, whose district included Panola County, proclaimed his authority but could not enforce it very far beyond his post. As long as this vacuum of authority persisted in Panola, Master Jack did not intend to relax his grip.[2]

In holding on to his black people so tenaciously, the old man may simply have been trying to wring a few last drops of profit from the institution of slavery before its inevitable demise. But he may have had something more in mind. There was hopeful talk among some Southern planters in those early summer weeks that the U.S. Supreme Court might nullify the Emancipation Proclamation, leaving the reconstructed Southern state governments free to restore slavery or at least to enact a gradual program of emancipation, perhaps with compensation to the slaveholders. Should this come to pass, those who were lucky and farsighted enough to hold on to their slaves would be rewarded.[3]

Whatever the motive, Master Jack and his family remained determined that no black person of theirs would escape the plantation. On Sunday, June

25, there was an incident that showed just how determined they were; and it was this that finally propelled Lou to make his break for freedom.

It happened as the McGehee clan returned from church. Most of the family members were in the carriages driven by Lou and George, and they took the main road home. Master Jack's son William was on horseback that day, however, and he took a different route that cut through the plantation. On the way he ran into some blacks from the neighborhood who had come to see the McGehee slaves. Sunday visiting in the quarters had always been tolerated by the McGehees, but now William grew suspicious. He demanded to know if the blacks had passes. When they replied that they did not, he ordered them off the premises. After Master Jack arrived at the Big House, William reported what had happened. Master Jack then summoned George and Uncle Peter, the foreman, and issued an order: no blacks from the neighborhood were to be allowed on the McGehee plantation without a pass from their owner, and any who showed up were to be brought to the Big House for interrogation.[4]

After George left the house, he found Lou and told him of the new rule. It was obvious to both men that Master Jack, worried that news from the outside world might make his slaves restless, now intended to seal them off completely. Lou looked at George and said:

"If we listen to them we shall be here until Christmas comes again."

"What do you mean?," George asked.

"I mean that now, today, is the time to make a start."[5]

Quickly they assessed their situation and devised a plan. They knew that they would not be able to keep their flight a secret for long. The McGehees would learn of it and would dispatch armed pursuers, probably with bloodhounds. The more time they had between their departure and the family's discovery of it, the better. It would be relatively easy to get away from the plantation without being spotted by any of the whites. The problem was to avoid being spotted by the other slaves: they were so terrified of being punished for not reporting an escape attempt that they might run to Master Jack. Waiting until nightfall to slip away was out of the question. It was just two days past the new moon and the tiny sliver of silver in the night sky would provide hardly any light. Lou and George therefore agreed that the best time to try to get away would be late that afternoon, when the slaves had gathered for their religious service. There was one who would not be at the service, however, and who would likely see them fleeing. This was John Smith, who had to feed the livestock every evening. They decided to approach John, reveal their plan, and beg him not to report their escape until he was through with the feeding, which was usually around seven. To their relief, John agreed. This would give them a good head start.[6]

They decided also to go without their wives and Lou's baby. The two men would go alone, heading for Memphis. If they succeeded in getting there, they would try to enlist help from the Union army and then return to the plantation to rescue the others.[7]

They returned to their cabin and told their wives what they intended to do. Matilda broke down, crying and pleading with Lou not to take such a risk. Kitty was stronger. "I'll be ready," she said, smiling, when Lou and George assured her that they would return.[8]

The men made their final preparations. They would have to travel as light as possible, but Lou made sure to take along some of the money he had made at the saltworks. Then, as the sounds of prayer and song reached them, they said good-bye to the women and set out. Quietly they made their way from the quarters to the orchard, then through the orchard to the fields and woods beyond, and past the boundary of Master Jack's land. They headed west, aiming for the Mississippi & Tennessee Railroad about five miles away. Their route took them through more fields and woods, for they avoided roads. All the while they listened for the sound of pursuers behind them; but they heard nothing.[9]

They reached the railroad just north of the Como depot, then followed it northward a few miles to a point near the village of Senatobia. By now it was about seven-thirty, and the sun had set. They found a safe place to camp and settled in for the night, elated at their success.[10]

The sun rose the next morning at quarter to five and the men set off again, still following the track northward. They were no longer worried about being pursued. In the communities they were now passing through, slavery was obviously dead. They saw other black people tramping along, heading for Memphis, and saw wagons loaded with cotton going in the same direction. They learned that a detachment of Union cavalry was now posted at Senatobia—perhaps it was this that had provoked Master Jack to try to insulate his slaves from news of the outside world. Rather than approach this small federal force, however, Lou and George decided to continue on to Memphis.[11]

It was about two o'clock in the afternoon when the two men arrived at Hernando, having made fifteen miles since daybreak. There they discovered that a train of sorts was running that could take them the remaining twenty miles to Memphis. This stretch of the Mississippi & Tennessee line had been wrecked during the war, but since the surrender the railroad company had managed to repair the track and trestles and put a flatcar in operation, pulled by a team of horses.[12]

Lou and George paid for their passage and seated themselves on the car. The day was sunny, and cooler than it had been for some time, so their open-air ride to Memphis was pleasant. It was slow, however, and not only because the horses could not match the speed of a locomotive. They also could not cross the narrow trestles, so each time the car approached a stream the teamsters had to unhitch them and lead them down the bank and through the water while the passengers pushed the car to the other side.[13]

It was almost sunset when the car pulled into Memphis. Lou looked around in wonder. The city had grown and changed so much in the three years since he had left that it was hardly recognizable. Black people were everywhere, for the city had become a mecca for fugitives from the plantations of northern Mississippi, western Tennessee, and eastern Arkansas. Lou saw some he knew, earlier escapees from Panola or Bolivar. Like him, they were slaves no longer. They were being called by a new name now: freedmen.[14]

The next day was Tuesday. Lou and George spent that day and Wednesday asking around, trying to figure out the best way to get help and complete their mission. As they walked the streets, Lou continued to shake his head in wonder at the changes he saw. Since it had fallen to the Union army in June 1862, Memphis had drawn not only hordes of blacks but also white refugees in great numbers, not to mention Yankee soldiers and citizens. The city was now home to at least 40,000 people, maybe 60,000—nobody knew for sure. To Lou it had always seemed a busy place, but now it fairly hummed; the old Memphis was a sleepy village by comparison. As he and George passed down Front Row, the heart of the business district, he saw many unfamiliar establishments among the shops and business houses and hotels. All around him, pedestrians, wagons, drays, and hacks jostled with one another for room. The annoyances that Memphians had always had to endure, especially in the summer, were now magnified. There was the dust, for one thing. The city authorities had never seen fit to pave the streets. The principal downtown thoroughfares were sprinkled with water every day, but it did not help much: choking clouds wafted in from the unsprinkled streets beyond. Lou knew that the only relief from the dust came when it rained, but then the streets turned to slop. The insects were worse than ever now, too. Flies buzzed around by the millions, feasting on the mounds of horse and mule dung that littered the streets. Swarms of mosquitoes fattened on animals and humans alike.[15]

Lou also took time to visit the place where he had lived for more than a decade. He was shocked to find that Boss's magnificent estate had been seized by the Union army and used for a headquarters. The main structure was intact: the two-story whitewashed brick mansion with its columned veranda and balcony. But the years of Yankee occupation had taken a toll. The place was untended and run-down, and in other ways transformed. In an odd way, Lou felt a personal sense of loss. He had helped build this house with his own hands, had lovingly polished its gorgeous mahogany furniture, had carefully tended its splendid ornamental garden. He had swelled with pride when he had heard it praised as one of the city's showpieces. Certainly he had some painful memories of the estate—the daily cruelties of Madam, the brutal whippings in the barn, the death of his twin babies—but what he saw now was nonetheless sad. "[H]ow different it was from what it had been," he thought. "All was changed."[16]

By Thursday Lou and George had picked up enough information to begin organizing their rescue expedition back to Panola. The first step was to see the Union army officer responsible for dealing with the freedmen in this military district, Captain Thomas A. Walker. On their way to his office, Lou and George must have noticed the excitement in the streets. It was election day in Memphis: the city, which had been under military rule since the Yankee army came, was being returned to civilian control. The hack drivers were especially busy, for the candidates for office had rented dozens of carriages to convey voters to the polls. By the time the polls closed at five, almost 2,300 voters had made their choices—not a large proportion of the city's adult male population, to be sure, for the blacks and the former rebels could not vote, but enough to keep the hackmen occupied all day.[17]

At Walker's office Lou and George found a large crowd of blacks waiting. It was two hours before their turn came to see the captain. When they were finally called in, they found a tall dark-haired man about Lou's age (early thirties), wearing a blue officer's uniform and sitting at a desk. He began to question them. They explained who they were and what had happened to them since the war began, and told of Boss and the mansion. The conversation went on for several minutes before they were asked to state their business. Lou replied: "[W]e want protection to go back to Mississippi after our wives, who are still held as slaves." If he and George attempted it on their own, Lou added, the McGehees "will shoot the gizzards out of us."[18]

Walker had heard many such stories. Union army officials were well aware that some planters in the more remote areas were ignoring their decrees about emancipation. That very day, in fact, one of the Memphis newspapers had reprinted a circular, issued recently by the commander of the west Tennessee department, that took note of the many complaints received from blacks and warned the citizens that they must "acknowledge and act upon the full and permanent emancipation of the colored race."[19]

Walker had held the position of Superintendent of Freedmen in the District of Memphis for almost a year and a half now, a long tour of duty by army standards. In truth, he was not a career soldier but a teacher. He had enlisted in his home state of Ohio in 1861 and had seen a good deal of combat before being assigned to work with the freedmen. Perhaps he accepted the task willingly but eventually it wore him down. He sympathized with the men and women who jammed his office every day seeking aid, but the complaints and pleadings seemed endless and his ability to help was limited. And these office hours were only one of his headaches. There were more than 15,000 blacks living in Memphis, all under army authority and in some measure his responsibility. By 1865 he had grown sick of the job—"one of the most laborious and unthankful positions in the whole General Department," as he described it—and was anxious to return to duty with his regiment.[20]

The case of Lou and George was typical of Walker's frustrations. He could do basically nothing for them. For one thing, Panola County, Mississippi, was beyond his jurisdiction. And even if he had had the authority to intervene, he lacked the power: the army was demobilizing and was now spread quite thin. It would be impossible, as he explained to Lou and George, to dispatch a military force to every plantation in the South where blacks were being abused. Nevertheless, he could offer a bit of encouragement. There were unofficial ways to accomplish what could not be done officially. "I will tell you what you can do," he said. "There are hundreds of just such men as you want, who would be glad of such a scout." Lou and George understood. They thanked Walker and left the office.[21]

Outside, the two men talked the matter over. The best thing to do now, they decided, was to return to Senatobia and seek out the officer in charge of the detachment there. Perhaps he could help.[22]

The next day, Friday, they rented a wagon and a two-horse team and made their final preparations for departure. Among the provisions they packed were two bottles of whiskey.[23]

Early Saturday morning, July 1, they were off, southward bound. The day was hot, but mercifully there was no rain. The two men undoubtedly preferred a dusty road to a wet one under the circumstances, for they knew how Mississippi mud could slow a wagon to a crawl.[24]

By sunset they had reached a place called Big Springs, in the prewar days a favorite site for religious camp meetings. There they halted, built a fire, and settled in for the night. They were preparing to cook supper when a pair of Yankee cavalrymen rode up. The two greeted Lou and George, asked them what direction they were heading, and then got down to business. "Have you any whisky?" they asked. Lou and George pulled out a bottle and offered them a drink.[25]

As the bottle was being passed around, Lou asked the men where they were stationed. Senatobia, they replied. Lou and George then explained their situation, recounted their meeting with Captain Walker, and announced their intention to go to Senatobia the next day to ask the commanding officer for help. The soldiers listened with interest, and then one asked: "How much whisky have you?" Two bottles, George told him.[26]

"Now my friend," said one of the Yankees, "I am afraid if you go to the captain you will be defeated. But I'll tell you what I'll do. Give my comrade and me one of your bottles of whisky, and we will put you on a straight track. The reason why I say this is that our captain has been sweetened by the rebel farmers. He is invited out to tea by them every evening. I know he will put you off. But I will write a note to some comrades of mine who, I know, will bring you out safe."[27]

Lou and George consented at once to the deal, and handed over the bottle. The cavalryman scribbled a note, gave it to them, and told them how to find the two men it was addressed to. "They are brave," he added, "and the only two I know of that can help you." The soldiers then mounted up and rode off.[28]

It was about eleven o'clock the next morning, Sunday, when Lou and George pulled up outside the village of Senatobia. They left the wagon there, went on foot to the cavalry camp, and found the men they had been instructed to see. The soldiers read the note and questioned Lou and George a bit, then told them to return to their wagon and wait. They did so, and a little while later the soldiers joined them. They wanted to know more about the proposed expedition, including the distance to Master Jack's. After Lou and George had answered all their questions, the soldiers agreed to go. Lou gave them ten dollars each, with the promise of ten more if the rescue mission was successful. The soldiers then headed back to camp to bring out their horses—surreptitiously, so as not to be spotted by their captain, who was unaware of what they were up to. When they left, Lou and George climbed back into the wagon and set out. The soldiers caught up with them a couple of miles down the road.[29]

As the little rescue party entered the Como district, Lou and George grew nervous. They were now back in the land of slavery, and they were attracting a lot of ugly stares from the white people they passed. But they pressed on, comforted by the company of the two tough cavalry troopers with their revolvers and carbines.[30]

Just after sundown they reached the lane that led to Master Jack's. The soldiers spurred their mounts and rode ahead, through the grove and into the front yard of the Big House. The only person to be seen was a black man working at the woodpile. "Go in and tell your master, Mr. McG[eh]ee, to come out," one of the soldiers ordered, "we want to see him." The man obeyed. A moment later William McGehee emerged from the house and confronted the soldiers.[31]

Lou and George had by now reached the yard in their wagon. Lou saw that the critical moment was at hand. He was frightened. The soldiers were stout fellows, but there were only two of them, and William McGehee was just the sort of man who might challenge them. He was a twenty-nine-year-old hothead who had served four years in the Confederate army, ending his service in an elite combat unit, General Nathan Bedford Forrest's cavalry escort. And he had proved himself willing to use deadly force to keep his family's black people enslaved.[32]

The two soldiers, however, had been warned by Lou of the possibility of violent resistance by the McGehees and they had devised a plan. Their first words to William were: "We want feed for seventy-five head of horses."[33]

Lou heard William protest that he could not provide so much feed and heard the soldiers repeat their demand. He and George did not slow the wagon, but steered directly for the slave quarters. The soldiers followed them.[34]

William ran into the Big House in a fury and aroused the family. "It is Louis and George," he said, "and I'll kill one of them to-night." But when he told the other McGehees of the soldiers' demand, they were persuaded that the two troopers were but the advance scouts of a large force of Yankee cavalry. They convinced William to settle down and not do anything stupid.[35]

Lou and George pulled up to their cabin and got down from the wagon. Kitty was at the door. "I am all ready," she told them. She had been preparing for their return: the few belongings that the two families intended to take were ready to load, and there was food stockpiled for the journey to freedom. Lou and George immediately began loading the wagon.[36]

Meanwhile Master Jack and the circuit minister who boarded with him had come down to the quarters. The soldiers spotted them and rode up to them. "[W]hat are you doing here?" one of the troopers snarled. "Why have you not told these two men, Louis and George, that they are free men—that they can go and come as they like?"[37]

By now the quarters were in an uproar. The other blacks had come out of their cabins and were gathering around the wagon to find out what was going on. Lou and George finished loading; in their frantic haste it took only twenty minutes. They hurried their wives and the baby into the wagon and headed for the lane, escorted by the soldiers. The packed vehicle could not hold them all, so Lou walked alongside while George drove. Kitty sat at her husband's side; Matilda and the baby perched atop a mattress in the bed of the wagon. The five were followed by nine others, who had made an instant decision to join the escape.[38]

They halted at the Big House and waited a moment for Matilda's sister, Mary Ellen, to join them. She was Mary McGehee Farrington's maidservant. As she exited the house with her two children, Mary Ellen spoke some parting words to her mistress: "Good-bye; I wish you good luck." Mrs. Farrington replied angrily: "I wish you all the bad luck." Mary Ellen ignored the remark and joined Lou while her children scrambled into the wagon beside Matilda.[39]

The moon was only six days shy of full, so there was plenty of light for a night journey. The little band—now numbering nineteen, including the soldiers—followed the lane to the gate, turned onto the road, and moved off in the direction of Senatobia. In the rush to get away, few of the blacks had given a thought to clothing or provisions. Most were hatless and some, including Matilda and Mary Ellen, were barefoot. Only Kitty brought food, and fortunately she had enough for all.[40]

Until they were out of the Como district, the fugitives could not rest easy. It was possible that the McGehees would sound the alarm, organize posse, and try to overtake or ambush them. So they trudged along warily, the soldiers occasionally riding ahead to scout. They stopped just one time during the night, and then only because of an accident. As the wagon descended the steep bank of a stream, the mattress slid off into the water, taking Matilda, the baby, and Mary Ellen's children with it. The four were unhurt, but the horses got spooked and grew balky. It was an hour before they could get the wagon moving again.[41]

By the time the sun began to creep above the horizon, they had gone far enough to feel fairly safe. At that point, the soldiers said they must leave them; they had to hurry back to camp for morning roll call. But they assured the blacks that if the party had not arrived in Senatobia by the time roll call was finished, they would come back to see about them. Lou gave the two men the rest of their fee, and they trotted off.[42]

The blacks arrived at the cavalry camp about nine in the morning. There they halted, contacted their soldier friends, made breakfast, and rested. Later that day they resumed the journey, having decided to make Memphis their destination. That night they camped along the road and on Tuesday plodded into the city. They were "a pitiful crowd to look at," Lou recalled—filthy, exhausted, and hot, fanning themselves with palm leaves. An old black man who saw them was so moved that he ran into the road to greet them, exclaiming "Oh! here dey come, God bless 'em! Poor chil'en! they come fannin."[43]

As they neared the heart of the city, they realized it was the Fourth of July. People thronged the streets, blacks and whites, soldiers and civilians. Flags were everywhere—not the rebel banner that Lou had seen so often in the last four years, but the Stars and Stripes—and there were parades and bands playing. To the new arrivals from Panola, it was an unforgettable sight. It seemed almost as if the city had turned out to celebrate their escape from bondage.[44]

Freedom: it was an inexpressibly exhilarating feeling. But at the same time, Lou and the others were apprehensive. What would they do now? As the festivities swirled around them, they talked things over and began to disperse, each to seek his or her own path.[45]

Lou scouted around and found a room to rent. It would be crowded, for Mary Ellen had chosen to stay with him and Matilda. The next day he went job-hunting. Perhaps he remembered how busy the hacks had been on elec- day; in any event, he quickly found work as a hack driver. His employer nly glad to have him, for Lou was an expert at the reins of a carriage w his way around the city.[46]

14. Memphis river front at the time of the Civil War

In the days that followed, as he carried passengers here and there, Lou had a chance to visit every part of the city and talk to people and get a sense of what was going on. It was an exciting place to be, there was no doubt of that. He surely spent much of his time going up and down the busy street that led to the wharf. It was graded but still steep, a challenge to even the best driver. The scene down along the river was what really captivated visitors to Memphis. The city was the chief port between St. Louis and New Orleans, and rare was the steamboat that did not pay a visit on its way up or down. On any given day that summer one could see boats of all shapes and sizes moored along the wharf, rocking gently in the muddy water. Overshadowing the others were the great "floating palaces," multitiered and gaily painted, with enormous paddle wheels and towering smokestacks. One could also see along the wharf dozens or even hundreds of cotton bales, stacked and awaiting shipment—last year's crop, only now able to be shipped to market.[47]

Something was doing at the wharf all the time, but the arrival of a boat triggered a particularly colorful flurry of activity. As the vessel put in, hucksters and hackmen would crowd around to proposition the debarking passengers, their voices competing with the calls of the deck hands and the shouted orders of the captain. Newsboys would jump aboard even before the gangplanks descended, then scurry among the passengers hawking the latest issue of the *Memphis Bulletin* or the *Argus*. Once the boat was secured, stevedores would lug 400-pound bales to the dockside and push them up one plank while passengers and luggage and freight descended on another. Sunset brought no cessation of activity: illumination was provided by lanterns hung on poles all along the wharf, and the bells and whistles of arriving and departing boats could be heard through the night.[48]

When his work took him into the southern section of the city, Lou had a chance to size up the situation of his fellow freedmen. Here was concentrated the bulk of Memphis's black population. Seven hundred or so, mostly women and children, resided in a camp on President's Island that had been established by the army. It was the last one remaining of several "contraband camps" set up around Memphis during the war to care for fugitive slaves. But the majority of the city's freedmen lived in rented rooms or abandoned buildings or shanties in what was now being called South Memphis. Here a true black urban community was in the making, something that did not exist—could not exist—in Memphis in the days of slavery. There were newly founded black churches, led by black ministers. There were black businesses, including stores and restaurants and barber shops. There were black fraternal organizations, such as the Sons of Ham. And there were aspiring black political leaders—men like Joseph Caldwell, a drayman, and John Brown, a barber—who were speaking publicly to the freedmen and any whites who would listen, proclaiming the message that simple freedom was not enough, that the former slaves must have civil rights and even the ballot.[49]

Memphis's black community glowed with optimism and a sense of expectation in that summer of 1865. These were, for the most part, men and women who had fled the plantations and refused to return, for they were determined that freedom would mean more than just hoeing some planter's cotton for wages and taking orders from an overseer who likely as not still carried the same whip he wielded in the days of slavery. Their numbers were increasing daily, for the city seemed to offer not only protection from the tyranny of the planters and overseers but also opportunity. And yet, as Lou and anyone else who visited South Memphis could see, for most of the freedmen opportunity was proving elusive. Lou was lucky—he had skills beyond agricultural ones, and he had some money. Most of the ex-slaves in Memphis had neither, and they now sat in squalid hovels, many of them ragged and hungry and idle because there were nowhere near enough unskilled jobs in the city to accommodate them. For now they were willing to bide their time in the hope that something would turn up. So much depended on what the state and federal governments would do, on what kind of reconstruction the South was going to have. There were rumors that the plantations would be confiscated, broken up, and distributed to the freedmen so that they could become independent farmers. In the meantime, many spent their days drinking and gambling in the saloons that had sprung up in the South Memphis community. Some turned to begging or prostitution or thievery to make a living.[50]

Another thing apparent to anyone who walked or rode the streets of Memphis that summer was the fierce resentment of many of the whites toward the freedmen. The Irish immigrants, who competed with the blacks for the available unskilled jobs, were the most openly hostile. In the recent election the Irish had pretty much taken control of the city government, and now the freedmen faced an unfriendly municipal authority. Mayor John Park was an Irishman, as were over half the aldermen and ninety percent of the policemen. The Irish resented not only the burgeoning population of freedmen in the city, but also the black U.S. soldiers stationed at nearby Fort Pickering, who were seen often on the streets.[51]

Among the many others whose bitterness toward the freed blacks was apparent were the returned rebel soldiers. There were hundreds in the city that summer, many still wearing Confederate uniforms (shorn of brass buttons and military insignia, however, by order of the federal authorities), and a lot of them were as idle as some of the freedmen. They hung around sullenly on the street corners and in the saloons and hotel lounges, too cowed by the presence of the Yankee occupiers to start trouble, but glaring with hostility at every display of black freedom.[52]

There were others in Memphis, however, who regarded themselves as friends of the blacks. Among these were a small corps of Northern missionaries, many of them women, who had dedicated their lives to the enlightenment of the former slaves. Most had come to the city during the war. They were sponsored by humanitarian organizations such as the American Missionary Association, headquartered in New York, and the Western Freedmen's Aid Commission of Cincinnati. By the summer of 1865 missionaries were operating more than a dozen schools in Memphis where black children and adults were taught the three R's.[53]

Another who professed good will toward the freedmen had arrived in the city just one day after Lou and Matilda. He was a Union army general named Davis Tillson, who was assigned to head the Memphis office of the newly created Freedmen's Bureau, a federal agency intended to aid the Southern blacks in their transition from slavery to freedom. The Freedmen's Bureau superseded the army offices of freedmen's affairs, such as Captain Walker's, and possessed broad authority in all matters pertaining to the former slaves. General Tillson made it clear from the start that the blacks under his jurisdiction would have protection. "No person shall escape punishment," he warned, ". . . who is guilty of wrong or injustice to the Freed people." Within days of his arrival he called on Mayor Park to discuss the status of the city's blacks. When he learned that under existing Tennessee law no black testimony could be accepted in court, Tillson set up a Freedmen's Bureau court and ordered the city officials to turn over all civil and criminal cases involving blacks.[54]

These white Northern friends of the black Memphians were well meaning and in many ways admirable men and women, idealistic and progressive. And yet, as Lou surely began to sense during those summer weeks, their vision of the black race and its future was in some ways at odds with that of the blacks themselves. The missionaries, for their part, were patronizing and paternalistic. They viewed the blacks as childlike and heathenish, cursed with barbarous customs and unseemly manners, and badly in need of some lessons in middle-class decorum and self-control. Acquiring these qualities, one of the missionaries wrote, would "fit them to take care of themselves."[55]

General Tillson was likewise certain that the freedmen needed guidance. "Their ignorance," he said, ". . . makes them insensible to their best interests." They required the bureau's help in order to understand "what freedom means." He pronounced them deficient in the virtues of "neatness, thrift and industry," and he banned the sale of liquor to them. Tillson disapproved especially of the large number of black Memphians who sat idle while planters were clamoring for their labor and offering decent wages. There could be only one explanation, he insisted, for their reluctance to return to the plantations: they were lazy. In August he came to a decision. Unemployed freedmen would be forced to leave the city and find work in the countryside.[56]

Lou was in no immediate danger of expulsion for he was self-supporting. He was, in fact, making a pretty good living by the standards of black Memphis. Nevertheless, he was restless. Memphis was stifling, and not only because of the summer heat. Here, he was now convinced, his freedom could not be fully realized; and he knew that no other place in the South would offer any better opportunities. He must go north. He was not sure what he would find there, but he sensed that "somehow . . . it would be better for us."[57]

What finally spurred him to move on was a chance encounter with a man who had knowledge of Matilda's mother. Matilda had not seen her since the day in 1855 when they were separated in a Memphis slave market. After gaining freedom, the man said, she had gone to Cincinnati; but that was all he knew. Lou, Matilda, and Mary Ellen talked it over and concluded that even though the chance of finding her was slim, it was worth a try. They would go to Cincinnati.[58]

Before they left Memphis, they had a gratifying reunion with their soldier friends. The two troopers had come to the city on some business and went out of their way to hunt up Lou. They were glad to learn that he and the others were doing well. Lou could hardly express his gratitude for what the two men had done back in Panola. He regarded them as heroes. Only after they said farewell did he realize that he had never learned their names.[59]

It was mid-August when Lou and the rest of the family packed up their things, headed down to the wharf, and booked passage on a steamboat to Cincinnati. The boat took them northward up the Mississippi and then, at

Cairo, turned northeastward. As they made their way up the Ohio, Lou could look starboard and see the South he was leaving; on the port side was the North, and his future.[60]

The boat docked in Cincinnati. Lou and the others made their way from the wharf to the heart of the huge city, gazing around in awe and trepidation. It was an overwhelming place, and they were utter strangers on a nearly hopeless quest. The only thing to do was to start asking around. They approached one black person after another, Matilda giving her mother's name and description. Incredibly, one man they questioned said that he knew such a woman, and he gave directions to the house where she boarded. When they reached the place, they knocked on the door, and a moment later Matilda and Mary Ellen were joyfully embracing the mother they had not seen for ten years.[61]

SAMUEL AGNEW

THE EARLY DAYS OF SUMMER FOUND SAM AGNEW HARD AT WORK in his poppy patch, intent and hopeful. The time had come to see if his countless hours of labor in the patch during the winter and spring would be rewarded. For months he had battled weeds, fended off invading livestock, repaired damage from torrential rains, hauled water from the creek during dry spells, and spread swamp mud and cotton seed as fertilizer. Now the plants were flowering, the pink blooms clashing wildly with the green expanses of corn and cotton that surrounded the patch. On the first day of June, Sam counted 164 blooms, and more appeared in the days thereafter. Within each bloom was a hard little green capsule, from which the precious opium had to be drawn.[1]

Moving down the rows of poppies on his knees, Sam painstakingly scarified each capsule by slicing lightly into it with a blade. He did this almost every evening throughout June, Sundays excepted. In the mornings he would go down the rows again, carefully gathering the gummy opium that had seeped from the cuts overnight. Capsules whose wounds had healed were rescarified until nothing more came forth. "It is a wearisome business," Sam decided, "tedious and slow."[2]

It was also, in the end, a disappointing business. "The yield is small," Sam admitted, "—smaller than I anticipated." When the last drop of juice had been wrung from the poppies and dried, his father, Enoch, weighed the entire harvest on his apothecary scales. It came to barely more than an ounce. Sam recorded this tersely in his diary and never mentioned poppies again.[3]

Besides keeping him tired and sore, his labors among the poppies hindered his news-gathering, for from the patch he could not see the road. Still, by chatting with passers-by whenever he was back at the house, by pumping acquaintances for information when he ran errands off the plantation, and by poring over every newspaper he could get, he picked up a good deal of news and rumor. But neither he nor anybody else in Tippah County really knew what was going on. No less than the last weeks of spring, the first weeks of summer were a time of confusion, uncertainty, and trepidation.[4]

The threat of famine, for one thing, continued to haunt the county. The Agnews were better off than many: no one on their plantation, white or black, was starving. But the farm animals were on short rations and had been for some time. On June 11 Sam recorded another incident involving the mule Peter, who in May had fallen and thrown him. This time Peter got mired in muck when he stepped into a pond. Too weak to extricate himself, he had to be pulled out. "Pa's mules," Sam wrote, "are broke down by hard work and nothing to eat."[5]

The grain shortage in the community could not be remedied anytime soon. During the spring the Agnews and their neighbors had managed to get some corn from the counties to the south, but those sources were now depleted; one of the neighbors went down in the latter part of June to see what he could buy but returned empty-handed. The Yankee occupation forces were distributing corn to needy people at certain points in northeastern Mississippi—corn from Confederate government depots, captured at war's end—but none was being doled out in Sam's vicinity. With the war over, military restrictions on trade had ended, and more and more wagons could be seen heading north to Tennessee; but getting to La Grange or Memphis, the nearest Tennessee trade centers, meant a very long trek on very bad roads, and the amount of goods that could be hauled back and forth was limited. The winter wheat was ready for harvesting by early June, but none of the farmers had planted many acres in wheat; everybody was counting on the corn crop, which would not ripen until the fall—and which was now stunted and unpromising, hurt by lack of rain. Sam, like others in his community, was quite concerned. "[W]hat we are to do for bread," he wrote, "is more than I can tell."[6]

The political situation, too, was troubling. The county government was still in a state of suspension. Until it could be revived, roads and bridges would go unrepaired, the poor would go unfed, and the robbers and horse thieves who infested the county would go unprosecuted. The fate of the county government depended on the state government, likewise suspended since the war's end. The fate of the state government depended, in turn, on what the federal government would do. And so all eyes turned toward Washington, where the new president was formulating a policy of reconstruction.

Sam learned from a newspaper on June 7 that President Johnson had recently made his first major pronouncement on the subject. The Proclamation of Amnesty and Pardon granted political absolution to those who had supported the Confederacy. They had only to take an oath pledging their allegiance to the United States and their acceptance of emancipation in order to avoid punishment for their "treason." However, there were some rebels not included in this general amnesty. Leading Confederate military and civil officials were required to apply to the president for a special pardon, as were a few other categories of Southerners—among them anyone who owned taxable property worth over $20,000. That provision was clearly aimed at the planters, a class whom Johnson despised and whom he blamed for the breakup of the Union. This was something the Agnews would have to reckon with: before the war, Enoch had listed the value of his plantation as $23,500.[7]

On June 13 Johnson set in motion the reconstruction of Mississippi by appointing a provisional governor, William L. Sharkey, whose job was to see that a state constitutional convention was held and a new state government set up. This promised an early end to military rule and the speedy revival of local government. Sam and his fellow citizens were pleased by this development but remained apprehensive about the South's future. The U.S. Congress had yet to be heard from on the matter of reconstruction, for it had adjourned in March and would not convene again until December. It was heavily dominated by Northern Republicans, many of them members of the radical faction who wanted to punish the rebellious South.[8]

Like many others that summer, Sam closely followed newspaper reports about Jefferson Davis, for the fate of the Confederate president might well be a harbinger of things to come. Davis had fled Richmond when the city fell and had been captured by federal troops in Georgia on May 10. "I have long looked upon [him] as a good, able man," Sam commented on learning of his capture, "but he is unfortunate for in the hands of his enemies he will certainly hang." Rumors in early June seemed to confirm Sam's prediction. "I hope it is not so," he wrote. "If Davis is executed it will always be a foul blot on the escutcheon of the United States." As it turned out, the rebel leader was not summarily hanged, but his treatment was hardly lenient: he was imprisoned in a dank cell in an army fortress and shackled in leg irons. Sam was appalled by this news, and by the report that Davis was to be tried not only for treason but also for complicity in Lincoln's assassination.[9]

Another matter of great concern as summer began was what to do about the blacks—the freedmen, as Sam was now starting to call them. Beyond the fact that they were no longer slaves, nothing was certain. Those on the Agnew place continued to work, but only as they saw fit. Most of the necessary chores were getting done, including harvesting the wheat, tending the livestock, and cultivating the corn and cotton. But they were not getting done with anything like the efficiency of the old days, for the blacks could only be cajoled now, not commanded.[10]

The other thing Sam observed about the blacks, besides their disinclination to work like slaves, was their restlessness and sense of expectancy. They apparently had gotten the notion that the Yankees were going to see that they were rewarded for their years of unrequited toil. They seemed reluctant to settle down until they saw what the future held.[11]

Sam had an interesting encounter that set him to thinking about this. On June 9 a squad of Yankee cavalrymen came by the house and stopped at the front gate, and he went out to greet them. It struck him as a notable occasion—"the first time for me to meet and talk with wild Yankees since the war began." Northern troops had come by several times during the war, of course, but Sam had always hidden in the woods on those occasions. Now there was no reason to hide, and he was curious about his former enemies. As it happened, these soldiers had fought in the battle there the previous June, so they and Sam found much to talk about.[12]

As they chatted, Sam noticed that "The negroes left the field and came flocking to the house," eager to see what the Yankees had to offer. The troopers ignored them, however, and soon mounted up and rode off. Sam got a certain satisfaction from this. "In my opinion," he wrote, the blacks "were sorely disappointed that nothing was done for them."[13]

If June 1865 was a time of uncertainty and anxiety for Sam and his neighbors, it was also in some respects a time of joy. For one thing, families were still welcoming home sons and brothers and fathers who wore the Confederate gray. These latest returnees were mostly men who had been in Northern prison camps when the war ended; the Yankees had finally released them and made arrangements to transport them south. Sam was pleased to see many friends and loved ones among them, especially his young cousin John D. Agnew. John had been in the family's prayers for a long time. In 1861, just turned twenty, he had enlisted in the 32nd Mississippi Infantry, a regiment that went on to fight in some of the bloodiest battles of the war. Wounded by an exploding shell at Chickamauga in September 1863, he had recovered and returned to his unit, only to be captured near Atlanta in July 1864. Since then he had been imprisoned at Camp Douglas in Chicago. Released on June 17, he arrived home nine days later. "I was rejoiced to meet him," wrote Sam.[14]

Sam rejoiced, too, at the large congregations that now greeted him on his preaching rounds. Every Sunday he saw new faces, as well as familiar faces long missing. When he rode to the Corders' home on June 4, he found the place packed with the biggest crowd he had ever seen there. Anticipating an even bigger turnout the next time he came, some members of the congregation talked of moving the meeting outdoors and building a brush arbor for shelter. Sure enough, when Sam returned four weeks later, an arbor was in place. But the crowd was so large that not all could find seats in the shade. Sam was deeply gratified that his words were reaching so many, and he gave thanks to God.[15]

Sam's domestic circle, too, was a source of joy. Little Buddy, born in early March, had been sick during the spring, forcing Sam and Nannie to postpone his baptism. But now he was well, and on Sunday morning, June 18, his parents bundled him up, mounted mules, and carried him three miles through a light rain to Bethany Church. Sam's mentor, Uncle Young—James L. Young, the pastor of Bethany—performed the rite. Buddy was christened Enoch David, in honor of Sam's father.[16]

This was the first time Nannie had been off the plantation since early in her pregnancy. In the weeks that followed, she went on more outings, glad for the opportunity to catch up on neighborly visiting. When her brother William came up from Starkville to see her, they rode over to Uncle Young's house and spent the night. On another occasion she and Sam spent the night with Sam's widowed aunt Rilla, John D. Agnew's mother. Nannie always brought Buddy along on these excursions, but he was getting so big now that she asked her companions to take turns carrying him. By the time he was four months old, Buddy weighed twenty-three and a half pounds—only a pound and a half less than his father had weighed at that age, as Sam proudly noted in his diary. Buddy was teething by this time, too, which made for some restless nights for him and his parents.[17]

By July the weather had turned sultry, and life in Tippah County assumed its customary summer pace—slower, more languid. Only the robbers and thieves showed no sign of listlessness: their depredations continued unabated. With civil law enforcement still suspended and the Yankee occupation forces apparently unwilling or unable to restore order, some of the men of the community talked of forming, as Sam put it, a "secret organization to repress thieving." On July 14 a meeting was held in a neighbor's home, a vigilante company of thirty men was organized, and a captain and lieutenant were elected. Sam's father attended the meeting. Sam did not, but he gave the company his blessing: "I hope it will do good."[18]

The vigilantes did not ride for long. On the last day of July, local officials convened in Ripley and revived the Police Board, the county's administrative body. Among the first actions taken by the resurrected board was ordering the sheriff to see that the county jail was repaired and made ready to receive prisoners. In the weeks following, the sheriff went after lawbreakers and Tippah County's crime wave gradually subsided. At its next meeting, in August, the board took the first steps toward getting the county's roads and bridges repaired.[19]

The revival of county government came at the behest of Provisional Governor Sharkey in Jackson, who on July 1 proclaimed that persons holding local office in the state when the war ended could temporarily resume their duties after taking the amnesty oath prescribed by President Johnson. The same day he issued that proclamation, Sharkey began the restoration of state government by ordering an election for delegates to a convention that would revise the state's constitution and take other necessary steps.[20]

The election was scheduled for Monday, August 7. On that day, Sam mounted a mule and rode to the designated polling place for his precinct. Before he could cast his ballot, he had to take the amnesty oath. He transcribed it word for word in his diary that night:

> I, Samuel A. Agnew, do solemnly swear in the presence of Almighty God that I will henceforth faithfully support, protect and defend the Constitution of the United States and the Union of States thereunder, and that I will in like manner abide by and faithfully support all laws and proclamations which have been made during the existing rebellion with reference to the emancipation of Slaves. So help me God.

"I did not fancy the latter part of this oath much," he added.[21]

Tippah County was entitled to four delegates, and there being only four candidates, Sam voted for all of them. A week later, the convention began its work in Jackson. By the time it adjourned on August 24, it had amended the state constitution to recognize the end of slavery, had declared null and void the state's 1861 ordinance of secession, and had set October 2 as the date for the election of state and local officials. Sam closely followed the convention's proceedings in the newspapers, and looked forward to the reestablishment of Mississippi's government.[22]

If the political uncertainty that had clouded the late spring and early summer months was dissipating a bit, the food problem was not. By July Sam was convinced that a crisis was at hand. The animals on the Agnew plantation were growing more and more feeble; some of them, Sam noted, "are so weak that when they get down they can't get up." And it was not just the animals that he worried about now: the Agnews themselves were running short of food. The wheat crop was very disappointing. Enoch reported in early July, after it had all been gathered, that it was "not near enough" to meet the family's needs. At the same time, the Agnews' supply of bacon ran out, and Enoch was forced to call on neighbors for a loan. No one in the community had much of anything to spare, however. Sam's uncle, Joseph Agnew, for one, had very nearly emptied his larder by July and was actually facing the prospect of hunger.[23]

The only thing the Agnews could see to do for now was to go to Tennessee and buy provisions. Enoch had two bales of cotton on hand that he could sell there. On the evening of July 17, Sam helped him load the bales into a wagon. At nine the next morning, Enoch set out for Memphis, more than ninety miles away. His black foreman, Wiley, drove the wagon, and Sam's fourteen-year-old brother, Erskine, went along for the ride. If the roads stayed dry and the mules held up, they could make it to Memphis in four days.[24]

It was after dark on the twenty-eighth when the wagon pulled into the yard of the Agnew plantation, filled with provisions for the family and for a few of the neighbors who had asked Enoch to buy some things for them. Enoch had gotten thirty-four cents a pound for one of his bales and thirty-eight for the other—$300 or so in total. His purchases would keep the family and the hands supplied for a while, perhaps until the fall harvest.[25]

The question now was whether that harvest would prove adequate. The rainfall shortage that had plagued the crops in spring continued through the summer. Hardly a drop of rain fell on the Agnew plantation between July 18 and August 11. Toward the end of summer some showers came, but Sam was afraid they might be "too late to do [the] corn much good." The crop was "badly injured" and the yield would probably be light.[26]

Drought was not the only problem threatening the harvest. A sickness of some kind was killing the Agnews' mules. It was an ailment that Sam and Enoch had never seen before, and they were perplexed by it. It began with a large swelling on the animal's jaw or near its ear, which sometimes discharged a fluid. Whether the mules' weakness exacerbated this affliction was uncertain; in any event, it was quite deadly. The Agnews lost three mules in the space of two weeks. This meant three fewer animals available for the plowing necessary to cultivate the corn and cotton, and three fewer to haul the harvested crops in the fall.[27]

In July the Agnews also lost their only remaining horse. He was named Jin, and he succumbed not to the mysterious malady that felled the mules but to old age aggravated by hunger. Sam was saddened by this loss, for Jin had been on the plantation since Enoch bought him in 1856. By 1865 Jin was about sixteen years old and too frail to be ridden, although he could still do a little pulling. Mostly he just grazed in the pasture. On the morning of July 19, Sam went there looking for him but could not find him. Around noon some of the field hands found him dead and told Sam. "I went down and saw him. Hog[s] and buzzards and maggots are feeding on him. He was seen living yesterday evening and I think from appearances he must have died yesterday. . . . He has been my companion on many a long, lonely ride."[28]

Neither the Agnews nor anybody else in the community could afford to lose any more draft animals. They were already in short supply, for many had been given up over the last four years to the Confederate and Union armies. Thus there was great consternation when a report circulated during the summer that U.S. cavalry were going through the countryside seizing any livestock marked with the brand of the Union or Confederate army. According to the Yankees, these were the rightful property of the U.S. government, but the citizens had a different view of the matter. During the war, Union troops raiding northern Mississippi had sometimes abandoned their worn-out horses and mules, and in many cases citizens had taken possession of them and nursed them back to health. Citizens had also acquired and rehabilitated a number of decrepit animals belonging to the rebel army, some of them abandoned, some condemned by the Confederate government and auctioned off. None of the Agnews' animals bore a "US" or "CS" brand, but there were other farmers in the area who stood to lose a valuable horse or mule.[29]

Even if draft animals and rainfall had been plentiful, however, the Agnews and other planters would still have worried about the fall harvest because the labor situation was in turmoil. As the summer went on, the blacks seemed more unreliable than ever and the whites grew more and more exasperated. Many of the Agnews' farm hands, Sam wrote, were simply "doing as they please: they go off in daylight on their own business and are not giving their master's concerns any attention." As a consequence, Sam found himself taking on unaccustomed chores around the plantation: making a new rope for the well bucket, gathering and cleaning the loose bits of cotton scattered around the floor of the gin house. Even Wiley, the long-time foreman, was undependable now. Enoch reported that while he was in Memphis on his trading expedition, Wiley wandered off on his own, leaving Enoch and Erskine to tend to the wagon and mules.[30]

The whole black population, in Sam's view, was not only disobedient and "trifling" but maddeningly unsettled. Many were leaving the plantations and taking to the road. Even those who remained on their former owners' estates spent a good deal of time going about the district, visiting with friends and kin, having barbecues and picnics. In some districts, according to stories Sam heard, the blacks were not just restless but dangerously out of control. In the Starkville area, Nannie's home, they were reportedly "hold[ing] carnival" and "prowling through the country stealing."[31]

Some whites were reacting with violence. Nannie's brother William told Sam about such an incident on the McKell family farm near Starkville: one of the hands had left the place but then decided to return; when he did, the overseer "gave him a good whipping." This was a risky action. U.S. military commanders in the state had made it clear, through a series of proclamations reprinted in all the newspapers, that no physical abuse of the freedmen would be tolerated. These pronouncements were reiterated by agents of the Freedmen's Bureau, which was operating in Mississippi before the summer ended. And it appeared, from reports Sam heard, that the federal authorities were enforcing their word. "Was told that a gentleman of Aberdeen was recently fined $50.00 for slapping a negroe off the pavement," Sam noted on July 20, and "another was fined $25.00 for striking a little negroe. Rev. Mr. Brooks of Okolona was cruelly beaten by some Yankees because his wife whipped a little negroe recently." Sam was indignant. "The negroe is a sacred animal," he fumed. "The Yankees are about negroes like the Egyptians were about cats. Negrophilism is the passion with them. When they come to their senses they will find that the negroe must be governed in some way."[32]

There was no whipping on the Agnew place that summer. Sam and Enoch were sufficiently impressed by the threat of Yankee retaliation to dismiss any thought of physically coercing their unruly workers. But both were convinced that some measure of discipline must be restored or the plantation would go to ruin. Fortunately for them and other planters, the Yankees had no intention of letting the Southern economy suffer any longer from the derangement of the labor system.

"Negrophilism" was a gross caricature of the U.S. government's attitude toward the freedmen, as Sam himself recognized in his more reflective moments. In reality, federal authorities had many doubts about the newly freed slaves. They were especially skeptical about the blacks' capacity for self-discipline and were determined to see that they did not abuse their freedom by shirking work. From the various military headquarters and Freedmen's Bureau offices in Mississippi issued a stream of proclamations warning the freedmen against idleness. "[I]t must be clearly understood," a bureau official declared, "that belonging to a place and lying about without work does not entitle any one to wages, nor even to food." All who were able to work must do so, the Yankees decreed. But, at the same time, workers must be fairly compensated. To ensure justice to laborer and employer alike, contracts were to be drawn up, signed, and submitted to the federal authorities for approval.[33]

In obedience to this command, and because he could see no other way to impose any semblance of order on his plantation, Enoch called the hands together on the last day of July and, as Sam wrote, "broached the matter of hiring." Enoch made an offer; the blacks demanded more. No agreement was reached. "Pa's terms are not palatable to the negroes," Sam noted in his diary that night, "and I think he will have to make them some concessions."[34]

The next day, Enoch met with the hands again, and this time he gave in. The agreement involved no cash wages, for cash was scarce. Instead, the hands were to receive food, clothing, and shelter, and also one-tenth of the fall harvest, to be distributed among them. They also secured the right to a half-day off every other Saturday. For their part, they agreed "to be diligent honest and faithful as farm laborers." Sam recorded all this in his diary, adding "I think it very probable that some of them will fall short of their obligation."[35]

Negotiating with field hands was a new and unwelcome experience for Enoch: it galled him to bargain rather than to command. The blacks proved quite adept at using the leverage that freedom had given them. Being able to say no, with the threat of leaving in search of a better deal, was a powerful economic weapon. Enoch knew that if he refused to compromise, his laborers would likely desert him. Some already had: several were now living in Memphis. Moreover, he had heard that two others had been offered employment by a neighboring planter. Enoch discussed this last matter with Sam, who agreed that it was a disturbing development, perhaps heralding a future in which planters were all competing desperately with one another for labor. Hiring away a neighbor's hands, Sam declared, was "an unkind, unfriendly act."[36]

Sam spent the whole morning of August 2 drawing up contracts, one for each black family on the plantation. By the time he was finished, his fingers were aching. After dinner, he rode to the homes of two neighbors and brought them back to act as witnesses. Then he and Enoch summoned the hands to the rear portico of the Big House for the formal signing ceremony. Each of the nine black family heads—Wiley, Thompson, Arch, Eliza, Caroline, Franky, Tom, Big George, and Little George—signed two copies of his or her contract by mark. Enoch and the witnesses signed each copy, too.[37]

The other planters in the vicinity were likewise making contracts with their hands, Sam learned. But there was still the matter of federal approval. On August 12 Sam found out that the U.S. authorities were insisting on a single contract embracing all hands on each plantation, rather than separate family contracts. He and Enoch therefore had to draw up a new document and arrange another signing ceremony. They gave two copies to a friend who was on his way to Okolona, the nearest federal post. He returned a few days later with one copy endorsed and approved by an army major.[38]

In some respects, the Agnews' contract preserved the old system of labor: the field hands would continue to work in gangs under the direction of Enoch or his foreman, and all the blacks would continue to live in the former slave quarters. But whether this arrangement would be renewed after the end of the year, when the contract expired, was anyone's guess. On some plantations, freedmen were insisting on more independence. They wanted to move out of the quarters, rent a portion of the estate sufficient to sustain their family, build a cabin on it, and work it without day-to-day supervision. Few planters would willingly surrender that much control to their laborers, of course. Nor would many planters gladly accede to the other demands that were, with increasing frequency, being voiced by freedmen throughout the South: demands for land of their own, for civil rights, for the vote.[39]

Sam got irate at any suggestion that blacks might be entitled to something. For now, however, that matter was in abeyance. There could be no legislation on the status of the freedmen until the new state government went into operation in the fall and Congress met in the winter. In any event, there were more immediate matters to deal with, in Sam's view. Besides the labor problem, there was the continuing food crisis. And now there was another concern: sickness.

The dog days of summer were always an unhealthy time in Mississippi, but this season seemed especially bad. Sam filled his diary with news of illness. Luther Richey, a young neighbor who had only recently returned from a Northern prison camp, came down with a serious fever, perhaps related to the battle wound in his arm that had never completely healed. Uncle Joseph Agnew suffered an intense attack of diarrhea that laid him low for at least five days. Erskine spent three days "very sick with a high fever." Buddy broke out in hideous skin eruptions of a sort the Agnews had never seen. "What it is I know not," said Sam. He speculated that Buddy had contracted it from another infant, whose mother had visited the Agnews recently. Sam and Nannie dosed him with sulphur and applied sugar of lead to the sores, but it took him a long time to heal.[40]

There was so much sickness in the community that summer that the local physicians were overwhelmed, and Enoch, who had long ago given up the practice of medicine, was called on for help. But then he himself fell ill. He had been in poor health for many years anyway, the victim of a chronic form of diarrhea. When cholera struck him on the evening of August 5, the family feared for his life. Sam described his father's torments: "His bowells were acting and the pain was so great that he made loud moans. This was accompanied with nausea and vomiting. He was, to use his own language 'so sick.'" Some time after midnight the family decided to call in a doctor. Sam ran to a neighbor's home to borrow a horse, which he brought back and turned over to Thompson with orders to gallop to Guntown and fetch Dr. Borth. All that the family could do after that was try to comfort Enoch and wait anxiously for the doctor. They were greatly relieved when, a little before dawn, Enoch's symptoms began to abate. By the time Dr. Borth arrived at eight, he was no longer needed. But Enoch was left weak and dehydrated, and he remained bedridden for days.[41]

When he was not nursing the sick, helping Nannie tend Buddy, or doing chores around the plantation, Sam spent his time as he always had: visiting, reading, preparing sermons. He also worked in his tobacco patch, which had succeeded his disappointing poppy experiment as a useful pastime. Back in May he had transplanted 156 tobacco seedlings in a well-fertilized plot of land formerly used as a cow lot. The drought had taken a toll since then, but he still had well over a hundred plants. They demanded a lot of effort: there were always weeds to be chopped and worms to be picked off. The summer heat, however, kept Sam out of the patch except in the early mornings and late evenings.[42]

The first part of August began the laying-by season, when the ripening corn and cotton needed no further attention. In the rural South it was a time of relaxation and communal gatherings, a respite between the hard work of cultivating and the hard work of harvesting. Among the gatherings were "protracted meetings" at the churches, where preaching and baptizing and soul-saving went on for days at a time. Sam was cheered by news of joyous meetings being held in his vicinity: at Orizaba, Buncombe, Wallerville, Locust Grove, Lebanon, and Mt. Gilead. Among the nine people who underwent immersion at Mt. Gilead on August 20 was his friend James West. "James was baptized at Hopewell as an infant," Sam noted wryly, "but I suppose he did not think this was well enough done."[43]

Sam took part in no protracted meetings in those waning days of summer, but he kept up his Sabbath appointments. On August 27, the last Sunday of the month, he rode to the Corders' home. Waiting for him at the brush arbor was the largest congregation he had yet seen there. He had prepared two sermons for this occasion; he delivered both, with a half-hour break between them. The first was from Acts: "Believe on the Lord Jesus Christ, and thou shalt be saved." The second was from Isaiah: "The sinners in Zion are afraid. . . . Who among us shall dwell with the devouring fire? who among us shall dwell with everlasting burnings?" The congregation listened attentively to Sam's messages of salvation and damnation. Encouraged, he announced that he would return on the first Sunday of October and lead a meeting of several days.[44]

After the service he ate dinner with the Corders, relaxed and chatted with them until about five o'clock, and then rode home. Over the next few days he left the plantation only once, to visit Aunt Rilla and to check on a carriage wheel that Enoch had sent to a blacksmith for repair. On August 30, some travelers came by the plantation, parked their wagons just off the road near the garden, and camped for the night. They had some recent newspapers that they loaned to Sam. He stayed up late that night reading them. As he read, it began to rain. It rained through the next day and into the evening, and when he awoke on the first day of September the landscape was shrouded in fog.[45]

CORNELIA MCDONALD

JUST BEFORE SUMMER BEGAN, HARRY MCDONALD TOOK A JOB AS a farm laborer, working for a man named Reid who had an estate on the outskirts of Lexington. Cornelia tried to talk him out of it, but she could not deny that the family needed the money badly, and at last she gave in. She was never really happy about it, however. It hurt to see her son trudge off just after daybreak each morning and then slump home fourteen hours later, exhausted and grimy. Harry was not unused to hard work—he had spent much of the winter and early spring chopping wood—but this field labor was grueling. When he returned home at dusk he would collapse wordlessly into a chair, doze for a while, and then head upstairs to bed, too tired to join the family's evening get-togethers or even to read. He never complained, however, and he stuck to the work manfully despite the long hours, the increasingly hot weather, and the paltry wages.[1]

Cornelia was unhappy about Harry's job not only because it took such a physical toll on him, but also because she thought it degrading. Here was her first-born hoeing and plowing some planter's cornfield, side-by-side with blacks, when he should be in school preparing for a profession. Not only that, but Allan, the next oldest, had now taken a job, too, doing yard work and running errands for a family on the other end of town. And Cornelia herself, of course, was working as a private tutor. Just four years earlier the McDonalds had been ensconced among the South's propertied and cultured elite, possessed of land, slaves, money, self-sufficiency, and a fair amount of leisure. Now they were crammed into a rented house, laboring from morning to night, wearing patched and repatched clothes, counting pennies, and scrambling to make ends meet. Thinking about it made Cornelia sick at heart. "To see my noble sons, little daughter, and pretty little boys dragged down so low, how could I bear it."[2]

She felt even sicker when she contemplated the future. If her financial situation did not improve, the family might well slide further into society's depths. The house rent was coming due, and she had no money to pay it. Every bit of income was going to buy food and pay the cook. Even so, the family was not getting enough to eat, particularly Cornelia, who was growing noticeably thin and hollow-eyed. "At times," she recalled, "I was so weak from hunger that I could scarcely go up and down stairs."[3]

In her desperation, she took a gamble that she soon regretted. A man came to her one day offering to take over the cultivation of her garden if she would let him have the produce from half of it. With Harry and Allan both away all day, the garden was being worked solely by Kenneth, Roy, and Donald, who were small and woefully unskilled. Thinking it over, Cornelia calculated that she would get more in the long run from a well-tended half-garden than a poorly tended whole one. She therefore accepted the man's proposal. He let her choose her half, and she selected the one that included two apple trees.[4]

As the summer weeks went by and the garden yielded its bounty, Cornelia rued her decision. Her half produced little besides apples. She was not being cheated, she was certain of that: she kept an eye on the man and made sure he was devoting equal attention to the two sections. But for some unfathomable reason, hers failed while his prospered. As he hauled away basket after basket of ripe peas and other produce, Cornelia and the children ate beans and roasted apples.[5]

While the McDonalds and other families in Lexington struggled to sustain themselves, they struggled also to come to terms with the reality of Confederate defeat. The period of uncertainty following Lee's surrender ended on June 9, when a detachment of U.S. cavalry rode in and took possession of the town. This temporary occupation force was succeeded in July by a permanent force of forty soldiers of the 58th Pennsylvania Infantry. With the Yankees' arrival, martial law was in effect in Lexington.[6]

Slavery, which the local authorities had preserved more or less intact since the demise of the Confederacy, collapsed abruptly with the coming of federal troops. The occupiers decreed that no blacks were to be held against their will, and those who had been forced to labor without pay since the war's end must receive back wages for that time. Any whites who continued to resist emancipation would be arrested and jailed, the federals warned, as would all other "refractory persons."[7]

Even before the troops appeared, the people of Lexington experienced a Yankee invasion of sorts, but it was one they had not anticipated. Beginning not long after Appomattox, a number of Northern entrepreneurs rolled into town on wagons loaded with merchandise and proceeded to set up shop as tradesmen. Many of the townsfolk deeply resented this intrusion. The Reverend William Pendleton, husband of Cornelia's friend Ann Pendleton, spoke bitterly of the "Yankee adventurers" who came "to cheat our people out of their little remaining coin." By early summer an informal boycott was in the making. The Northern merchants, as Reverend Pendleton's daughter Rose reported in June, "have a great deal of custom among the negroes, but very little if any among the white people."[8]

The citizens reserved their fiercest hostility, however, for the occupation troops. They saw no reason why U.S. soldiers should be lording it over them, no reason why martial law should prevail in their town. They had accepted Confederate defeat and laid down their arms. While few regarded the reunion of the nation with any enthusiasm, no one was resisting federal authority. They wanted only to be left alone to restore order and prosperity to their community. Cornelia was one of many in Lexington who thought military rule gratuitous, despotic, and humiliating. "In every way possible the town people were annoyed and persecuted," she wrote, "I among the rest. Some new and oppressive prohibition or arbitrary command [was] inflicted on us every day."[9]

By word and gesture, Lexington's citizens let the Yankee soldiers know they were unwelcome. Cornelia was an old hand at this sort of thing. Back in Winchester during the war, she had earned a reputation for standing up to the enemy soldiers who periodically occupied the town. A neighbor of hers there described her as "daring in her audacity," and "one of the talking heroines." Her audacity was carefully gauged, however: while she made it clear to the Yankees how she felt about them, she always stopped short of the kind of brazen remark that would provoke retaliation. She was a master of the cold stare, the condescending voice, the subtle insult.[10]

In the eyes of Lexington's occupiers, the smoldering hostility displayed by citizens like Cornelia only proved the need for a military presence in the town. What they saw as they patrolled the streets in the summer of 1865 was a sullen, unsubdued mass of rebels who, if left to their own devices, would undoubtedly try to reenslave the blacks and probably try again to overthrow the U.S. government. Lieutenant Colonel Cecil Clay, commander of the military subdistrict that included Lexington, was outraged at their behavior. They are "impudent and insulting to officers and soldiers," he wrote, and "There are many . . . who openly glory in the part they have taken in the rebellion." In his view, anyone who did not sincerely embrace the national government was defying it, and he saw "very little real affection for the Union" in this section of Virginia. "The inhabitants of Lexington," he added, "are perhaps the most bitter."[11]

In truth, the conqueror's hand rested lightly on the citizens of Lexington. The townspeople may have been "annoyed," as Cornelia claimed, but they were hardly "persecuted." With the war over, the federal army relaxed its stern policy of retribution and destruction aimed at bringing Southern citizens to their knees. The first contingent of occupation troops in Lexington did commit some depredations in and around the town and taunted the inhabitants to some extent—even Colonel Clay admitted they "were rather a hard party"—but for the most part the soldiers posted in the town during the summer were restrained and well disciplined. They seized no private property and occupied no citizens' homes, although Colonel Clay did require them to confiscate all U.S. and Confederate government property in the citizens' hands and did give them permission to take possession of any public building they needed. Nor did the occupation troops interfere in the citizens' attempts to make a living and get the local economy back on its feet, except to make sure they did not abuse their black laborers.[12]

All things considered, the little Yankee force in Lexington was something less than tyrannical, and Cornelia—who had experienced truly harsh and destructive Union army rule in Winchester—knew better than most that this was so. Now and then the troops even won the citizens' gratitude, as, for example, in late July, when they rounded up all the unemployed freedmen in town and put them to work cleaning the streets. The editor of the *Lexington Gazette* remarked on that occasion that the federals deserved "double thanks for thus ridding the town of two nuisances—idle negroes and dirty streets."[13]

If the oppressions of Yankee rule in Lexington were more symbolic than otherwise, injuring honor and pride more than anything else, they were nonetheless galling to the citizens. In July the town was shaken by a controversy that aggravated the citizens' resentment, even as it confirmed the Yankees' belief that these people were still rebels at heart.

The controversy involved the Reverend Pendleton, rector of Grace Episcopal Church and former chief of artillery in Lee's army. A man of great dignity and aristocratic bearing, he was also among the most bitter and unyielding of Lexington's ex-Confederates. Writing to a kinswoman two months after Appomattox, Pendleton characterized the victorious Union army as a host of "German, Irish, negro, and Yankee wretches [who] invad[ed] our homes under the impulse of Northern envy and malice, stimulated by fanatical madness in some, lust of power and plunder in others, and iniquitous passion in all, though sought to be covered over by the shallow preten[s]e of virtuous devotion to constitutional liberty." Regarding the justness of the Confederate cause, he told another correspondent in June that "my convictions remain wholly unchanged." The secession of the Southern states was a proper response to "the great wrongs inflicted . . . by their Northern copartners, in . . . flagrant violation of the compact of union." He now accepted defeat, but only grudgingly: "As it has . . . pleased the Almighty Ruler of the world to permit us to be overwhelmed, I . . . am willing to submit myself peaceably to an authority which, whatever I think of its justice, I cannot resist to any good purpose." At the same time, he continued to hope "for some ordering in the future by which divine Providence may yet enable us to achieve the independence which is our birthright and of which we have now been despoiled by a mighty combination."[14]

As one of Lexington's most prominent citizens and stoutest champions of the Southern cause, Pendleton took it upon himself to defend the townspeople against military misrule. The Yankee troops had been in town only a month when he fired off his first letter of protest to the commanding officer. "On my way from church yesterday attending several ladies," he wrote, "I met two of your soldiers. They so occupied the foot walk as to compel the ladies to yield the way and walk round to avoid them." He knew of similar incidents of "disrespectful obstruction" by the troops, he said, and he advised the commander that such "offensive conduct" was "irritating to our people."[15]

Four days later Pendleton dispatched another protest to the same officer. This time he had been personally offended, and grievously so. He had gone to the cemetery on the south end of town to visit the grave of his son, Alexander "Sandie" Pendleton, a Confederate officer mortally wounded in battle in 1864. To his horror, he found that it "had been very recently desecrated by a serious mutilation of the head-board. This indignity has, I have no doubt, been perpetrated by some of your men. I found three of them in the grave yard at the time of my visit, one of them indecently exhibiting himself under a call of nature near the gate."[16]

Pendleton also voiced his protests from the pulpit, and in doing so he sparked a conflict with the military authorities that disturbed the town for months. On Sunday, July 9, he preached from the Beatitudes: "Blessed are the poor in spirit." In his sermon he spoke of the material as well as spiritual poverty that now afflicted his homeland, and he pointed a finger of blame: "The spoliations of iniquitous power and the atrocities of devastating enemies, have spread this experience through our beloved South." Those responsible would ultimately be punished by a just God, he assured the congregation, and the righteous would be vindicated.[17]

He never mentioned Yankees specifically, but the sermon's message was obvious to his listeners, including whoever subsequently reported it to the military. The following Sunday, three federal army officers were seated in the pews. Pendleton nevertheless delivered his sermon just as he had prepared it, including passages in which he alluded to the occupiers as "representatives of the Gigantic power which oppresses the land" and spoke of the destruction that God invariably inflicts on an ungodly kingdom, especially an "Infidel blasphemous, atrocious tyranny . . . in its pride of power."[18]

This was too much for the military authorities. Shortly after the service ended, a sergeant and three armed privates marched into the church and confronted Pendleton in the vestry. The sergeant told him he was under arrest. Despite his insistence that he "be treated with propriety," he was locked up in the guardhouse. There he penned yet another letter to the commanding officer, protesting his confinement in a filthy and uncomfortable cell—the guardhouse was a converted corncrib—where he was forced "to listen to the ribaldry and profanity of your common soldiers." Released after eight hours, he was summoned the next morning to an interrogation by several officers. He refused to answer questions and condemned his persecutors' "ungentlemanly conduct."[19]

The next Sunday, Grace Episcopal was closed by order of the federal authorities. Pendleton was told that it would remain closed until he agreed to make no more seditious or insulting remarks in the pulpit and agreed to offer a prayer for the president as part of the service. He was also told to stop signing his letters "Late Brigadier-General and Chief of Artillery, A. N. Va., C. S. A."[20]

He was prepared to give in on every point except the prayer, the exact wording of which the federals prescribed, based on that traditionally offered for the U.S. president in the Episcopal Church. To the rector this was a matter of principle. Four years earlier, the Southern dioceses of the church had ordered that the customary prayer be replaced by one for the Confederate president. Since the Confederacy no longer existed, Pendleton now omitted that prayer, but he insisted that he could not restore the former one without approval from his diocese, which had not yet acted on the matter. And besides, as he wrote in yet another letter to the authorities, "cordially as I can and do pray God to guide the Pres[ident] into all wisdom and usefulness, I cannot ask unconditionally for his prosperity, irrespective of his course."[21]

By now the Yankees had had enough of the rector's protests. A formal order was issued: if he held church services in violation of their decree, he would be arrested, tried by a military commission, and punished. Pendleton thereupon suspended services.[22]

Not all of Grace Episcopal's congregants approved the rector's course. In the opinion of some, he had provoked the authorities, he was being obdurate, he should back down in the interest of the church. But the majority applauded his stand, as did most other citizens of Lexington. As Sunday after Sunday passed and the pews and pulpit of Grace Episcopal remained empty, the town seethed with resentment over Pendleton's treatment as well as all the other perceived injustices of Yankee rule. In no other part of the subdistrict, the commander noted, was there so much "hatred [of] the Gov[ernment] and its Officers."[23]

Cornelia despised the Yankee intruders as much as anybody else in Lexington, but she was too preoccupied to brood over their misdeeds. The struggle to provide for her family was absorbing nearly all her energy. It was wearing her down, too, and not just physically but emotionally. As the summer went on, she grew increasingly anxious and depressed. In later life she would remember this as a time of "tormenting anticipations." She was becoming obsessed by the fear that she and the children would "descend to the lowest level" and end up in "squalid poverty."[24]

Her thoughts that summer were haunted also by a ghost. It was that of her husband, Angus. He had died in December 1864, and she grieved deeply for him still. That she had not been at his side in his last hours made the pain of losing him keener. She had been denied a final farewell, denied the comfort of his last words. Although she had hastened to Richmond at his summons, she had arrived one day too late. What she found there—an image burned forever into her memory—was his corpse, "stretched on a white bed

15. Angus McDonald in 1852

with a large green wreath around his head and shoulders, enclosing them as in a frame."[25]

Angus had suffered in his last years, and that too preyed on Cornelia's mind. The man she had married in 1847, although old enough to be her father, was a robust six-footer, handsome and strong, with a forceful presence. But by 1860, severe rheumatism was taking a toll on him, and he declined precipitously during the war. By 1863 he was a feeble, pain-wracked old man, emaciated and crippled, unable to mount a horse or even dress and undress without help. When Cornelia saw him that year after an absence of many months, she was stunned: "I at first could not believe that wreck was my husband."[26]

Angus had suffered in spirit as well as body. A proud and ambitious man, he had dreamed of winning glory in the war. The Confederate government had high hopes for him, too. He was a West Point graduate who had spent two years as a U.S. army officer and five years as a western adventurer—just the kind of man to help lead the Confederate army to victory. When the war began, he was commissioned a colonel and given command of a cavalry regiment. He proved a disappointment, however. He failed to win the confidence of his troops, and they grumbled about his leadership to the point of demoralization. He also failed on the battlefield. In a minor engagement in northern Virginia in October 1861, his troops were routed by the enemy and fled in panic, abandoning their baggage train. Angus held himself blameless, arguing that the enemy had ten times his number, but his superiors considered his performance disgraceful. Recognizing that his career in the field was at a dead end, and that in any event he was too infirm for such a command, he asked to be relieved. His request was granted, and thereafter he was assigned to desk jobs. He was left with "a wounded spirit," as Cornelia wrote, bitter about his tarnished honor and his frustrated dreams.[27]

Angus's visage and voice crept into Cornelia's thoughts again and again through the melancholy seasons of 1865. One day in early summer, around the time of her forty-third birthday and not long after the eighteenth wedding anniversary that Angus did not live to celebrate, she borrowed a horse and rode fifteen miles into the countryside to the place where he had been taken captive one year earlier. She had not visited the site until now, but she knew every detail of the story. When the Union force under General Hunter invaded the upper valley in June 1864, Angus, who was then serving as post commander of Lexington, prepared to leave town to avoid capture. He managed to secure an army ambulance for his journey and had a mattress and blankets loaded into it, along with his official and personal papers, a trunk of clothes, and several guns. Harry was to serve as driver. As the Yankees approached and the small Confederate force holding Lexington prepared to withdraw, Angus said good-bye to his family. The ambulance then set off, with Harry at the reins and Angus lying in the back. It was the last time Cornelia saw her husband alive.[28]

Harry and Angus headed south, trying to stay ahead of the advancing enemy columns. Late in the day they stopped at the home of an elderly man named Wilson, who put them up for the night. The next day they heard that the enemy was in the vicinity. Wilson then gathered some of his valuables and set out with Harry and Angus in search of a refuge.[29]

They found a secluded, wooded spot on a mountainside not far away and made camp there, intending to stay hidden until the Yankees left the area. On the morning of their third day in the woods their luck ran out. A local man whom Wilson knew to be a Union sympathizer stumbled on their campsite and eyed them suspiciously before passing on. That afternoon they heard the sound of approaching horsemen, and then a voice demanding their surrender. A fence ran along the edge of the woods they occupied, and beyond it was a field, only recently cleared of trees and still littered with stumps. In the field there, just sixty yards away, they saw three Union cavalrymen. Harry grabbed a gun and fired, knocking one of the soldiers from the saddle. The other two retreated, taking the wounded man with them. Angus, Wilson, and Harry immediately decided to move to a new place of concealment. Before they could get away, however, the Yankees reappeared in strength and again demanded their surrender.[30]

Although they were only two old men and a boy against nearly two dozen federal cavalrymen, Angus insisted they make a stand. They took cover and began firing. The troopers dismounted and returned fire. Angus and Harry held their ground even after Wilson was cut down by a bullet and Angus was wounded in the hand. At last, however, Angus recognized the futility of resisting. He called out that he was surrendering, and he and Harry laid down their guns.[31]

The federal soldiers took them prisoner, burned their belongings, and led them away in the ambulance, leaving Wilson for dead. After several days traveling northward under guard with a number of other captives, father and son were separated. Harry soon escaped and made his way home, but Angus spent the next five months in various Yankee prisons. What remained of his health was destroyed. Exchanged in early November, he was transported to Richmond, where he was taken in by relatives. He died less than four weeks later.[32]

Nature had not yet hidden all traces of the little skirmish on the mountainside when Cornelia visited the site in the summer of 1865. "There were the piles of ashes still where the trunks had been burned," she noted, "with leaves of books and scraps of paper lying about. The prints of their footsteps were still there, and marks of the bullets on the fences and trees." Before returning home, she went to see Wilson. His family, having heard he was killed, had gone to recover his body the day after the fight, only to find him clinging to life. Although the ghastly head wound he suffered cost him an eye, he survived. Perhaps he thought Angus's decision to make a stand was more foolish than valiant; if so, he did not tell Cornelia.[33]

Haunted by memories and consumed by anxiety, Cornelia sought the comfort of friends. She had many in Lexington, but only two—Mrs. Powell and Mrs. Dailey—whom she felt comfortable pouring out her heart to. After Mrs. Powell's husband returned at war's end, the couple moved away. Cornelia thus turned more and more to Mrs. Dailey, who was, like herself, a refugee from Winchester. Their friendship had begun there, and she and her husband had helped Cornelia get settled in Lexington in 1863. Cornelia felt close to her not only because of their long friendship, but also because her situation was almost as bleak as Cornelia's own. She was without her husband in the early summer of 1865, for he was away seeking employment, and she and her children were, as Cornelia wrote, "in a great state of distress, being even for a time without bread." One day Cornelia called on her and found her in tears. She had just sent one of her most treasured possessions—a silver bowl that had been her mother's—to the mill to be swapped for a barrel of flour.[34]

Cornelia saw other friends that summer, including Ann Pendleton and her daughters, Madge Paxton, and Anne McElwee, but she would never admit to them how desperate things were in the McDonald household. Partly it was because they were friends of recent vintage and there was still a touch of formality in their relationship, a bit of distance. But mostly it was because of Cornelia's pride. While few if any of her friends were financially comfortable at this time, all except Mrs. Dailey were better off than the McDonalds. If Cornelia confessed her poverty, they would of course come to her aid; but she could not stand the thought of being a charity case, an object of pity. She would never let her children starve, of course, but it had not yet come to that. Until it did, she would keep up appearances. When friends stopped by her house, she recalled, "I would sit and talk to them, and be as cheerful as I could." When they left, she would "go up stairs and throw myself on my knees and cry to God for food."[35]

She was already nearing the limit of her physical and emotional endurance when disaster struck. It happened on a morning in July. She was working in the kitchen, which was in the basement. A kettle of boiling water hung in the fireplace—the house had no stove—and she was preparing to take it up to the dining room to wash the breakfast dishes. This was normally the duty of Susan, the cook, but she was at the moment busy elsewhere in the house. Rather than lug the kettle to the dining room, Cornelia emptied it into a dishpan, took the pan by the handles, and started up the steps.[36]

Somehow the dishpan slipped from her grasp, dumping the boiling water on her right foot. She screamed, ran up the steps to the back porch, and then into the house and up the stairs to her bedroom. There she removed her right slipper and then her stocking. "[O]n taking off the stocking," she recalled, "all the skin came with it."[37]

When the shock wore off, the pain set in. A doctor confirmed that the burns were severe. For the next several weeks she was confined to bed, suffering terribly. "I could not turn in the bed, and could not endure . . . the slightest jar. A door shut too suddenly, would occasion a nervous shock and intense pain."[38]

Friends rallied to help her. Many sent food, and once she was well enough to receive, they called frequently. Madge Paxton, especially, proved to be a saint. She came every morning bearing an orange or a bunch of grapes or some other cheery little gift, and while there she would straighten up Cornelia's sickroom and bathe and dress little Hunter. When Nelly came down with diphtheria, Madge tended her as if she were her own, carefully washing out her throat each day. Harry and Allan were a great help, too, staying home to minister to their mother, lifting and carrying her as needed until she was able to get around on crutches.[39]

However welcome and necessary the help from the two older boys, it entailed a financial sacrifice that the family could not afford. Every day Harry and Allan spent at home was a day they earned no wages. Not only that, but Cornelia's own income was abruptly cut off by her infirmity. Until she healed considerably, she was unable to continue giving drawing lessons.[40]

Even as she recovered from her injury, she slipped further into depression. The family's store of food was nearly exhausted, and there was little money to buy more and none to pay the cook. The house rent was overdue and the landlord was losing patience. There were also doctor bills to pay, and, with fall approaching, the family would need to lay in a supply of firewood for heating. On top of all that, Mrs. Dailey moved away, leaving Cornelia "forlorn and undone," with "no one . . . to whom I could confide any part of my misery." Things had seemed bleak before, but now they seemed hopeless.[41]

One day toward the end of summer she hit rock bottom. As she sat at the dinner table staring at the usual fare of bean soup and bread that she had grown thoroughly sick of, she "was seized with utter despair. I felt that God had forsaken us." She left the table, lay down on the sofa, and remained there for hours, overwhelmed with "unbelief and hopelessness." Horrible thoughts came to her, thoughts she could not suppress. "I desired at that moment to be done with life, for no one seemed to care for us, whether we lived or died." It was all she could do to keep from falling on her knees and uttering "the impious prayer that God would destroy us."[42]

Her deep faith soon reasserted itself. She remembered "the goodness my God had shown me in the former dark hours I had passed through . . . [and] with that remembrance came the resolve, 'Though He slay me, yet will I trust in Him.'" Before the day was done, she had climbed from her pit of despair.[43]

The experience frightened her badly, nonetheless. Fearing more "attacks of the Tempter," she vowed to keep herself so busy that she could not "dwell in thought for a moment on my own miseries." As soon as she was able, she resumed her tutoring. Harry and Allan returned to work, too, and the restoration of the family's income, although more a trickle than a stream, helped boost Cornelia's spirits. And then one day she unexpectedly received a package from some old friends in Winchester, gifts of clothing: underwear for her, shoes and frocks for Nelly. It cheered her to be reminded that she had "friends who had not forgotten me."[44]

As summer ended, she thought of the season ahead. Autumn had always been for her a time of joy and peace, when she would take long walks in the countryside, relishing the mellow sunlight and the crisp air. She did not anticipate such joy and peace this autumn, however. Despite her resolve, she could not wholly banish the dark visions from her mind. "[A]lways the thought of the desolation of our penniless home was before me, and my heart ached."[45]

JOHN ROBERTSON

JUNE OF 1865 WAS WARMER THAN USUAL IN EAST TENNESSEE. The heat, and the thin haze that always came with it in that part of the country, seemed more like July or August weather. Had John Robertson not firmly renounced the habit of cursing that he had picked up in the army, he would now have been damning the heat, and damning the bad luck that made it necessary for him to sweat each day in the fields. Uncle Allen was still sick, cousin Jacob was still confined to bed with a broken thigh, and the younger son was too little to help, so the farm work now fell to John. The books he had borrowed to help him prepare for the Methodist ministry sat unopened in his room.[1]

These June days were long as well as hot. Any farmer who was not at work by five in the morning, when the sun was already over the horizon, and not still working fourteen hours later, was considered no-account. Those hours were filled with toil, for if the corn plants were not diligently tended they would be choked by weeds. And the weeds were relentless: the row of corn that was hoed or plowed one day would be overrun again a few days later. The farmers all looked forward to the laying-by in late summer, when the corn would be tall and strong enough to survive on its own and the weeds could be ignored.[2]

Even with all the demands of field labor, however, John found time to visit Tennie. Her mother's farm adjoined Uncle Allen's, so it took John only a few minutes to walk over; often he would eat his midday meal there. Tennie's mother, the widow Robertson, always made him welcome, and when he joined the family at the table, she insisted he say grace.[3]

Toward the end of the month, John volunteered to do some work at Tennie's place, figuring it was a good excuse to spend more time there. Mrs. Robertson had a twelve-acre field of wheat that was ready to be harvested and had hired a man to do it. John joined him in the field early on the morning of June 26 and the two went to work. Slowly they waded through the golden expanse of ripe wheat, sweeping their cradles in a wide arc from right to left, and laying the sheaves on the ground to be gathered later. John was an old hand at this kind of work, for his father had raised wheat during the years John was growing up in Greene County.[4]

His companion in the field was a recently returned Confederate soldier named McPherson. He was a young man, but the war had taken a toll on him and, as John observed, "he could not stand hard work." By ten o'clock it was already blistering hot, and poor McPherson was suffering. He stripped down to his underwear and kept going until one, when his cradle broke. He then put on his clothes and left, telling John he was going home to get another cradle. "[T]hat was the last I saw of him."[5]

John kept working, but not too hard. He had no intention of charging Mrs. Robertson for his labor and thus felt no obligation to exert himself. "I was in the house about as much of my time as I was in the field," he wrote. "Tennie was good company and I would rather be pestering her than cutting wheat." It took him days to finish the job.[6]

The only thing besides Tennie to which John gladly devoted time during these summer weeks was the Sunday school at Blue Springs Church. He was especially excited about the grand ceremony that the congregation decided to stage to celebrate the success of the school. He was appointed to the committee that planned the occasion, and he took the responsibility seriously. Sunday, July 2, was the day designated, and it turned out to be a beautiful day. The event began in the morning with a procession: John, Tennie, and the other officers and teachers of the school were in front, followed by the students, and then everyone else who wanted to take part. The choir lined up, too. Once assembled, they all marched solemnly down the road away from the church for half a mile, then turned around and marched back, circled twice around the church, and finally filed inside and seated themselves. Several speakers were to address the crowd, one of them being John himself. While the others were speaking, John passed among the pews collecting donations for the school library.[7]

An unpleasant incident marred the occasion. One of the speakers, a minister named Bever, was a unionist who decided to take this opportunity to express his feelings on "the war question," as John termed it. "This spoiled our Celebration. Many left the house while he was speaking; when I got up [to speak] many of them returned." Put "in a bad humor" by the Reverend Bever's indiscretion, John cut his own address short.[8]

This was one of the few times "the war question" had intruded into John's little corner of Roane County since he had moved there the previous fall. The neighborhood's unionists and secessionists generally tried to get along with each other. Not all east Tennessee districts were so harmonious. Many were deeply divided, and some were so riven by hostility that they were dangerous places to live—especially for rebels, who were heavily outnumbered in all but a few parts of the region. The wave of prosecutions, ostracism, intimidation, and violence set in motion by embittered unionists against their rebel neighbors during the spring showed no sign of slackening in the summer. Many of its victims were now leaving east Tennessee, seeking sanctuary in other regions.[9]

Some were fleeing to middle or west Tennessee, where rebels predominated. But no part of Tennessee was completely comfortable for rebels, for the state government was controlled by unionists of the most unforgiving sort, chief among them Governor Brownlow. Most of the former Confederate states were now being politically reconstructed under President Johnson's authority, and thanks to his lenient policy of amnesty and pardon they would soon be back in rebel hands. Not so Tennessee: its government had been restored in the last weeks of the war, and the rebels had been allowed no part in it.[10]

Governor Brownlow now proceeded to ensure that his enemies would remain powerless. In June, at his behest, the legislature passed a law that barred anyone from voting who had not been a loyal unionist from the beginning of the war to the end. Brownlow justified it with the fierce and uncompromising rhetoric that was his trademark. Rebels were "traitors," he declared, and being stripped of their political rights was the least they deserved. He recounted the suffering of unionists under the Confederate regime, and their continuing persecution in areas where they were a minority. Justice for these victims, he said, as well as their safety and the safety of the Union itself, demanded that the "bloody hands" of the rebels be kept from the ballot box. "[T]he spirit of Rebellion . . . still exists and must be defeated."[11]

Like every other rebel in Tennessee, John Robertson detested Brownlow—"the *basest of all wretches*," he called him. The voting law was of no direct concern to him, however, for he was not much interested in politics and was too young to vote anyway. But there was another effort under way at Brownlow's instigation, this one outside the realm of government, which could well affect John's future.[12]

Brownlow was an ordained Methodist minister. Although he had long ago given up circuit-riding in favor of journalism and politics, he had remained active in the Southern Methodist Church. When secession and war came, he had publicly condemned the ministers of his faith who sided with the Confederacy, and when the Holston Conference—the governing body of the church in east Tennessee—formally endorsed the rebel cause and expelled a number of unionist ministers, Brownlow vowed revenge.[13]

Now he had the power to make good on his vow. His plan was to reorganize the Holston Conference as a thoroughly unionist body, align it with the Northern Methodist Church, seize all property held by the conference, and expel the rebel ministers. On June 1, a group of unionist Methodists assembled in the town of Athens and, with Brownlow's blessing, took the first steps. Declaring themselves the legitimate Holston Conference, they resolved that "those who entered into the late rebellion and imbibed the spirit thereof, are guilty of a crime sufficient to exclude them from the kingdom of grace and glory, and must not be admitted into this Conference, save upon full confession and thorough repentance."[14]

East Tennessee's rebel Methodists, especially those of the cloth, thus faced an uncertain future. John Robertson would have to reckon with this turmoil in his church. There was nothing he could do about it for now, however. Even if he could soon get back to his books, his ordination would be years away. And besides, there was something much more pressing on his mind.

His anxiety about Tennie had by now rendered him utterly miserable. "I could not sleep," he wrote. "Sometimes when in her company, I had hope and thought she loved me; but at other times I had doubts." He could resolve this agonizing uncertainty at any time by declaring his love and asking for her hand. But he was afraid to, for rejection would bring only greater misery.[15]

By July he had decided he could go on no longer. He would confront his beloved and accept his fate. Late in the afternoon of July 9, he walked over to Tennie's. "I made my way very slowly," he recalled, "as with a weary step." She met him at the door with a smile, as always, and they seated themselves in the usual place, close together on the little front porch. To John's great relief, Mrs. Robertson went off to call on some sick neighbors. He liked her, but wanted no interruptions this day. For two hours he and Tennie sat, but John was unusually quiet. Several times she asked him "what was the matter, or, if I was sick; why I talked so little, and why so sad."[16]

It was sundown when at last he mustered his courage, took her hand in his, and said the words he had prepared:

"Tennie, I have one request to make of you, and I hope God may help you to decide for your own good. It will not take me long to make it, and it is this: Will you consent to be my wife? to share both my joys and sorrows through life? I love you, and you only do I love. I promi[s]e before God to ever strive to make you happy. This is all any man can promi[s]e, and I make the request and promi[s]e from my heart."[17]

As he spoke the final words, she gripped his hand tightly and laid her head against his chest. But before she could reply, he told her she must wait. He had taken her by surprise, and thought it only right to give her time to think. He would return in six days, he said, and hear her answer. They said good night, and he walked home in the twilight.[18]

He spent those six days cutting grass in Uncle Allen's meadow and gathering it into a haystack. He was only a little less miserable than before. Tennie's unspoken response to his proposal had given him hope, but still he feared that her answer would be no. He could think about little else, and the days passed with excruciating slowness.[19]

When the fifteenth came, he did not wait until evening. He left the meadow at noon and walked to Tennie's. They greeted each other with unaccustomed solemnity. She invited him to sit and then joined him, but neither spoke much. It was Tennie's mother who finally broke the ice, with a bit of horseplay. John was nervously fingering a silver dollar he carried, and she made as if to take it from him. "[S]oon Tennie joined in the play," John recalled. "They got it from me but I got it back." Mrs. Robertson then left them alone.[20]

John took Tennie's hand and asked if she had made her decision. She replied without hesitating: "Yes, Dear John, if you think I can make you happy, I *am yours.*" As she spoke, she fell into his arms.[21]

"My feelings at that time I can not describe," John wrote. "None but those who have been lovers know the joy of experienceing love. I had now all I desired. Tennie had vowed before God she would be my companion, what more could I wish." They held each other for a long time. When he left, he gave her the silver dollar as a keepsake.[22]

They set no wedding date, for they were still quite young and were content to wait until John had progressed farther in his career. Fortunately, he now had more time to devote to his studies. About three weeks earlier, toward the end of June, his uncle James Robertson had moved in with Uncle Allen. With him came his wife, Margaret, their six children, and a long-time friend of John's named Grig Register. They had moved from Greene County, where John's parents still lived. Their arrival filled Uncle Allen's house to near the bursting point, but also provided other hands to work the farm, relieving John of that responsibility.[23]

John did not go back to his books full time, however, for he had by now concluded that he needed to earn some money. Disliking manual labor, he sought the only other kind of work he was qualified to do, which was teaching.

There were no public schools in Roane County, only subscription schools. The way a teacher got a position was by announcing that he was "getting up" a school and then trying to persuade parents to enroll their children and pay the tuition. In the last days of June, John went around the area soliciting subscribers. Before the month was out, he had enough to start a school and had secured a suitable building.[24]

He began in mid-July with seventeen students. More came to enroll as the laying-by freed them from the fields, and eventually he had thirty-eight—sixteen of them his cousins. Most were rambunctious youngsters, but one was a married woman. "None of my scholars were far advanced," John noted. What they needed, and what he proceeded to give them, was simply the three R's along with a little geography.[25]

July gave way to August. Five days a week John was at his post in the hot, crowded classroom, explaining the mysteries of spelling and long division, listening to awkward recitations, and trying to keep order. His Saturdays were his own. He spent them with Tennie, or studying, or at Blue Springs Church, or helping out on the farm. The Sabbath was devoted to Sunday school.[26]

Thus would John's weeks have passed until midautumn, when the subscription school term was to end, had events not taken an abrupt turn in late summer. Perhaps it was inevitable that the troubles afflicting so many other communities in east Tennessee would at some point spill into John's. The wooded ridges that bordered his little world were high and steep, but they were no defense against intruders. In August intruders came and changed John's life forever.

The ordeal began on a Saturday. John was at Uncle Allen's, but the other men of the family were away. Late in the morning a band of six horsemen, all armed, rode up to the gate. He saw them through a window. Grabbing his pistol and stuffing it partway down into the leg of his boot, he headed out the front door, ignoring the pleas of the women to stay inside.[27]

When he asked the men their business, he noticed that "they seemed puzzled to know what to say or do." After a few moments they requested directions to a neighbor's house and, when John told them, they rode off. "I was glad to get rid of them on such easy terms," he recalled. He recognized one of the men. He was a unionist named Hale who lived not far from John's home in Greene County.[28]

In the back of John's mind had long been the fear that his brief career as a rebel vigilante would return to haunt him. The home guard outfit he had ridden with for several months in 1863 in Greene and Washington counties had made itself notorious among the local unionists. "[W]e would go out of our bounds," John admitted in retrospect, "and do things we ought not to do." What they did was terrorize unionist families, plundering their homes, threatening them, and arresting any man or boy suspected as a Tory guerrilla. The more elusive suspects they set traps for and tried to waylay. John knew that some of these unionists were itching for revenge; twice someone had attempted to murder him from ambush on his father's farm. It was for this reason that he exiled himself from Greene County after the Yankee invasion gave unionists the upper hand.[29]

He could not be certain that this disturbing encounter with armed riders had anything to do with all that. The men had said nothing to suggest that it did, and Hale had given no indication that he even recognized John. Perhaps it was just coincidence that had brought Hale more than a hundred miles to Uncle Allen's gate.

John's relief at the departure of the horsemen was short-lived. An hour later they returned, and again he armed himself and confronted them. This time Hale called him by name and said he was there to collect a debt John's father owed him. John knew the debt had been paid long ago, and he said so, adding that even if it had not been paid, it was no responsibility of his.[30]

The men then said they would like to have some dinner. John replied that they were welcome to come into the house and eat. They declined, saying they would rather he bring the food out to them; they would wait at the spring nearby. "I feared they were trying to draw me away from the house to abuse me, and perhaps kill me," John wrote, "but, determ[in]ed to stand them the best fight I could, I took the dinner to the spring."[31]

He stood by as the men ate, watching them carefully and staying close to a large tree, "expecting to make it serve me as a breast-work, should they attack me." All the while they whispered among themselves, but he could not make out what they said. At last they stood up and mounted their horses. As they galloped off, they yelled and fired their pistols into the air. John then returned to the house, to the great relief of the women, who had heard the shots and feared he was dead. He concluded that he "had run a narrow escap[e]," and that only his boldness had saved him.[32]

During the week that followed, he heard nothing more of this gang and he taught school each day without incident. He did, however, take the precaution of getting in some target practice with his pistol. By the end of the week he had used up all his ammunition, but he planned to get more at a store near Blue Springs Church. He would be attending a service at the church on Saturday and would stop by the store afterward.[33]

When Saturday came, he set off for Blue Springs on foot, leaving the pistol behind. As he passed the home of the Raby family, Mr. Raby hailed him. There was a gang of unionists looking for him, he warned John, and he "had better watch out." John promised to do so and went on. As he neared the church, he saw a group of horsemen coming down the road toward him. He was able to jump over a fence and into a thicket before they spotted him, and they passed on. He could not get a close look at them.[34]

He entered the church and took a seat, and the service began. It was interrupted momentarily by some late arrivals. John turned to look and saw that they were the gang he had confronted at Uncle Allen's the Saturday before.[35]

After the service those in attendance chatted for a while outside the church. John was talking with the minister when a man waded into the crowd on horseback and stopped in front of him. He was a stranger and was wearing a pistol.

"Why how are ye Mr. Robertson?" he said.

"I am well sir. But how come you to know me? I don't know you."

"Why my name is *Bacon*, just from your Pa's. I have seen you many a time."

"I have no recollection of you Sir at all."[36]

Bacon then invited himself to go home with John for dinner. John did not like the idea, but decided not to object. He set out apprehensively, accompanied by Bacon and two other armed and mounted men who seemed to be his companions. Eventually the other two rode off, leaving Bacon and John alone. As they continued down the road together, the one on foot and the other on horseback, Bacon chatted so amiably that John began to relax. Perhaps there was no danger after all.[37]

There was a point where the road passed through a stretch of thick woods. As they entered it, Bacon suddenly stopped, pulled out his pistol, cocked it, and curled his finger around the trigger.

"What do you mean by treating me in that way?" John demanded.

"*I mean to blow your brains out right here*," Bacon replied.

"You will give me your cause first, wont you?"

"Because you bushwhacked me in Washing[ton] Co. sir."

"I never bushwhacked you in Washington sir."

"*You are a d—d l[ia]r, and here you'll die.*"

John again protested his innocence. Bacon pointed to a hole in his sleeve, saying it was made by the bullet John had fired at him from ambush two years before.

John kept talking. Boldness had saved him a week ago; perhaps it would do so now. "If you wish to kill the innocent and answer for it at the day of Judgment," he said, "crack away."

"You d—d rebel you, you're too m[ea]n to live anyhow."

"Don't you expect to answer for this when you come to die?"

"That don't concern me now, so prepare to die!"

"Sir I am ready, more so perhaps than you are."[38]

At that remark Bacon seemed to lose some of his nerve. Abruptly he announced that he would let John live if he gave up his pocket watch and pistol. John was wearing his watch in plain sight; how Bacon knew about his pistol he could guess. He replied that he would see about it when they got to Uncle Allen's, and the two continued on their way.[39]

John was carrying a walking stick and kept looking for a chance to use it on Bacon, but the man kept his pistol drawn and cocked and his eyes on John. Maybe, John thought, he would let his guard down while at the house and could be disarmed.[40]

When they arrived at Uncle Allen's, John abandoned all hope of overpowering Bacon, for he was suddenly outnumbered. Bacon's two companions were waiting inside the house. No adult family members were at home, only some of the younger cousins, along with Tennie, who was visiting. After John and Bacon entered the house, Tennie and the children fled, scattering into the woods.[41]

John tried one last ploy. Hoping he might simply wear the men out with delays, he insisted that he was going to sit down and have his dinner before he did anything else. And so he did, eating slowly and deliberately. But the three showed no sign of impatience as they stood over him with guns drawn. Finally, seeing no other way out of the situation, John finished his meal and reluctantly surrendered his watch and pistol.[42]

The ordeal was not quite over. As they pocketed their loot, the men swore at John, saying "We have not taken any of your blood yet, and we're going to have it." One of them picked up John's walking stick, remarking that it would do just fine to beat him to death with.[43]

John grabbed a chair and made ready to defend himself with it. "You will not kill me by inches," he said fiercely. "If you strike me you will have to kil[l] me, or die." The men looked at John and decided to press the matter no further. They left the house, mounted up, and rode off.[44]

Tennie soon reappeared. She said she had run to the home of a neighbor and pleaded with him to come help, but he had refused, saying he was afraid. John was grateful to her. "She had showed her fidelity as a true lover in the fray. She had done all she could, but could give me no help. This only served to bind us more close, and dearer to each other if possible."[45]

The next day was Sunday. John stayed away from Blue Springs Church, missing Sunday school for the first time. That night he learned that a band of unionists had shown up at the church looking for him and declared their intention to kill him.[46]

They would likely come again to Uncle Allen's, he reasoned, and they might well come after him at his schoolhouse, too. He would have to hide out for a while. He knew of a place to go. Tennie had recently begun teaching a school of her own in a community five miles away; she boarded there, coming home each Friday evening and returning early on Monday. John decided to go with her and stay in that area until his own community was safer. Uncle Allen agreed to take over his teaching duties for the time being.[47]

John stayed away for a week, then returned and went back to the classroom. He had no further visitations from the "Lincolnites," as he contemptuously called them, but he remained uneasy. If they were determined to kill him, there was nothing he could do to stop them—nothing, that is, except go where they could not find him. Through the waning days of August, he agonized over his plight. By September, he had decided he must leave.[48]

PART FOUR

FALL AND ANOTHER WINTER

JOHN ROBERTSON

John Robertson would have left east Tennessee early in September but for the rain. It began falling around the second day of the month and continued with hardly a letup for two weeks, drenching the ridges and hills and inundating the bottom lands. The wagon that was to haul his belongings to the train depot was no match for the muddy roads, and so his departure was postponed.[1]

He had little to do while waiting for the weather to clear. He had closed his school on September 1—halfway through the three-month term he had planned—and farm work was pretty much at a standstill as long as it was raining. Tennie was away at her school five days out of seven. John thus had a lot of time to think things over, but he did not reconsider his decision to leave. To stay would be to risk his life. The armed gang that had twice accosted him had declared their intention to kill him. Where they were now he did not know; but even if they had left Roane County, they could return at any time, and they knew where he lived, where he went to church, and what paths he walked. Appealing to the authorities for protection was pointless: they could hardly guard his remote community against an elusive band of vengeful unionists, even if they were so inclined—which they probably were not, for they were all unionists themselves.[2]

John's new home would be in Iowa. His uncle Jim Robertson, who had been living with Uncle Allen since June, had decided to seek his fortune there and had persuaded John to go with him. Iowa was far, far away, but John had no close family or friends outside east Tennessee and concluded that, as long as he must live in exile among strangers, he might as well "be 1200 miles from home as 150."[3]

He did not especially relish the idea of living in the North, a "distant clime, where I had but little assurance of enjoyment, and where, I had been told, the hearts of the people were as cold as the climate." That those people were also his former enemies bothered him little. He had no quarrel with them now, and he anticipated no real trouble from them. The ironic fact was that he was much safer in Yankeedom than in his east Tennessee homeland. Northerners had no love for rebels, but neither did they seek bloody vengeance against them.[4]

It was having to leave Tennie that he dreaded most. When he told her of his decision to go, she did not try to dissuade him. She knew as well as he that his life was in danger, and in any event she was not the sort to argue with him. They did not seriously discuss the possibility of her going with him. John thought himself too young to marry—he had turned nineteen in April—and even if old enough, he was in no position to support a wife and family comfortably. There was no other choice, he concluded sadly: he and his beloved would have to separate. Their plans for the future remained intact, however. He promised he would one day return to claim her as his bride, and she promised she would wait for him.[5]

The rain let up after the second week of September. By Sunday, the seventeenth, the roads were passable, and John and Uncle Jim agreed that they would leave the next day. That evening John walked over to Tennie's for a last visit. It was "a gloomy sabbath to me," he recalled, "and not less g[l]oomy to someone else." The weather had turned cool and Mrs. Robertson had a fire going in the parlor. Her younger children were gathered around the fireplace, carrying on happily. John took a seat next to the armchair where Tennie sat. Hours passed, but neither said much; not even the cheery fire and the frolicking children could lift their spirits. "Occasionally a smile would light upon [our] lips, but a deep sigh would follow." After a while someone suggested singing, and a hymnal was brought out. John loved to sing, but tonight his heart was not in it, and after a few hymns the book was put away. Then Tennie fetched a Bible, and John joined the family in their nightly prayers. It was very late when at last he said good night and left.[6]

He returned early the next morning for a final, brief farewell. Tennie met him on the porch. He took her hand and looked into her eyes. "I will return," he said.

"Never fear me," she replied. "I will prove true." They kissed, and he left.[7]

When he got back to Uncle Allen's, he found a crowd of neighbors gathered to say good-bye. "Whole families were there to see us start," John remembered, "large and small old and young." The party bound for Iowa numbered ten in all: John, Uncle Jim, his wife, Margaret, their six children, and a family friend named Newton Mullens. Two wagons were on hand to haul them and their luggage to the railroad station at Sweetwater, eight miles away. Once the wagons were loaded, they said their good-byes. "I gave Uncle A[llen] my hand in sorrow," John recalled. "I regret[t]ed to part with him [for] he had been a friend to me. . . . [F]or the first time in [my] life on parting with a friend, a tear rolled down my cheek."[8]

It was well into the afternoon when they finally got away. The wagons, driven by neighbors, carried John and his nine companions eastward over the ridge to Blue Springs, where more friends were gathered to say farewell, and then headed southeast. It was almost dark when the party got to the Sweetwater depot. After unloading their baggage they found themselves with several hours to kill, for the train was not due until midnight. They ate the cold supper that they had brought along, then laid down pallets on the waiting room floor for the sleepy children, who ranged from a toddler to a thirteen-year-old. John and Mullens wandered around the little town a while, then returned to the depot.[9]

John stretched out on a table in the waiting room and tried to sleep, but could not. After a while he went outside to the platform. For a long time he paced back and forth along its length, melancholy and pensive. He thought about his parents in Greene County. He had not seen them in over a year and wondered when he would see them again. He thought about his commitment to Christ. That brought a measure of comfort, for, as he reminded himself, no matter how far from home he journeyed, he would always have "one friend who never forsakes those who do his will." Mostly, though, he thought about Tennie.[10]

The noise of the approaching train interrupted his reverie. He looked down the track and saw the locomotive, with its huge headlight, "glaring like a demon through the darkness." Quickly the adults roused the children and gathered the luggage. As the train came to a stop, hissing and screeching, John took his valise in one hand and the littlest child in the other. Stepping up onto the end platform of one of the passenger cars, he squeezed through the door, made his way down the center aisle, and found a seat. The others climbed aboard, too, and a few moments later the conductor clanged the brass bell and the train moved out.[11]

South and west they headed, along the track of the East Tennessee & Georgia Railroad. Barely had they stowed their bags and gotten the youngsters settled when the train stopped at Athens, ten miles from Sweetwater. John had visited this town once or twice in the past to peddle the cigars he and Uncle Allen had made. When the train pulled out and left Athens behind, continuing on its southwesterly route, he realized that he was now farther from home than he had ever been.[12]

The interior of the long low-ceilinged car in which he rode was dimly illuminated by a lamp. There was nothing to be seen from the windows, for the night was moonless and pitch-black. John sat silently, rocking ever so slightly with the motion of the train and listening to the iron wheels clatter rhythmically over the rails.[13]

After a while, Mullens, who was sitting beside him, decided he needed cheering up. "Come John," he said, "don't be grievin[g] about that sweet heart a[l]ready; stir up and don't be so drowsy."

John was in no mood for banter. "It is true I feel gloomy," he replied stiffly, "but as for me being grieving, I believe you are mistaken."

"Well stir your stump," Mullens chirped, "and let's talk about them devils up in Green[e] County."

"Up in Green[e] County?"

"Yes," said Mullens, "them we're running from."

Now John began to get very annoyed. He no more wanted to talk about the unionist gang than about Tennie. He wished Mullens would shut up. "For my part," he said sharply, "I am not running from any devils as I know of."

Mullens persisted jovially. "Well it looks mighty like it the way this old train jogs along; it's more like flying."

To this John declined to reply. Mullens finally gave up and eventually dozed off, leaving John alone with his thoughts.[14]

He was still awake and brooding when the eastern sky began to brighten with the rising sun. It was around 5:30 and the train was approaching Chattanooga. To the left lay Missionary Ridge and ahead, beyond the city, towered Lookout Mountain. These were the renowned battlefields where, in November 1863, Ulysses S. Grant's forces had dealt smashing blows to the rebel Army of Tennessee, breaking its siege of the city, sending it reeling back into Georgia, and opening the way for Sherman's later campaign against Atlanta. Chattanooga had remained an important Union army post from that time until the end of the war, and it was even now garrisoned by Yankee

16. Chattanooga at the time of the Civil War. Lookout Mountain looms in the distance.

troops. It had also become a haven for slaves who had deserted their masters in the wake of Sherman's army. Thousands still resided in the city or in a settlement they had established nearby known as Contraband.[15]

At the Chattanooga depot, John and his party collected their baggage and got off the train. They would have to change to another to continue on their way, and it was not scheduled to leave for an hour. As he waited, John gazed around the depot. He was revolted by what he saw. Not only was the place crowded and noisy and disorderly, but it was also teeming with blacks. He had seen few or none since his stay in Knoxville back in January, and he would just as soon never see any again.[16]

He heard voices raised in anger not far from where he stood. Turning to look, he saw a white man and a black man arguing. In a moment they were pummeling one another. To John's disgust, the black got the better of the white and thrashed him. Before that fight was over, another broke out nearby. "[T]his did not concern me," John remarked, "as it was between two negroes."[17]

There was worse to come. Not thirty feet away he saw "two big, rusty negroes" in U.S. army uniforms. They were members of the Yankee garrison, assigned to patrol the depot. As John watched, the soldiers moved in to arrest a white man for some infraction. He resisted, but to no avail. "[G]athering him like dogs would a sheep," John wrote, "one by each arm, they drug him off to prison," both cursing profanely the whole time. John boiled with anger. "O how I wanted to shoot them down, like an old hunter would a panther." He was glad when the train whistle blew, signaling the passengers to board. "I longed to be off from this place where negro equality was being [en]forced so rigidly."[18]

The train chugged westward, skirting the base of Lookout Mountain, and traveled twenty miles or so before dipping southward into Alabama. John and his companions marveled at the scenery along this stretch. In places the track was cut right into a mountainside. On one hand would be a nearly perpendicular wall of rock hundreds of feet high, and on the other a ravine equally deep, into which it seemed the careening locomotive might tumble at any moment.[19]

Nearing Bridgeport, the train crossed the Tennessee River on a long wooden trestle. After a breakfast stop in Stevenson, it headed north, now on the track of the Nashville & Chattanooga Railroad, and soon reentered Tennessee. Everywhere along this route were reminders that it had been one of the Union army's vital lifelines in subduing the Confederacy. At frequent intervals stood stout blockhouses and redoubts, empty now of Yankee soldiers and cannons but still imposing.[20]

By noon the train had passed through the rugged middle Tennessee highlands and into the fertile lowlands. This was a world far different from what John had known in east Tennessee. It was a world of great plantations and great wealth—or had been, before the war. Remnants of it survived: from his car window John saw stately mansions surrounded by broad, level fields of ripe cotton; in the fields, gangs of black men and women were at work. But he saw, too, large stretches of abandoned land, fenceless and overgrown, and the charred ruins of houses and barns. Middle Tennessee had been smitten harder by the hand of war than almost any other region of the South, and the scars would be long in healing.[21]

The train stopped in Murfreesboro in midafternoon but was soon on its way again. Just north of the town John saw more vestiges of war. An immense circular earthwork was located here—Fortress Rosecrans, built during the latter part of the conflict by the Yankee occupation forces. Fully a mile across and three in circumference, it was big enough to hold an army. Within it, and for a thousand yards around it, every tree had been cut down. John got a close-up view of this great ugly sore upon the land, for the railroad track cut directly through it.[22]

Not far beyond the fortress, the train passed the Stones River battlefield where, in the winter of 1862–1863, one of the war's bloodiest engagements was fought. Evidence of its ferocity was visible still: tree trunks mutilated by Minié balls and shells, and row upon row of graves. "What a scene of death and bloodshed must have been here," John thought. He was especially moved at the sight of the final resting places "of those who had bravely fought in both armies; thousands of them buried here far from home and friends with only a small board to tell where they lay and many not even that." He was reminded that, but for the grace of God, he himself might be lying in such a grave.[23]

It was about five o'clock when the train rolled into the Nashville & Chattanooga depot on the south side of Nashville. Now they would have to change trains again, and to do so they must get to the city's north side, where the Louisville & Nashville depot was located. Stepping down from their car, they found themselves in the midst of a crowd even denser and unrulier than that in Chattanooga. Hurrying passengers, importuning hack drivers, shiftless loafers, and others of all sorts, black and white, jostled for room on the platform and inside the depot.[24]

Pushing their way through the mob to the street, John and the others boarded a big mule-drawn omnibus for the crosstown trip. As the vehicle wended its way along the streets, John gazed around in awe. Nashville was by far the biggest city he had ever seen. It had been a sizable place even before the war, but after the Yankees captured it and made it a primary base of operations, the population mushroomed. Even with the end of the war and the demobilization of the Union army, the military presence in Nashville remained strong. It seemed that wherever one looked there was an army barracks, hospital, quartermaster depot, or repair shop, and soldiers were everywhere, many of them black. No section of the city, however, saw more military activity than Smoky Row, the rowdy brothel district near the river. During the war it had achieved legendary status among Union soldiers, who patronized it by the thousands, and it was still going strong. Besides dozens of whorehouses, it boasted a large proportion of Nashville's four hundred saloons.[25]

On the city's highest hill stood the massive, domed state capitol, which the Northern occupiers had turned into a citadel bristling with cannons, but which now was stripped of armament and back in the hands of the state government. As the omnibus trundled past it, John reflected bitterly on Tennessee's political situation. A few minutes later he caught sight of the state penitentiary. "My only wish was that . . . all fit subjects in the state was in it; and that Brownlow the most base of all could be . . . transfer[r]ed from the State mansion to it. If this was done I felt that I could return home and live among friends at peace." Then the graves he had seen earlier in the day came to his mind, and he was seized by a premonition: "som[e]thing within told me that those extensive graveyards was not yet complete, and that there must yet be another conflict to add to their dimensions, before justice was given to all."[26]

When the omnibus halted at the Louisville & Nashville depot, John and the others got out. The scene inside was just as chaotic as at the Nashville & Chattanooga depot, but they would not have to endure it long, for the train to Louisville was to leave at 6:45. Mingling with the other sounds here were the cries of newsboys hawking the *Nashville Daily Press and Times*, which many passengers bought because it printed the Louisville & Nashville timetable every day. Those who purchased a copy that day, and who had the time and the inclination to peruse the classified advertisements, read this poignant notice, one of many such to be seen in Southern newspapers in the postwar months:

> $200 REWARD
>
> During the year 1849, Thomas Sample carried away from this city as his slaves, my daughter Polly and son George Washington, to the State of Mississippi, and subsequently to Texas, and when last heard from they were in Lagrange, Texas. I will give $100 each for them to any person who will assist them or either of them to get to Nashville, or get word to me of their whereabouts, if they are alive. Any information concerning them left in this city at my place, so that I can get it, will be liberally rewarded.
>
> Ben East[27]

It was dark when the train steamed out of the station, carrying John and his companions northward. The others were soon asleep, but he remained wakeful and pensive. Not until the train was well into Kentucky did he finally doze off. He awoke at a little after five in the morning, and a few minutes later the Louisville depot came into view. "Here as usual we found it difficult to get out of the train for 'nig[g]ers.' . . . [T]hey had forgot how to get out of the way of white people." Another omnibus ride brought the travelers to the south bank of the Ohio River, where a ferry was available to take them to the other side. The sun was well up when John stepped off the ferry in Jeffersonville, Indiana, setting foot for the first time on Northern soil.[28]

There was a half-hour wait for the train to Indianapolis, and John spent it gazing back across the river at Louisville, wondering when he would see the South again. At boarding time, the party decided, for the children's sake, to sit in the ladies' car, where smoking, spitting, and unseemly behavior were prohibited. The train had just set out when, as John put it, "I was insulted for the first time on the trip."[29]

It happened that he was wearing a gray suit that resembled a Confederate uniform. He had not previously given it a thought, but now he noticed that some of the other passengers were staring at him unpleasantly, and he soon guessed the cause. Stubbornly he decided to ignore them. "I had a blue suit in my vali[s]e which wo[ul]d have pleased them better, but I did not feel disposed to chang[e] uniform merely to gratify them."[30]

An assistant conductor entered the car, took a hard look at John's outfit, and confronted him officiously:

"Have you a wife in here?" he asked.

John wanted to reply that that was none of his business, but instead merely said "No sir I hav'nt."

"Well what are you doing in the ladies' coach?"

"I have some little girls here to take care of."

"Where is their parents?"

"There they are."

"Well give them to their parents, and you get to another coach."

"I have a right to stay here and intend to do it."

"Well get out of here, or I'll put you out."[31]

Rather than cause a scene, John left the car and went to another. He sat there stewing, determined not to let this "impertinent yankee" get the better of him. When the senior conductor came by, John told him what had happened and said he was going back to the ladies' car. The conductor said it was all right with him.[32]

Back in the ladies' car, he found that a man had taken his place. "I ordered him out of my seat which he hesitatingly obeyed." When the assistant conductor came through again, he gave John a "sour look . . . but said nothing." John then settled back in his seat, "smartly elevated at the thought of outwit[t]ing a yankee for once."[33]

The train continued northward. The landscape John saw now was quite unlike anything he was accustomed to, and he scrutinized it skeptically. "It seemed to be to[o] low and flat, to be healthy." Indianapolis, which the train reached in the early afternoon, likewise failed to impress him. It "is a large city," he wrote, "but I was not pleased with its appearance." Compounding the city's ugliness, in his eyes, was its reputation as a hotbed of radical Republicanism. He had nothing but contempt for "such an aboli[t]ion 'hole.'"[34]

North of Indianapolis, two tracks ran side by side for a distance, and here John and his fellow travelers had some excitement. Their train left the city simultaneously with another on the parallel track and, as John recalled,

> This gave occasion for a very nice race across the flat prairie. Off both trains went at full spe[e]d for several miles[;] it was hard to tell which was going to be winner. The passengers of both trains [were] poking themselves half out of the windows, yelling, [w]hooping and waving their hats, hollowing at the top of their voices for their engineer to "put on more steam." Citizens were flying from their dwellings to the front yards to see the race.

At last John's train slowed, conceding victory to its rival.[35]

Two and a half hours after nightfall the travelers reached the southern tip of Lake Michigan, whose shoreline the train then followed toward Chicago. John found the sight breathtaking. Ships glided back and forth over the vast stretch of water, their lanterns visible for miles through the darkness. Most spectacular were the great, multitiered passenger steamboats, their many windows ablaze with light. To John they looked like "larg[e] and fine mansion[s] floating on the water's s[u]rface."[36]

It was midnight when they got to Chicago. At first John was disappointed that he would not see the city by day, but he felt differently when he saw that the streets were brightly illuminated by gas lamps and still pulsing with activity. For the next hour or two he walked the streets enthralled. The city struck him as a place of enormous contrasts: on the one hand there was "beauty and magnificence"; on the other, "all kinds of wickedness." Saloons were everywhere, and passing them he heard from within "the most profane epithets." In the space of a few blocks he observed "every mode of swindling which could be thought of or invented. . . . [G]ambling tables were to be seen surround[ed] by groups of profligate and drunken men. Occasionally the police would stroll through the streets picking up such as they could catch."[37]

From Chicago they traveled westward through the heart of the Illinois prairie. It was after dark on September 21 when they arrived at a village on the eastern bank of the Mississippi River. Leaving the train, they boarded a ferry that took them across to Burlington, Iowa. There they secured lodging at a hotel, allowing them at last to catch up on their sleep. The next day they resumed their westward train journey, after saying good-bye to Mullens, who was setting out in a different direction to seek his fortune.[38]

Late that night they arrived in Oskaloosa, Iowa, where Uncle Jim intended to make his new home. "Thus ended our long and toilsome journey of twelve hundred miles," John wrote, "after a lapse of exactly four days, or 96 hours, after leaving Sweetwater."[39]

It took them some time to get settled. Uncle Jim hunted around for a farm to rent, had no luck, and soon moved on to Springfield, twenty miles away in Keokuk County, where he found what he was looking for. Meanwhile, John hired out as a laborer and worked for several farmers around Oskaloosa. After a few weeks, however, he joined Uncle Jim and his family in Springfield.[40]

What really drew John to that village was not the prospect of being with kinfolk but of going to school. As small as it was—John guessed there were not more than 500 inhabitants—Springfield nevertheless boasted a fine public high school. Hungry for more education, he enrolled in November and threw himself into his studies energetically. Among the courses he took were algebra, composition, elocution, and dictation. "I don't think ever a poor fellow studied harder than I did," he recalled. "Midnight generally found me with book in hand." He boarded at Uncle Jim's, a quarter-mile from the school, earning his keep by chopping firewood and doing other chores around the farm. He rarely missed class and never fell behind in the lessons.[41]

Springfield also boasted a literary and debating society that met each Friday night. John attended a meeting soon after his arrival and decided "It was a good institution, well calculated to make an orat[o]r of a young man if there was any such trait about him." He joined at the next meeting and a week later got his first experience of formal debate, taking the floor to argue in favor of knowledge over wealth as "the greatest influence" in society. The following week the question was "Which is the greatest man? Gen. Grant or Gen. Sherman?" John volunteered to take Grant's side—somewhat reluctantly, "not being a lover of either of the 'great men.'" Leaving it to his two teammates to praise Grant, he lit into Sherman. That general's famous march through Georgia and the Carolinas, proclaimed John, exemplified nothing better than "the bloody and detestable code of the savage. . . . Men [were] shot down, women [were] insulted and abused, depredations committed contrary to all rules of civilized warfare. . . . I ask, in the name of God, what honor can you tie on behind this degraded man?" When the debate concluded and the audience declared the winning team, John felt proud. "The unanimous voice of the house . . . was, 'hurra[h] for Gen. Grant.'"[42]

John's developing taste for argumentation found another outlet in religion. There were two churches in Springfield. One was Methodist, and John joined it soon after he arrived. The other was Campbellite and, as John soon learned, its members were waging a campaign to win souls away from his church. They proselytized aggressively, with some success, for they were well informed on doctrine and could out-argue most of the Methodists. John decided to answer their challenge. He borrowed some books from his minister to brush up on Methodism and started attending the meetings of the Campbellites to learn where they stood. Seeing him in their church, they thought they might be gaining a convert, but, as John wrote, "The more I heard them preach the further I got from their doctrine." He was especially put off by their emphasis on baptism, a ritual they insisted on performing even when the creeks and ponds were icy: "This was more faith in water than I could muster," he remarked. Before long he was taking on the Campbellite minister himself in lengthy, animated private discussions, contradicting him point by point.[43]

Rarely did John encounter any hostility on account of his Confederate service. While he made no secret of it, neither did he boast of it, and he kept his sentiments on current political affairs mostly to himself. His rule in these matters was "to attend to my own business and let every body else alone as near as possible." Finding that this was so, the citizens of Springfield responded in kind. Now and then, especially when wearing his gray suit, he would notice people staring at him and whispering among themselves; and once he overheard some boys snickering behind his back about the "Rebel" in their village. But generally the people accepted him. For his part, he came to like these Iowa Yankees pretty well—especially after he realized they were not all Republicans, much less radicals. There were many "good hearted clever people" here, he decided, and in no time at all he had a number of friends.[44]

He never felt, however, that he was one of them. In fact, the longer he stayed in Springfield, the more he was struck by how different these Northerners were from him and his fellow Southerners. It was not just their politics and accents, he noticed, but also their manners and character. For one thing, there was the brusque way they addressed strangers, so unlike the courteousness that prevailed in the South. "The first I noticed of this was in Indiana," John wrote, "when the train conduct[o]r spoke so abruptly to me as if I was a dog. I afterward found that this . . . was nothing uncommon amongst Northern people." Responding politely to such rudeness got him nowhere, he found. "I soon learned how to turn the cold shoulder too and others said I was going to make a 'good yankee' before a year."[45]

Even those who were not strangers to him often displayed an aloofness that John found puzzling. "You might meet them in the road 40 times a day, or pass their house I don't care how close, they would never salute or speak to you. . . . I always liked to see a man tend to his own business, but they attend to it to[o] close." He was even more perplexed by the lack of visiting and meal-sharing. "I have known families to live there one year and even more, and there had never been one of their neighbors in their house. Ev[e]ry family has its own neighbors they visit and revisit, but never add new neighbors to their circle. Two or three neighbors are as many as any of them want." Furthermore, "If a neighbor comes in about dining time or while they are dining, they are but seldom asked to eat, nor do they expect to be asked. . . . A stranger is never invited to eat."[46]

It was the storekeepers who really irritated him. Instead of simply stating the price of an item and letting the customer take it or leave it, they would name a wildly inflated price and then expect the customer to dicker. "If they saw [that] you would not give their price they would begin to fall, but you could never get them in sight of cost. They would lie all the time and offer to swear to every word they said. . . . [T]hey think lying and cheating is honorable." John learned their tricks, however, and was soon haggling as shrewdly as any Yankee.[47]

There were two Northern traits he found admirable. One was the willingness to support a good public school system. Although he got tired of hearing them "laughing and making sport of the ignorance of the South," which they did frequently, he had to admit that "as a general thing the Northern people is the best educated."[48]

The other thing he admired was that Northerners, at least those he lived among, "do not drink so much ardent spirits. A drunkard is looked down upon, and is almost drum[m]ed out of society. It should be looked upon in this way in all States." John himself had not touched liquor in more than a year and had pledged never to do so again. "It is one of the most debasing practices a man could engage in. It makes of him a slave."[49]

The one thing he could not get used to in Iowa was the weather. "The cold Northwestern winds were very disagreeable, and some mornings I found it very hard to face them going to School." A snowfall came in late October, far earlier than he was accustomed to, and others came frequently thereafter. The snow always remained on the ground for days or weeks, for the sun was no match for the cold.[50]

In mid-December a freezing rain left everything thickly coated with ice for many days. John was dazzled by the stark beauty of the scene—"The prairies were like a vast Ocean covered with ice," he wrote—but he found himself almost immobilized. The younger people of the village simply strapped on their skates and went about their business, but John did not know how to skate and feared that if he tried, he would break his neck. He affixed metal cleats to his boot heels as the older folk did, but still had trouble getting around. The first time he slipped and fell, he hit his head hard on the ice and skinned one side of his face from ear to chin.[51]

As busy as he was in the last weeks of the year, his thoughts still turned frequently to home. He missed his family and ached with longing for Tennie. Iowa was not a bad place, all things considered, he thought, but "I had left my heart in Tenn[essee]."[52]

The last day of 1865 was a Sunday. "The weather was cold and disagreeable," John recalled. There would be worse to come before this winter was over, he knew. How many more Yankee winters he must endure before he could go home, he did not know.[53]

CORNELIA MCDONALD

ON SEPTEMBER 9, 1865, AN OFFICE OF THE FREEDMEN'S BUREAU opened in Lexington, Virginia. The white residents of the town, who had been seething with resentment ever since the Yankee occupation force arrived in June, were thus provoked anew.[1]

The agent in charge of the office was First Lieutenant C. Jerome Tubbs of the 58th Pennsylvania Infantry. A New Yorker by birth and a house carpenter by trade, the thirty-three-year old Tubbs had served in the Union army since 1861. He had endured long stretches of dull garrison duty in North Carolina and Virginia, punctuated by intervals of hard campaigning. He had dealt with a lot of rebels, in and out of uniform, and he had little sympathy for them.[2]

It took Lieutenant Tubbs no time at all to size up the citizens of Lexington and Rockbridge County. They were, in his view, unrepentant rebels of the worst sort. "Holy Water would as easily spring from a rock," he remarked caustically in a report, "as loyal sentiments from their Rebellious hearts." He was convinced, moreover, that the citizens had malevolent intentions toward the blacks. While he admitted that a few were "well disposed and willing to help the freedmen in making an honorable living," he believed that most "try to take every advantage of the freedmen they can, and only wish the troops were withdrawn [so] that they might execute their diabolical scheme of wholesale slaughter of the poor freedmen. Occasionally one is bold enough to speak out plainly that as soon as the *damned Yankees* [leave] they will shoot [the blacks] like dogs."[3]

The day he assumed his new post in Lexington, Tubbs began issuing orders. "[A]ll difficulties between the whites and Freedmen will be reported at this office without delay," he commanded. He would see to it that the former slaves were treated justly. He had his orders printed as handbills and posted them around the town.[4]

The citizens of Lexington sized up Lieutenant Tubbs no less quickly than he did them. In their eyes he was an arrogant, meddling little tyrant. Cornelia McDonald was among the many who regarded him with utter contempt. She thought his high-handed pronouncements not only humiliating to the whites but also provocative to the blacks, encouraging them "to be impudent and aggressive."[5]

Not long after Tubbs arrived, Cornelia had a run-in with him. One afternoon he appeared on her front porch and began questioning her. He was "a clerky looking man," she observed, with "an impudent manner." He demanded to know who had torn down a handbill that he had posted on her fence. Cornelia had seen Roy do it, and so she summoned him to the porch, assuming that Tubbs would dismiss the incident when he saw that the culprit was a nine-year-old. Instead, he proceeded to scold the boy harshly. Roy evinced neither contrition nor fear, but merely stared at Tubbs with a "mocking face and fiery black eyes." Tubbs grew furious. He threatened to punish Roy and then turned on Cornelia: "You must learn how to control your children," he fumed, "and I can tell you that if the offense is repeated you may find yourself in the Old Capitol prison."[6]

At that moment Harry came riding by on a horse he had borrowed to run an errand. Noticing the trouble on the porch, he went around to the backyard, dismounted, and then walked through the house to the front door, horsewhip in hand. He moved toward Tubbs, raised the whip, and growled "Get out of this house, you rascal." The lieutenant, who stood only five and a half feet tall, looked up at Harry, and then, as Cornelia put it, "hastened away . . . effecting a rather disorderly retreat."[7]

Although Tubbs backed down from a physical confrontation with Harry, he carried out his official duties vigorously, investigating every report of trouble between blacks and whites in his jurisdiction and seeing that justice was done. Hardly a day went by that he did not adjudicate a complaint of some sort. Wages and labor contracts were a frequent source of contention. One day in October, for instance, a man named Hector Perry came to the office claiming that he had never been paid for the work he did for Mathney Perry, his former owner, during the spring and early summer, during which time he was still being held as a slave. The bureau's rule in Virginia was that anyone still enslaved when the war ended was entitled to wages beginning with April 10, 1865, the day after Lee's surrender. Tubbs immediately dispatched a message to Mathney Perry, telling him to pay Hector Perry eight dollars for each month he had been forced to work without wages beyond April 10 or face arrest. "This employing of the Freedmen and refusing to pay them," Tubbs added sternly, "will not be tolerated." Mathney Perry showed up at the office the next day to protest, but Tubbs was unmoved. In the account book where he carefully recorded every case he investigated, he noted the outcome of this one: "Mathney Perry agreed to pay in a few days, but thought it hard to pay his own servants."[8]

As the autumn progressed, Lieutenant Tubbs saw plenty of evidence supporting his belief that the whites could not be trusted to deal fairly with the freed people. Fraud was commonplace, there were instances of violence, and it also appeared that the law was being used as a weapon. In October, the Rockbridge County court took up a burglary case involving a black man named William Gwyn. Although martial law was technically in effect, the occupation authorities generally let the civil authorities handle criminal matters of this sort. The fate of Gwyn raised questions about that policy, however. He was charged with taking clothing and food from the home of a white man—specifically, two pairs of pants, four shirts, two pairs of socks, a pair of drawers, a coat, a vest, and a ham, the whole valued at fifty dollars. After denying him the jury trial he requested, the court convicted and sentenced him. The sentence was five years in the penitentiary.[9]

Evidence of this sort encouraged Lieutenant Tubbs to keep a vigilant eye on Rockbridge County's whites. But at the same time, he endeavored to be scrupulously fair. Even as they reviled him, the whites had to admit that Tubbs often took their side. One day in September, for example, a freedwoman named Martha Smith came to him complaining that her employer, Jacob Nicely, refused to pay her. After questioning Nicely, however, Tubbs concluded that Smith "had told a wil[l]ful bare faced lie" and was "a worthless servant and of a disreputable character." He dismissed the charge.[10]

Tubbs was also determined to monitor the blacks' moral rectitude. As was true of many other Yankees, his sympathy for their plight was tempered by a certain skepticism about their character. Dealing with their domestic problems consumed a good portion of his time. A typical instance involved Emily Banks, who came to him with a complaint that her husband, Elick, had deserted her and was going to wed another woman. Tubbs duly summoned

Elick, who insisted that Emily was unfaithful to him and that he therefore considered the marriage over. Tubbs proceeded to deliver a lecture on conjugal duties, informing Elick that "he must not quit his wife and marry another woman—but must support the one he has already got."[11]

The arrival of the officious Lieutenant Tubbs added to what was, in the eyes of Lexington's white inhabitants, an already oppressive federal presence. There was also a U.S. Treasury agent in town, who was making himself obnoxious by going from house to house and farm to farm demanding that the citizens turn over any U.S. or Confederate government property they held, particularly horses. And, of course, the federal army garrison was still on hand, forty men under the command of Major Robert Redmond, who was no more tolerant of impenitent rebels than was Tubbs.[12]

Redmond was particularly incensed at the behavior of the Reverend William Pendleton. After Grace Episcopal Church was closed by army directive, Pendleton began holding Sunday services in his home for a small invited congregation, and Redmond was convinced that he was using these occasions to incite hostility against the federal government. Pendleton continued, moreover, to annoy the military authorities with haughty letters of protest. Although Redmond was powerless to interfere with the rector's private services, he firmly refused to reopen the church and missed no opportunity to put Pendleton in his place. After receiving yet another letter from the rector in September detailing why he could not in good conscience offer the required prayer for the president, Redmond replied curtly: "Your quibbling would be impertinent were it not contemptible."[13]

Pendleton was not the only prominent ex-Confederate in Lexington whose behavior the Yankees were watching during the fall. There was a newcomer whose influence on the citizens was potentially far greater than the rector's. He arrived in town on a September afternoon, a gray-haired, gray-bearded man in a gray suit, riding a gray horse. He came to assume the presidency of Washington College. He was Robert E. Lee.[14]

That Lexington was the new home of the Confederacy's greatest hero was a matter of enormous pride to the citizens. It had come about quite fortuitously. When the war ended, Washington College found itself on the brink of extinction. The student body had enlisted in the army en masse in the spring of 1861, and for the next four years the institution had limped along as a preparatory school for boys under military age. It had suffered badly during General Hunter's raid in 1864—library books were stolen or destroyed, laboratory equipment wrecked, windows and doors smashed—and when the federal garrison troops arrived after the war, they seized some of the college buildings for offices and barracks and did a good deal more damage. On top of all that, much of the college endowment was in now-worthless Confederate bonds. The school needed not only funds, repairs, and students, but also a president, for the last one had been run out of town in 1861 because of his Union sentiments.[15]

In the summer of 1865, a member of the college's board of trustees happened to learn that Robert E. Lee—who had remained in Virginia since the surrender, first in Richmond and then on a farm west of the city—was looking for a job. Sensing an opportunity, the trustees acted boldly. On August 4 they held a meeting and unanimously elected Lee president of the college. They then sent him word of their action, hoping he would consider the matter seriously, but well aware that he would have many other, and certainly more lucrative, offers.[16]

Other leading citizens of Lexington seconded the trustees' appeal to Lee. William Pendleton wrote to his old commander, acknowledging that the town was "a place of no great importance" but assuring him that he would find it congenial and reminding him that, as president of the college, he would perform "an important service to the State and its people." Former governor John Letcher, back home in Lexington after six weeks in a federal prison, likewise encouraged Lee to come. "You can do a vast amount of good," he wrote, "in building up this institution, and disseminating the blessings of education among our people."[17]

Lee mulled it over for nearly three weeks. A man of deep religious convictions and a profound sense of duty, he finally concluded that Providence was calling him to Lexington, and he accepted the summons. Packing some clothes in a saddlebag and dispatching his other belongings by canal boat, he set out on his beloved horse, Traveller. He went alone, intending to send for his family when he was settled. After a four-day journey, he arrived in Lexington on September 18. The citizens were anxiously awaiting his arrival, but because he was not expected until the nineteenth, there was no formal welcome of any sort when he got to town. That suited the modest Lee just fine.[18]

The McDonalds were among the first to see him, for he rode into town from the north, on the road that became Main Street. Allan spotted him and ran to his mother's room to tell her, and Cornelia watched reverently from her window as the great man passed, dignified as ever in his bearing, bowing slightly and doffing his hat to acknowledge the greetings from men and women on the sidewalk. He rode on up the street toward the Lexington Hotel, where he intended to stay until the college president's house was made habitable. Allan followed him and, while Lee was making arrangements for lodging, he plucked some hairs from Traveller's tail. These he proudly showed to his mother, vowing that when he married he would give them to his wife to wear in a breastpin.[19]

On October 2 the college officials held a very simple inaugural ceremony for the new president in a second-floor classroom, Lee having vetoed their plan for a grand ceremony replete with a band and a chorus of girls wearing white robes and flower head-wreaths. He went to work immediately thereafter and soon established a routine. Rising early each workday morning, he would breakfast in the hotel at seven and then walk to the college chapel, where one or another of the town's ministers was usually on hand, at his invitation, to lead a brief devotional service. From eight until two he would work in his office or attend to duties elsewhere on campus, then return to the hotel for dinner and a short nap. If there was no late-afternoon faculty meeting or other business, he would mount Traveller and go for a ride in the countryside. After a light supper he would read until ten and then retire to bed.[20]

He did not seek the adulation of the local folk, but of course he received it. He could go nowhere without being hailed and cheered. Sometimes he was greeted with the rebel yell, there being any number of his former soldiers living in the town and county. This behavior Lee discouraged, for he was sensitive to the scrutiny he was getting from the local military authorities and, indeed, from the whole nation. Southerners were looking to him for guidance; Northerners were watching to see what example he would set. For his own part, Lee genuinely accepted defeat and sincerely pledged his loyalty to the federal government; he was no Pendleton, bitter and prickly and unreconstructed. Publicly and privately, Lee urged his fellow ex-Confederates to put aside their hostility and get on with the business of rebuilding the South. "I think it the duty of every citizen," he wrote in his letter of acceptance to the college trustees, "in the present condition of the Country, to do all in his power to aid in the restoration of peace and harmony. . . . It is particularly incumbent on those charged with the instruction of the young to set them an example of submission to authority."[21]

Lexington was by now becoming something of a model for those who, like Lee, were anxious to rebuild the South. Not only did Washington College survive and prosper—it had fifty students by the time Lee took office, a hundred by year's end—but so also did the Virginia Military Institute. The institute had been even more disrupted by the war than had the college, for General Hunter's troops had burned much of it to the ground in June 1864, and it had remained closed from that point on. But under the leadership of its long-time superintendent, Francis H. Smith, it was resurrected in October 1865—although by order of the federal occupation authorities the cadets were forbidden to wear uniforms or to drill with muskets.[22]

The reopening of the two institutions made Cornelia more melancholy yet, for it reminded her anew of the depths to which her family had sunk. Many of her friends were enrolling their sons in the schools; Harry should be among the students, Cornelia thought, but she had no money to pay his tuition or buy him decent clothes. Not one of her children was getting any education now, in fact, and none had gotten much for a long time. No public school was operating in Lexington, and it would be humiliating for a McDonald to go to one anyway. Private academies were open, but they were expensive. Cornelia had tried all through the war to give lessons to the children when they could not go to school, but she had little time for that now, what with her private drawing instruction and the housework; and, in any event, the children were now occupied with helping around the house or working for wages.[23]

Contemplating the family's plight, which seemed to her "more and more hopeless every day," brought Cornelia to the verge of another emotional breakdown like that she had suffered in August. There was not enough money for food now, let alone firewood and rent. She and the children were hungry much of the time, the weather was turning cool, and the landlord was running out of patience. Angus's estate was still in legal limbo and would probably remain so for years; Cornelia had written to a lawyer about it, but had gotten no encouragement. Moreover, her closest friends had moved away, and she now had no confidante, no one to whom she could pour out her heart and confess her nightmarish visions of the future, visions of a life of penury and homelessness and degradation. Again she sank into despondency, a gloom that even the autumn beauty of the Shenandoah Valley could not dispel. "I could scarcely lift my heavy eyes to the blue hills, or endure the light of the lovely sunsets. The sight of the smooth, peaceful river gave me no joy of heart."[24]

One evening in October she left the house, hoping that a stroll up Main Street would lift her spirits. It did not. As she passed along, she glanced in the windows of homes and saw contented families sitting around cheery fires. "[I]t made me feel all the more desolate."[25]

She walked on, past the courthouse and the Presbyterian church and the hotel, past the stores and artisans' shops, until she reached the south edge of town. On her left was Lexington's cemetery, and she turned and entered it through the open gate. It was as serene and beautiful as ever, although the rose bushes that bordered it and lined its walkways were bare of blossoms now. White marble headstones and monuments crowded the grounds. These marked the older graves; the newer ones, including the many that held the remains of Confederate soldiers, had temporary wooden markers. Near the center of the cemetery was the resting place of Stonewall Jackson, a clover-covered mound of earth no different from any of the other soldiers' graves except for the tall pine pole that rose next to it, on which a Confederate flag had once waved.[26]

Cornelia sought out the grave of Sandie Pendleton, the rector's beloved son, Stonewall Jackson's trusted adjutant, and one of the most popular and capable young officers in the Army of Northern Virginia. When he died of a battle wound in the fall of 1864, a few days before his twenty-fourth birthday, the army had grieved, as had the town of Lexington. Cornelia had done her best to comfort his mother and sisters during that sad time. They had done the same for her several weeks later, when Angus died.[27]

She sat down next to Sandie Pendleton's grave, feeling "wretched and forlorn." The headboard—mutilated back in July by Yankee soldiers, to the shock and disgust of the Pendleton family—cast a longer and longer shadow as the minutes passed. Silently she sat, "trying to regain courage and hope," until it grew cold and nearly dark. Then she rose, went out through the gate, and headed home.[28]

She had not gone far when she met Ann Pendleton, on her way to visit her son's grave. Even in the dim light, Ann could see the distress on Cornelia's face. "What can be the matter," she asked Cornelia. "Come home with me now, I will go back."[29]

Touched by Ann's concern and unable to contain her misery any longer, Cornelia burst into tears. Ann took her hands and insisted she tell her what was wrong. The pride that for so long had kept Cornelia from speaking frankly to her friend now collapsed. "We are starving," she sobbed, "I and my children."[30]

Ann's reply left Cornelia astonished. "Comfort yourself," she said. "I meant to have come and told you that help is coming for you. You are to re-

17. Lexington Cemetery, resting place of Stonewall Jackson and Sandie Pendleton. The large stone cross marks Pendleton's grave, where Cornelia McDonald sat despondently on an October evening in 1865. Erected sometime after that year, it replaced the wooden marker defiled by U.S. soldiers.

ceive a sum of money in a few days." As Cornelia stifled her weeping, Ann explained that there existed a certain fund for the benefit of needy and deserving people, and, through the influence of her husband, one hundred dollars had been secured for Cornelia and another hundred for Sandie Pendleton's widow. More than this, Ann refused to reveal. "You must not ask where it comes from," she said.[31]

That night Cornelia went to bed "with a happy heart and a thankful one." The next morning came further proof that, as she put it, "God was . . . good, [and] that with the trial he provided the needful help." She had been too depressed lately to do much visiting, but now, buoyed by the news from Ann, she decided to pay a call on her friend Mrs. McElwee. As it happened, Mrs. McElwee had just bought a quarter of beef, and she insisted that Cornelia take a roast. Cornelia was overjoyed. Wrapping it in paper and holding it tightly under her shawl, she hurried home. She and the children had it for dinner that very day. Less than a week later, Mrs. McElwee returned Cornelia's call and brought more welcome news. She had received an inheritance from her brother, who had been killed two years earlier at the battle of Chickamauga, and she offered Cornelia $300 as a loan. "I accepted it," Cornelia wrote, "and with a light and happy heart set about making provision for the winter."[32]

The weeks that followed brought her more good fortune. Her stepson Edward, his terrible facial wound now healed and covered by a beard, came to town bringing word that he had discovered an old bond owned by Angus and had cashed it in. He gave Cornelia a portion of the money, enabling her to pay the house rent. Edward's generosity did not end there. He, his brother William, and their sisters Susan and Flora had recently moved in together on a rented farm in Clarke County, in northern Virginia. Edward was working the farm, William was teaching school, and Susan and Flora were keeping house. They offered to take in one of Cornelia's older boys and see to it that he got an education. Before fall ended, Allan packed his clothes and headed off to Clarke County. By then Cornelia's little girl was back in the classroom, too. Mary Pendleton, Ann's daughter, started a school in town and offered to take Nelly as a pupil.[33]

Despite the signs that she was under the protection of a caring Providence, Cornelia continued to have moments of doubt and despondency, for her financial plight was by no means resolved. As December approached, she again grew depressed and began avoiding company. When the other ladies in town enthusiastically volunteered to help get the college president's house in shape for the impending arrival of Robert E. Lee's wife and daughters, Cornelia declined. "[H]ow could I go among them with my sad face and sorrowful heart," she thought. Once again, she became "wholly occupied with my own trouble and distresses."[34]

While Cornelia struggled with her worries, the town was disturbed by more conflicts. In early December, the Reverend Pendleton at last received permission to resume services at Grace Episcopal. Major Redmond had no hand in this, however; permission was granted by Captain Henry Robinson who now commanded the post. Pendleton made no promise to use the prescribed prayer for the president, but had merely persuaded Robinson that the time had come to relax the proscription. Services did not resume for long. When Lieutenant Colonel Cecil Clay, commander of the military subdistrict, got wind of Robinson's action he immediately overruled it. Two days later, on December 17, Clay dispatched a letter directly to Pendleton. The church would stay closed, he told the rector firmly, until the proper prayer was given.[35]

Even as the citizens of Lexington fumed over this news, they were provoked by what they regarded as yet another instance of Yankee interference.

Since the war ended, they had seen their town "invaded" by Northern merchants, a federal army garrison, a U.S. Treasury agent, and a Freedmen's Bureau agent. Now, in December, more interlopers arrived: Yankee teachers who intended to set up a school for blacks.

When the school opened on December 12, the freedmen flocked to it eagerly, young and old alike. By year's end, 115 were attending day classes and 226 were attending night classes. The teachers, one of whom was a woman, were sponsored by the American Missionary Association, a Northern humanitarian agency. Freedmen's Bureau agent Tubbs, whose duties included assisting the teachers and monitoring the progress of black education, wrote enthusiastically in his December report: "We have a large and flourishing school conducted by able and efficient teachers with the cooperation of some highly intelligent freedmen."[36]

The reactions of Lexington's whites to this new intrusion ranged from disgust to outrage. Few believed that educating blacks would accomplish anything useful. It would merely give them big ideas, the whites insisted; there was no surer way to ruin a good servant or field hand. No sooner did the school start than some citizens claimed to see a change in the blacks. Mary Pendleton wrote her sister that it was now harder to get and keep servants. "They are all so busy getting an education they cannot work for white folks. I wish we could get two strong efficient Irish girls."[37]

Few condemned the blacks, however, for wanting an education; white hostility was directed mostly at the meddling Yankee teachers. A good number of whites went out of their way to snub or harass them, hoping thereby to send them packing back to the North. Lieutenant Tubbs was convinced that only the presence of the army garrison prevented outright physical assaults. The female teacher, Julia Shearman from Brooklyn, New York, was subjected to torments of all sorts beginning the day she arrived in town. "Never did I walk the streets of Lexington without rudeness, in one form or another," she recalled bitterly. "Ladies glorified in compelling the Yankee woman . . . to step into the mud for their accommodation; the boys of the aristocratic school of the place hooted every time I passed them. . . . I have been awakened from my sleep, in the dead of night, by horrible serenades, performed under my window, by these same gentlemanly young men. I have taught an evening school while brickbats were being thrown by them at the windows." Epithets of the lowest sort were hurled at her. One she heard over and over was "Damn Yankee bitch of a nigger teacher."[38]

Cornelia was too preoccupied with her family's survival to be much concerned with this new controversy that erupted in the waning days of the year. The cold darkness that descended on the town early each evening was as nothing compared to that which enveloped her heart. Her faith in God's goodness was strong, but it could not altogether silence the cruel mockery of the Tempter who told her she had been abandoned and there was no hope. And so she entered upon another winter of uncertainty, wondering if it would ever give way to spring.[39]

LOUIS HUGHES

THE REUNION OF MATILDA AND MARY ELLEN WITH THEIR MOTHER in Cincinnati at summer's end was little short of miraculous. Many former slaves were trying to trace their lost loved ones in the postwar months, but few families that had been separated for as long as Matilda's would ever meet again. To the further astonishment and joy of the two women, they found that their older sister was living with their mother. They had last seen her in the Memphis slave market ten years ago, when they said their good-byes. They now learned that she and their mother had been sold to different masters and taken from Memphis, but had managed to escape after the Yankee invasion in 1862 and had made their way back to the city. By coincidence, both had gotten jobs as nurses in one of the Union army hospitals in the city, and there they found each other. Later during the war they moved together to Cincinnati. Matilda saw the hand of God at work in this reunion of her family against all odds, and she gave thanks.[1]

Lou, Matilda, their baby, and Mary Ellen and her two children now crowded into the one-room apartment rented by Matilda's mother and eldest sister. With so many people moving into Cincinnati that fall, the city's residential buildings were teeming. Jobs were scarce, too, and it must have been apparent to Lou that getting along in Cincinnati was not going to be easy.[2]

Newcomers like Lou and his family found the size and strangeness of this place overwhelming. The Queen City of the West, as the inhabitants proudly called it, now had a population of about 200,000, three or four times that of Memphis. The narrow streets—which were all either cobblestone or paved, unlike those in the Southern towns Lou had known—were filled with vehicles and noisy with the ringing of streetcar bells and the clopping of hooves. In the heart of the city, around Fourth and Vine, traffic jams routinely blocked the thoroughfares, forcing pedestrians to walk a block out of their way to cross. The sidewalks were as congested as the streets. On many corners, vendors had set up little wooden stands where they sold peanuts, candy, fruit, and newspapers. Shoppers and tradesmen had to step around these and other obstructions as they made their way about the city. They also had to pass by knots of idle men who hung out on the corners ogling women and had to make way for the ragged street preachers and other eccentrics who wandered the streets.[3]

The crowded Queen City was plagued with sanitation problems beyond anything Lou had ever seen in the South. The municipal authorities kept street-cleaning crews at work, and the crews were reinforced by the hogs that ran loose in violation of city ordinances. Together, crews and hogs managed to keep the main thoroughfares more or less clean, but in the numerous alleys the refuse accumulated unchecked: garbage, filth, dead dogs and cats. No one was surprised when the city experienced an outbreak of dysentery that fall; everyone watched nervously for signs of typhoid and cholera, too.[4]

At every turn Lou could see other indications that he was now in a different world. In the city's vacant lots, boys and young men were playing something called baseball, a popular sport that had not yet made its way to the South. Down at the river, construction crews were beginning work on a bridge that would stretch across to Covington, Kentucky. It would be the world's longest suspension bridge, a triumph of Yankee ingenuity and industrial might and, to some, a symbol of the reunification of North and South.[5]

There were unfamiliar sounds as well as sights, particularly the accents that Lou could hear in the conversations on the sidewalks and the cursing of the wagon drivers. He was undoubtedly familiar with the Irish brogue and the Midwestern twang; those could be heard in Memphis, which was fairly diverse as Southern towns went. But here there were many other accents; and there were languages spoken that Lou did not understand, including German, the native tongue of many of the city's inhabitants.[6]

Another thing that struck Southern visitors to Cincinnati such as Lou was its distinctive districts. Every Southern town of any size had its main business district, of course, and in Memphis and other places there were now all-black residential areas. But otherwise the various sections of any given Southern town tended to be undifferentiated: in each, houses stood next to shops, blacks lived alongside whites, and the hovels of the poor sat beside the mansions of the rich. Cincinnati was starkly different. It seemed a kind of patchwork, each section having a peculiar character and function. The downtown was divided into a commercial and manufacturing district along the river and a retail and financial district a little farther up. On each flank of the latter district was an exclusive, upper-class residential enclave. Beyond the downtown, as one headed away from the river, was an area embracing the homes of the old-stock, white, middle-class residents. On the city's outskirts lay the neighborhoods of the poor, the Germans, the Irish, and the blacks.[7]

Some of these outlying neighborhoods were very disorderly places. Lou had undoubtedly seen a good deal of underclass rowdiness in Memphis, but nothing like what was now before him. Brawls erupted frequently in Cincinnati's numerous saloons and gambling houses, often spilling into the street. Even when no fights broke out, the vice dens reverberated all night long with the sounds of raucous amusement. The worst problem in some sections was not the men but the boys. They roamed in gangs, engaged in petty theft, got into scuffles, and built bonfires in the streets at night. The police seemed unable to do much about it.[8]

Bucktown, the black neighborhood on the city's east side where Lou and his family probably lived, was the roughest part of town, as well as the most run-down. Stabbings and shootings were common in the saloons and gambling houses there, and muggings made the streets unsafe day and night. The neighborhood was also densely crowded, and more people were moving in every day, many of them refugees from the South like Lou. Some of the newcomers could not secure rooms and had to live in shanties in the alleys.[9]

Lou and his family had a room, but nothing more. They could not afford more spacious accommodations unless Lou found a job. At first glance, Cincinnati seemed to be full of opportunities for working men. Business of all sorts was booming. The city wharf, in particular, was busier even than the one in Memphis. Cincinnati had emerged before the war as one of the nation's great river ports, thanks in large part to its trade with the South. The war had cut off most of that trade, but with the coming of peace Cincinnati's merchants reestablished their Southern connections. Now, every day saw the arrival of giant steamboats from Memphis, Natchez, or New Orleans, each piled high with cotton bales—sometimes seven, eight, even nine hundred or more on a single vessel. Unloading these bales, hauling them by wagon to the railroad depot, and stowing them aboard freight cars for their journey to the mill towns of New England required an army of laborers.[10]

A tour of the streets along the waterfront revealed a multitude of men at work in other sorts of jobs. Thousands of them sweated in the city's manufacturing establishments, for Cincinnati was one of the nation's great industrial as well as mercantile cities. Even before the war, its many meat-packing plants had earned it the nickname of Porkopolis. Wartime demand had multiplied and diversified the city's industrial output, as manufacturers responded to the government's call for food, uniforms, muskets, and cannons for the armies of the Union. Moreover, the government set up facilities of its own in the city and hired civilians to work in them, including several military hospitals and nearly two dozen army warehouses.[11]

But now the war was over. The military contracts were being canceled and the government facilities closed. Workers in factories, hospitals, and warehouses were being laid off. At the same time, men and women were flooding into the city in search of homes and jobs—not only Southern freedmen like Lou and Matilda, but also discharged Union army veterans and recently arrived European immigrants. These hopeful newcomers all saw Cincinnati as a place to begin their lives afresh. But the crowded city could not accommodate so many people and so many dreams. Many of the new arrivals were, like Lou, getting frustrated.[12]

This is not to say that the mood of the city was sour. There was much optimism that fall among Cincinnati's newcomers and old residents alike, a sense that the triumph of the Union had ensured a bright future for themselves and for the nation. Lou could not help being struck by this mood. In Memphis there had been lots of talk about a bright future, but the public optimism was tempered by the former Confederates' sense of defeat and the former slaves' uneasiness about reconstruction policies. Cincinnati, by contrast, glowed with a feeling of victory and the certainty of God's continued favor.[13]

The city's celebratory mood reached a climax about a month after Lou's arrival, when General Ulysses S. Grant paid a visit. The great hero of the Union was on a tour of the North, and Cincinnati prepared a grand reception for him. On the morning of September 23, the mayor and several dozen other dignitaries boarded the *C. T. Dumont* and steamed downriver about fifteen miles to North Bend. They met Grant at the train station there and then ushered him aboard the boat. Everyone in the welcoming party was impressed by the modesty of the hero, who wore a plain wool hat and brown duster and carried his own valise. At the wharf in Cincinnati, carriages were waiting. The 7th National Guard Regiment and the city police force were also on hand, and they escorted the general and the city delegation to Pike's Opera House, where a large audience was assembled. Grant stepped up to the stage and gave a brief speech, thanking the people of the city and commending their "loyalty . . . to the cause we have been fighting for the past four years." Then it was back to the carriages and a parade through the city, led by a marching band. All who were there that day agreed that Cincinnati had never been more festive. Signs of welcome hung everywhere, and buildings sported red, white, and blue bunting. Thousands upon thousands of citizens jammed the sidewalks or leaned out of upper-story windows, straining their necks and cheering excitedly as the general came into view.[14]

Even as the people of Cincinnati toasted their victory in war and hailed their great hero, they turned to confront the future and the new problems it presented. Two of these were particularly controversial in the city that fall: labor and race.

Cincinnati had a tradition of labor activism. During the war, when many men exchanged their work clothes for blue uniforms, the city's labor unions had been relatively quiet. In the summer and fall of 1865, when the soldiers mustered out and returned to the city to resume their trades, they found that wartime inflation had far outpaced wages. The result was a resurgence of union activity. In the weeks following Lou's arrival in the city, evening meetings were held by the Journeymen Tailors' Association, the Bricklayers' Union, the Carpenters' Union, the Journeymen Plasterers' Association, the Gas-Fitters' Union, and many others. At these gatherings, workers talked late into the night about their current plight and how to remedy it.[15]

The labor militancy that rocked Cincinnati that fall was something altogether unfamiliar to Lou. Southern cities, including Memphis, had their workingmen's associations, but they were mostly relics of an earlier era, when manufacturing was done in small artisan shops, and masters, journeymen, and apprentices lived as well as worked together. There were still such shops and craftsmen in Cincinnati, but manufacturing in the city was increasingly dominated by highly regimented factories with fifty or a hundred or more workers, most of them unskilled machine-tenders and all of them overseen by impersonal supervisors. It had long been an article of faith among Northern laborers that if a man worked hard, he could acquire a skill and property and eventually be his own boss. But the coming of the factories called that assumption into question: such a system of labor seemed to many workers nothing better than "industrial slavery."[16]

When Cincinnati workingmen went on strike that fall—as the journeymen stonemasons and boot makers did in September, demanding a raise—they were seeking not only to put more meat on their tables, but also to secure their vision of the future. Higher wages alone were not enough. Many in the city were also calling for a truly radical reform: an eight-hour workday. This represented not simply a desire to work less, proponents insisted, but to become better citizens, for the extra leisure time would be devoted to self-improvement. "Eight Hours For Work, Eight Hours For Sleep, and Eight Hours For Mental and Moral Improvement," was their battle cry.[17]

The moving force behind the eight-hour campaign was an organization called the Trades and Labor Assembly, whose mission was to bring all of Cincinnati's workers together in one giant city-wide union. This was a herculean task, given the antipathies that had long divided the city's labor force. Skilled workers looked down on the unskilled; the Germans and the Irish disliked each other; male laborers refused to associate with the women and children who were employed in many of the factories; and the whites wanted nothing to do with the blacks.[18]

White-black antagonism was not confined to the labor movement. Cincinnati had a long history of racial friction. The city had witnessed at least four antiblack riots, most recently in July 1862, when Irish dockworkers reacted to competition from black laborers by going on a two-day rampage, screaming, "Let's clear out the niggers!" No one would be surprised to see more such trouble, for the influx of freedmen only aggravated the racial tension. The city's Democratic newspaper, the *Daily Enquirer*, did its best to provoke white resentment, using editorials to remind workers that "[t]he negroes are coming" to take away their jobs. Emancipating the slaves, the editor told his readers, was "the most foolish and unsound measure that has happened in this country." And every day on the city's streets there were arguments and scuffles between black and white men, any one of which could, under the right circumstances, explode into a riot.[19]

Cincinnati's blacks were not without friends. White Republicans, who outnumbered Democrats by almost four to one in the city, were for the most part moderate on racial issues. Many had been active in the antislavery movement before the war and, although few would concede that blacks were inherently equal to whites, all endorsed emancipation wholeheartedly and deplored the race-baiting of the Democrats. Some now even advocated allowing Ohio's black men to vote. There were, moreover, whites in the city who were willing to give tangible aid to the black race. The Ladies' Freedmen's Aid Society of Cincinnati, formed in January 1865, solicited donations of secondhand shoes, clothing, and eyeglasses. Some of these items were sent to a contraband camp in Tennessee, and others were directed to a home for sick and orphaned freedmen that the society maintained in Cincinnati.[20]

Whites and blacks came together one evening in early autumn in Greenwood Hall, one of the city's auditoriums. The occasion was an address by Henry Highland Garnet of Washington, D.C., a minister and former slave who had earned a reputation as a spokesman for his race. In a measured yet passionate tone, the Reverend Garnet told his audience of his vision of the future of America's blacks. They would not seek vengeance for the wrongs done to them in the past, he predicted. Nor would they stridently demand legal equality; but they deserved it and, in the fullness of time, they would surely receive it. He reminded his listeners that when the war began, whites who rallied around the Union banner had at first rejected the idea of enlisting black soldiers in their cause. But before long they had found it necessary to call on those great reserves of black strength, and the tens of thousands of black men of the North and South who responded to that call had helped achieve the glorious triumph of the Union. Now, Garnet reasoned, those who cherished the great ideals of the American republic—liberty and equality—would before long find it necessary to grant full citizenship and the ballot to the nation's blacks, so that they could be enlisted in the continuing struggle to bring those ideals to full fruition. "The colored race ha[s] been recognized as soldiers," he declared; "they must now be recognized as men." He praised Abraham Lincoln as "the best friend of freedom," a leader who had moved the nation in the right direction. Lincoln's successor was proving to be stubborn and contrary, Garnet said, but he had no fear that President Johnson would obstruct America's progress, for "[h]e who should stand in the way of God's providence would be crushed to pieces, and the Lord would raise up some one who would carry out [H]is purposes."[21]

The Cincinnati that welcomed the Reverend Garnet and General Grant was a city of charity and optimism, but even so it was not the city Lou Hughes had hoped for. After several weeks he still had no steady work, and he and his family were living in nearly intolerable accommodations. And he had seen enough of Cincinnati to convince him that neither problem was going to be solved if he stayed in the city.[22]

By midautumn he and the four women of the family decided to move on. Somewhere they heard that there were opportunities in the town of Hamilton, Ohio, twenty miles north. So one day in the latter part of October they packed up their belongings and made their way to the newly constructed depot of the Cincinnati, Hamilton, & Dayton Railroad, an imposing, four-hundred-foot-long building that stretched between Fifth and Sixth streets on the west side of town. There they boarded a train for the short trip to Hamilton.[23]

It was an unpretentious town on the banks of the Miami River, home to nine or ten thousand people, the governmental seat and economic center of Butler County, a farming district. The first thing many visitors noticed about it at this time of year, when the weather grew cool, was the coal soot that drifted down from the chimney tops and covered everything outdoors—a "miniature snow storm in black," one observer complained.[24]

The new arrivals found a place to live and moved in. Lou searched for steady work but finally had to settle for odd jobs, mostly whitewashing fences and buildings. Matilda and her mother and sisters spread the word around town that they were available to do laundry, and they soon had a good deal of business.[25]

There were some troubling things about Hamilton that undoubtedly became apparent to Lou as the weeks passed, besides the depressing dinginess of the place. For one thing, the town seemed to be in the grip of a crime wave. It was nowhere near as dangerous as Bucktown, to be sure, but there were enough burglaries and muggings to alarm the law-abiding citizens. At a public meeting in November, some of those citizens demanded that the town council create a night police force and put lawbreakers to work on a chain gang. The editor of Hamilton's newspaper, the *True Telegraph*, pointed out that towns all across the northern United States were experiencing a similar surge of villainy and showing other signs of moral decay. It was a consequence of the war, he said. While the soldiers had struggled on the battlefield, those at home had relaxed civic discipline, allowed churches to decline, and indulged in a "reckless spirit of extravagance and luxury."[26]

Another disturbing thing about Hamilton was the racial atmosphere. The residential segregation that Lou had seen in Cincinnati was reproduced here in miniature. All but a handful of the 200 or so black inhabitants were clustered in one ward of the town. Hamilton was, moreover, predominantly Democratic, and there was much hostility toward blacks. The newspaper was vehemently racist. One had to read no further than the motto that adorned the paper's masthead to learn the editor's guiding principles: "White Supremacy—State Sovereignty—Federal Union—DEMOCRACY." In his columns he told crude racial jokes, railed against Republican proposals to provide better schools and the ballot for Ohio's blacks, warned that "negro equality" meant "white degradation," and bemoaned the continuing influx of freedmen. Ohio, he said, was becoming "a vast almshouse for the negro paupers of the South."[27]

Before long Lou grew restless again. As the days passed and the soot-covered leaves of Hamilton's trees drifted to the ground, his thoughts turned more and more to another place: Canada. Before the war, a good number of slaves had fled there with the help of Northern abolitionists. Lou had eavesdropped on occasion when Boss read aloud newspaper accounts of the Underground Railroad. Everybody in those days knew that Canada was the only real haven for black runaways, the one place in North America beyond the reach of the Fugitive Slave Law. One of Boss's slaves, Tom, who had been a close friend of Lou's, had actually escaped to Canada in the 1850s. Having secretly learned to write, Tom had forged a pass, gone down to the Memphis wharf, and gotten a job on a steamboat. Eventually he made it to New Orleans and from there sailed to Boston. After reaching Canada, he had had the temerity to send Boss a letter notifying him of his new address.[28]

Now that slavery was abolished, many of the Canadian fugitives were returning to the United States. But Lou was not convinced that any former slave was truly safe in America. "We did not know what might come again for our injury," he wrote, and to him Canada was still the only refuge. He talked the matter over with Matilda and her mother and sisters, and all agreed that they should go to Canada.[29]

By the time they had made up their minds to leave Hamilton, December had arrived and with it came Lou's first Yankee winter. The trees were starkly bare, and there was a frigid crispness in the air unlike anything he had ever felt in Mississippi, Tennessee, Alabama, or Virginia. And there were sights he had perhaps never before seen: ice skaters gliding over the frozen river basin, and store windows radiant with Christmas displays of toys, candy, and fireworks.[30]

It was late in December and there was snow on the ground when Lou and his family climbed aboard a train at the Hamilton depot for the journey north. From Hamilton they traveled to Detroit. There they boarded a ferry that went across to Windsor, Ontario. It was Christmas day. As Lou stepped off the ferry and onto the Canadian shore, he felt that he was a free man at last.[31]

SAMUEL AGNEW

NOT LONG AFTER THE MORNING FOG LIFTED ON SEPTEMBER 1, IT began to rain. Soon it was coming down in torrents, blown by furious winds—"the biggest rain we have had in a long, long time," Sam Agnew wrote. The roads dissolved into bottomless muck and the creeks rose fast; even the little branch that ran near the Agnew plantation was "half up saddle skirts deep." More rain came that night, and still more over the next two days. People stayed indoors, and farm chores and neighborly visits were postponed. No one complained, however, for the deluge seemed to herald an end to the drought that had threatened the corn and cotton. Now there was a chance that the crops could be saved.[1]

The rain gave way to heat, as stifling as any that July or August had inflicted. As the roads dried and Sam resumed his usual rounds, he found himself constantly in a sweat. Early mornings offered some relief, but evenings offered none: he and everyone else in Tippah County sweltered on their porches and in their beds.[2]

On Saturday, September 9, Sam packed some clothes and set out on a mule for Ebenezer Church, twelve miles away. A protracted meeting was to commence there that day, and he had agreed to take part. He left at eight in the cool of a cloudy morning, traveling at an easy pace, but by the time he reached his destination the heat was oppressive and his clothes were soaked.[3]

He remained at Ebenezer for nearly a week, staying with various friends and acquaintances in the area. Uncle Young was also there, and the two took turns leading the services. Some days Sam preached in the morning, other days in the evening. He was gratified by the response of the congregation: "[I]t is cheering to the minister to behold large numbers looking and listening intently to the words of life." Twenty-six new members were added to the church in the time that Sam was there, and one who had previously withdrawn came back into the fold.[4]

During the midday dinner breaks, Sam caught up on news and gossip. There was much talk of the upcoming state election. A number of local office-seekers dropped by the church, in fact, while the meeting was in progress. "The candidates are thick around Ebenezer these days," Sam remarked. And of course there was talk of the incessant problems with the blacks. Everyone agreed that they were pretty much worthless now, idle and disobedient. Some were altogether out of control, or so it was reported. Down in Oktibbeha County, Sam learned, there was "a good deal of excitement," for the freedmen were "'cutting up' generally."[5]

Frequently the dinner conversation turned to illness and death. The sickly season would not be over until the crisp days of midautumn. On his third day at Ebenezer, Sam heard that little Harvey Hawthorn, a boy who lived in his own community, had died of the "flux"—dysentery. Others in the Hawthorn family were down with it, too. This was very disturbing news. Everyone remembered the terrible flux epidemic of 1857 that had struck in late summer and raged well into the fall, taking many lives. Sam prayed that the community would be spared another such blow.[6]

He heard more reports of illness in the days following his return home. There was typhoid in the area now, and cholera. The saddest news concerned a friend, Joseph Sanford. For some reason known only to God, Sanford's digestive system had abruptly quit working. "He has not had an action on his bowells now for 10 days," Sam wrote on September 28, "and although most powerful purgatives have been administered they have not moved him." There was little hope for the poor man's recovery, and he had resigned himself to death. Sam despaired of his friend's soul, for "He has been careless and made no pretensions of religion."[7]

Sanford's agony came to an end on the last night of September. Sam learned of his death the next day, and that evening attended his funeral. "It was after dark by the light of the moone which now shine[s] brilliantly. . . . I believe it is the first burial I ever witnessed by moonlight."[8]

Late in the morning of October 1, just after he heard about Sanford's death, Sam rode to the Corders' home to preach. This was to be the beginning of another protracted meeting, but it proved an inauspicious start, for the congregation was small. In the days that followed, the turnouts were even more disappointing, and on the fifth Sam reluctantly brought the meeting to a close. It had been a mistake, he decided, to start so late in the season. "The people are busy in their farms and hence only a few come to Church." Harvesting had in fact been underway for a couple of weeks. The hands on the Agnew plantation went into the fields to begin picking cotton on September 20.[9]

The busy pace of fall farm work slackened momentarily on election day, October 2. Sam canceled the morning sermon at the Corders that day so he could vote. He rode to the precinct polling place early and found a big crowd already there, waiting for the polls to open. The voting began at ten o'clock and proceeded slowly, for the ballot was lengthy. Every state and local office had to be filled, from governor, legislators, and congressmen down to sheriff, county clerk, and local magistrates. Sam voted for twenty-five candidates in all.[10]

Political excitement had run high in the weeks leading up to election day, and the competition for offices was fierce, for this restored government of Mississippi would bear immense responsibilities. Assuming that the powers in Washington continued to allow the former Confederate states to reconstruct themselves, the men elected on October 2 would shape Mississippi's postwar world.[11]

In the days following the election, Sam picked up news of the outcome. The governor-elect was Benjamin G. Humphreys, a planter and lawyer by profession who had commanded a brigade of Mississippi infantry in Lee's army. As a Confederate general, he was excluded from President Johnson's general amnesty for rebels, but he had taken the oath of allegiance to the United States and then run for governor with the hope that the president would grant him a special pardon—which Johnson did, three days after the election. Humphreys was to be inaugurated on October 16, and the new state legislature would convene the same day.[12]

The governor-elect was a man of conservative political temperament, a former Whig and a stout opponent of secession until the outbreak of war in the spring of 1861. The same was true, for the most part, of the other newly elected state officers. The Mississippians who went to the polls on October 2 overwhelmingly repudiated the extremist Democratic "fire-eaters" who had led their state out of the Union. They hoped that the people of the North would grasp the import of this election and thus recognize that their former enemies had accepted defeat and were now ready to resume their place in the Union. Sam was among this great majority of Mississippians who looked forward to sectional reconciliation. If the North proved as forgiving as the

South, he believed, and proved willing to let the South find its own solutions to the problems it now faced, all would be well.[13]

As he followed the election news and the progress of the harvest, Sam prepared himself for a temporary loss within the family circle. Nannie, who had not been down to Starkville to see her family since the summer of 1864, was planning a visit. She intended to take Buddy along, for her widowed mother and most of her other kinfolk had never seen him. Her brother James, who came up on October 4, would escort her down on the train.[14]

Early on the afternoon of the tenth, she, Buddy, and Sam set out in a mule-drawn carriage driven by Wiley, the black foreman. James followed on a horse that Sam had borrowed. They reached Guntown by four o'clock, unloaded the baggage at an inn, and then sent Wiley back home with the carriage. Sam wandered around town a while, picking up news, before he and the others settled in for the night at the inn.[15]

They got up long before daylight and made their way to the Guntown depot, Sam and James lugging Nannie's trunk. The train lumbered in a little after sunrise, wheels screeching and boiler huffing. While James loaded the baggage, Sam found some empty seats in the rear passenger car. He ushered Nannie and Buddy aboard and said good-bye. When the car was out of sight, he returned to the inn, ate breakfast, and then mounted the horse and headed home alone.[16]

The next day, while he was at his desk working on a sermon, an unexpected visitor appeared. His name was Captain Rice, formerly of the Confederate army. He had come to retrieve the body of his brother, a rebel soldier who had been wounded in the battle of June 10, 1864, and had died that night in the Agnews' house. The body was buried under an oak tree near the front gate. Captain Rice had first visited the grave in February 1865 while on military duty, and Sam had met him then.[17]

The captain's return journey this autumn had been a long one. He had traveled south from his home in Lauderdale County, Tennessee, to Memphis, and then east by train to Corinth, Mississippi, where he had hired a carriage for the thirty-mile trip south to the Agnews. With him, besides the hackman, was an undertaker he had picked up in Memphis. Also in the carriage was a new metallic coffin.[18]

After Sam greeted Captain Rice and learned his business, he summoned two of the field hands, Thompson and Arch, who agreed to exhume the body. With pick and shovel they dug down until they exposed a wooden coffin, which they lifted out and pried open. Sam and the others stood by solemnly. "The body was much decayed and blackened and not recogni[z]able," Sam observed. "What a mass of filthy corruption is the human body when in the grave." The corpse was then transferred carefully to the metal coffin.[19]

By the time the task was finished and the coffin was sealed tight, the sun had sunk below the horizon. Sam invited Captain Rice and his companions to spend the night. The three guests arose the next morning well before daylight in order to get an early start. After breakfasting with Sam by candlelight, they secured the coffin in the carriage and headed back to Corinth. Sam watched them go, knowing that he might have more such sorrowful visitations in the future, for there were other soldiers' graves nearby.[20]

By now it was mid-October and harvesting was mostly finished on the plantation. The hands had been picking cotton for more than three weeks and corn for more than two. The cotton demanded far less of their time than it had in the past, for Enoch had devoted little acreage to it this year. A state law in effect when he had begun spring planting restricted cotton-growing in favor of food crops for the Confederate war effort. Three bales would be about all he would get this fall; before the war, he had normally produced eighty or ninety.[21]

On the morning of October 17, Sam went to the fields to pick cotton. He did it for no other reason than to shame the blacks, who on the sixteenth had done what he regarded as a poor day's work. "I told them that I was no great picker but I knew that I could beat what they did that day." Attaching a long cloth sack to his waist as the field hands did, he moved down the rows plucking the bolls that had ripened since the last time the field had been gone over. Periodically he emptied his sack into a large basket at the edge of the field. By noon he had gathered over thirty pounds of cotton without really pushing himself, whereupon he quit and returned to the house, satisfied that he had made his point.[22]

The last boll of cotton was picked the next day. Field work was not over, for there was still some corn to be gathered and winter wheat to be planted, but these labors were lightened by the arrival of fall weather. Days were cool and clear now, and nights chilly. The leaves of the oak tree by the front gate turned a fiery red, those of the hickories nearby a brilliant yellow. Sam loved this time of year. "Poets might go into raptures," he wrote, "celebrating the beauties of autumn."[23]

When the last of the corn was gathered and Enoch tallied it up, the Agnews had reason to give thanks. The threat of famine was now over, at least on their plantation. The rains of late August and September had revived the parched fields, and they yielded a generous harvest. Enormous heaps of corn now sat in the Agnews' storage buildings ready to be shucked and shelled. There would be plenty for the family and the hands, and also for the hogs when it was time to pen them up for fattening. The other livestock were already enjoying the bounty of the corn fields, for the leaves that the hands had stripped from the stalks before harvest time provided tons of fodder. The mules were getting stronger now, and the beef cattle fatter.[24]

Even as the Agnews gave thanks, however, they worried about the harvests yet to come, for the labor situation on their plantation was more unsettled than ever. The blacks insisted on working at their own pace and often shirked tasks that did not benefit them directly. When reprimanded, they responded with complaints of their own. Sam witnessed one such altercation between his father and Arch on November 9. With cotton- and corn-picking at an end, Arch had been assigned to make rails for fencing, but over the course of four days he split only 120. When Enoch scolded him, Arch replied that "he could not make rails on 'beef and molasses' and not enough of them." Enoch was furious, "and told him plainly that he would have to do better or leave the place."[25]

The imminent expiration of the contract between the Agnews and their hands was another source of contention. The blacks were unhappy with the contract and wanted a different arrangement for next year. In late November Enoch met with Big George to discuss the matter, and they wound up arguing. Enoch was prepared to pay the hands a set amount of cash for every bale of cotton the plantation produced, which was agreeable to Big George, but the two had very different ideas about the laborers' duties and the employer's authority. "Pa wants his hirelings to do anything he wants," Sam wrote. "George wants to hire to make a crop only. Pa wants a crop not only made but the farm to be kept up, fences prepared and fire wood got &c." Neither would budge, and the negotiations ended acrimoniously.[26]

The real problem, as Sam came to see, was that the blacks did not want to work as laborers at all, for "They have an idea that a hireling is not a freeman." What they wanted was to obtain land and live as independent farmers. They chafed under the Agnews' control and resented working for their benefit.[27]

Sam regarded this dream of yeoman independence as absurd. Freedmen would never be able to get along on their own, he was certain, for they were too ignorant and foolish and lazy—especially the Agnew hands, who were undoubtedly "the most worthless in the whole country." They ought to reconcile themselves to dependency, quit complaining, do as they were told, and show their former masters proper respect. He was getting fed up with them, and sometimes found himself wishing they would all pack up and leave. Meanwhile, he was doing more and more chores around the place, including chopping wood and shucking corn, simply because it was easier to do them himself than to wrangle with the blacks.[28]

Whenever he talked with other planters, he heard of similar problems. "The inefficiency of negroes is a subject of general complaint." Many planters were convinced, moreover, that their workers were being stirred up by agitators. The culprits most frequently named were the black U.S. army troops posted in the state, who were reportedly encouraging the freedmen to disobey and urging them not to sign contracts for 1866, claiming that the federal government was going to give them land before the present year was out. These troops were also harassing white people, it was said. Sam heard one such story about a planter named Copeland who lived near Guntown. "It seems that Copeland drove off one of his negroe women and would not let her have her things. She reported him [to federal authorities] and a colored sergeant with a detachment of colored brethren were sent to right the matter. Copeland was cursed and abused by these blacks. One . . . looked at Copeland and said I know you are a d—d rascal by the look of your eye." Sam was incensed: "Such things are hard to bear."[29]

A growing number of whites were not just angry about the racial situation but frightened. There were persistent reports from all over the state that the freedmen were plotting some sort of uprising, perhaps abetted by the black troops and their Yankee officers. These rumors were fueled by the increasingly common sight of freedmen carrying rifles and shotguns. When questioned, they invariably insisted that they were just hunting, but whites were skeptical. Sam was disturbed to learn that several of the Agnew hands had been seen in the woods with guns. "They have no use for them," he wrote, "and they ought to be taken from them."[30]

The rumors multiplied and fed on each other as the weeks passed, and by November many sections of Mississippi were in a state of panic. The freedmen were stockpiling weapons and ammunition, it was said, and were going to rise up on Christmas Day and seize control of the plantations. Some planters were sending their families to safety in other states and preparing to defend their lives and property. Governor Humphreys ordered the local militia to muster in any county threatened by insurrection.[31]

As the rumors intensified, Sam scrutinized the behavior of the Agnew hands. Although he saw nothing ominous beyond their having guns, and heard of no other suspicious activities in his community, he remained watchful. Scares of this sort had been common before the war, and Sam knew that they almost always proved to be unfounded, but no one could afford to dismiss this one out of hand. With slavery gone and the blacks unleashed, anything seemed possible.[32]

In the latter part of November came alarming reports of a planned "outbreak of the negroe population" in Sam's own county of Tippah. The plot was apparently extensive and well organized. "[T]here is a central committee at Ripley," Sam heard, "and delegates from every neighborhood in the county. The Central Committee receive their instructions from some Yankees." The plan was "to rise about Christmas and kill all the white men and boys." It was supposedly uncovered by a white man who had disguised himself in a U.S. army uniform, won the conspirators' confidence, "and ascertained their plans, numbers and supply of arms."[33]

Once the authorities were apprised of the plot, the county militia sprang into action, fanning out through the countryside in search of insurrectionists and weapons. Dozens of blacks were taken into custody. "One was killed," Sam learned, "because he ran and would not surrender."[34]

At two o'clock in the morning of November 24, a squad of militiamen descended on the Agnew plantation and forced their way into the blacks' cabins to search for weapons. Less than twelve hours later the same squad reappeared and again invaded the cabins. All together, five guns were confiscated, one of them a rifle "shortened so as to answer for a pistol," as Sam noted suspiciously. Every freedman's cabin in the neighborhood was likewise raided. No one was arrested, but many guns were seized. "Some of the negroes take this move in high dudgeon," Sam wrote, "and say they thought they had equal rights with a white man to bear arms."[35]

In the days that followed, Sam anxiously sought more news. The blacks being held in the county jail in Ripley were interrogated thoroughly, he learned, but the authorities could find no evidence of a conspiracy and soon let them go. The frantic rumors persisted for a while, but then died down. By December things were quiet again.[36]

Although he remained convinced that disarming the blacks was a prudent measure, Sam eventually concluded that this Tippah County insurrection scare was groundless. The conspiracy rumors "were only the creations of the imaginations of timid people." As the panic subsided, he reflected ruefully on one of its potential consequences: "the negroes must think that the white people are afraid of them."[37]

Similar spasms of hysterical reaction gripped communities throughout the state in November. Once calm was restored, Mississippians turned their attention to other matters. Among the most important was the progress of the new state legislature, which had been in session since mid-October. The legislators had much to do. The state's government was bankrupt, its economy deranged, its transportation network a shambles, its indigents desperate for relief. All of these problems had to be addressed and the state's course toward the future set.[38]

No issue was more pressing, however, than that of race. What role the freedmen should play in the postwar world was an enormously important and difficult question, now further complicated by the uprising scare. President Johnson's position was that the white people of the South, acting through their restored state governments, should be free to define the place of the black race as they saw fit, as long as they did not try to reestablish slavery. Southern whites knew, however, that they must also reckon with the demands of Congress and the Northern public. Few were willing to grant the freedmen anything like equality, but between chattel slavery and full citizenship there lay a vast terrain where the blacks might be situated.[39]

The racial statutes enacted by the Mississippi legislature during the fall, known collectively as the Black Code, seemed to Sam and most other whites a reasonable solution. The freedmen were granted certain basic rights: their marriages and other contracts would be legally recognized, they could bring civil suits and criminal charges before the law, their testimony would be accepted in court cases involving a black. They would not, however, be allowed to serve on juries or testify in any case to which a black was not a party. Nor would they be allowed to vote. They were also denied full economic freedom: none would be permitted to rent or lease farmland; any who were unemployed, even temporarily, would be prosecuted as vagrants and forced to work to pay off their fine; any who quit before their labor contract expired would be arrested and sent back to their employer. With the insurrection scare in mind, the legislature also outlawed "seditious speeches" by blacks and barred them from owning guns or bowie knives.[40]

Sam followed the legislative proceedings closely in the newspapers. He was also keenly interested in the pronouncements of the Freedmen's Bureau, which had authority to intervene in matters involving blacks. From what Sam could tell, the bureau officials in Mississippi accepted the premise that something less than full equality was sufficient for the Negro race, and they seemed more or less satisfied with the Black Code. In particular, the bureau seemed to endorse the notion that compulsion was necessary to get the blacks to work. In a published statement addressed to the freedmen, the head of the bureau in Mississippi explained why he supported the state's new vagrancy law: "I cannot ask the civil officers to leave you idle, to beg or steal. If they find any of you without business and means of living, they will do right if they treat you as bad persons and take away your misused liberty." Bureau officials furthermore warned the blacks that there would be no government distribution of land, no "forty acres and a mule." Dismiss that false rumor, they advised, hasten to sign contracts for next year, and labor dutifully for your employer.[41]

Sam wondered how much good these lectures would do. The freedmen remained restless, and even with the Black Code in effect, they had enough leverage in labor negotiations to frustrate the planters. Those on the Agnew plantation continued to haggle over every task and talked of leaving at year's end if they did not get what they wanted.[42]

The freedmen were not the only restless spirits in postwar Mississippi. As the fall progressed, Sam noticed a great many white people on the move, particularly young men of the poorer sort. They passed frequently on the road that ran by the plantation, many on foot, nearly all strangers to the county, some from distant parts of the South. While there was nothing threatening about them, they seemed as unsettled as the roving freedmen Sam saw so often. A number of them stopped to inquire about renting or sharecropping land. Among these were two former Confederate soldiers named Sutton and Wardlaw. They were from McNairy County, Tennessee, they told Sam, but they could live there no longer, for the unionists who dominated their community had sworn to run the former rebels out. Others whom Sam met seemed not so much uprooted by the war as liberated by it, sensing in the turmoil of the postwar months new opportunities to make their way in the world.[43]

Some of these fortune seekers and refugees had left wives and children at home, intending to send for them once they found a place to settle. Talking with them, Sam was no doubt reminded how much he missed Nannie and Buddy, who had been with Nannie's family in Starkville since early October.

He celebrated his thirty-second birthday on November 22 without them, but he was cheered by the knowledge that they were scheduled to return by train the next day. Wiley drove him to Guntown in the carriage to meet them. The train arrived a couple of hours after dark with Nannie and Buddy on board. Sam greeted them joyfully, but his spirits fell as soon as he saw his baby's face, which was "much disfigured by an eruption. . . . The left cheek was almost a solid black scab, and the right looked very sore." The little fellow had suffered from this affliction almost the whole time he was in Starkville, but Nannie had never mentioned it in her letters.[44]

They spent the night at the inn down the street from the depot, but Sam got little sleep for worrying about Buddy. First thing the next morning, he consulted a doctor in town and was relieved to learn that the condition, while uncomfortable, was not dangerous. It was called milk scab and would clear up on its own.[45]

They lingered in Guntown no longer than necessary, for Nannie was anxious to be home and Enoch needed the mules to get his cotton to market. Once the crop was all picked, cleaned, and dried, Enoch and the hands had run it through a gin to remove the seeds and then compressed it into bales using a big screw press. Three bales weighing about 400 pounds each were now bagged and ready for sale.[46]

On November 27, the Agnews' big farm wagon set out for Memphis with the cotton. The driver was a hired white man. Enoch, whose health was poor, did not go along in the wagon but, instead, took the train. He returned a week later, having sold the cotton for forty-four cents a pound—considerably more than he had gotten for the two bales from the 1864 crop that he had sold back in July, but less than he could have gotten if he had made it to market earlier in the fall. Two days later the wagon returned, laden with supplies.[47]

Wintry weather arrived in the second week of December. When Sam looked out his window early on the eighth, he saw thick frost, and on the thirteenth came a cold north wind. The next morning was frigid. "[E]ven my ink is a solid mass," he noted. "Old winter has been slow coming but he has come at last." On the sixteenth there was snow. It fell for two hours, then gave way to a heavy mist that froze as it descended, wrapping the tree branches and twigs in dazzling cocoons of ice.[48]

Another cold snap a few days later ushered in hog-killing. Enoch summoned the hands on the morning of the twenty-first and the work began.

They slaughtered, cleaned, and butchered eighteen hogs that day, which amounted to more than 2,000 pounds of pork. The next day, Sam helped Big George and Little George with the salting and packing. "It was very cold work," he wrote, "handling cold, frozen meat."[49]

The blacks worked willingly on these disagreeable tasks because they would get a share of the pork. But otherwise they showed little interest in plantation chores as the end of the year approached, and consequently almost daily some new dispute erupted between them and the Agnews. They had by now cast off every last trace of deference, and they responded hotly to the Agnews' complaints. They were being worked too hard, they told Enoch, and he had better ease up if he expected them to sign with him for next year. Even the younger ones were now openly defiant. Sam found himself boiling with anger one day when Tiny, the stableboy, ignored his order to fetch a mule, leaving Sam standing at the front gate. "My orders have no force," he fumed in his diary that night. The whole lot of them, from the youngest to the oldest, were "disobedient, idle and puffed up with an idea of their own excellence." He would put up with their insolence no longer, he vowed, and he hoped his father would quit trying to negotiate with them. "If I owned this place I would drive them off before tomorrow night."[50]

On December 19, while he was in Guntown on an errand, he picked up some news that suggested things were only going to get worse. Congress, which had convened earlier in the month, had refused to seat the newly elected senators and representatives from the former Confederate states. This amounted to a rejection of President Johnson's reconstruction policy and cast doubt on the future of the Southern state governments set up during the summer and fall. Certain members of the Republican majority in Congress were saying that the traitorous rebels were being let off too easily and that the freedmen were being oppressed. A joint committee had been formed to investigate conditions in the South and advise Congress on a proper reconstruction policy. The more Sam heard about these proceedings, the more discouraged he got: "there is nothing favorable to us."[51]

It soon became apparent that a great many people among the Northern leadership and public were appalled by what the white South had done, with President Johnson's approval, in the months since the war ended. What the former Confederates regarded as an honest effort on their part to accept defeat and come to terms with the new realities was seen in the North as defiance and intransigence. In the fall elections Southern voters had repudiated the extremists who had been at the forefront of secession and, instead, had chosen the more conservative of their old leaders—men such as Benjamin Humphreys of Mississippi. But in the eyes of Northerners, a reluctant rebel was still a rebel. Why, they asked, did the defeated South not turn to its loyal unionists for leadership? White Southerners also believed that they had dealt fairly and reasonably with the freedmen: they had granted them certain rights, withheld others they were unsuited for, and endeavored to restrain their primitive impulses and make them productive members of society. But when Northerners read reports about the Southern states' Black Codes, they saw a thinly veiled attempt to restore slavery. And when they read of the autumn insurrection scare, which had gripped not just Mississippi but the whole South, they saw a campaign of white terrorism against an innocent and helpless race. The ex-rebels had much to answer for, in the North's view, and it was by no means certain that the South was ready to resume full partnership in the Union.[52]

As Sam glumly followed the news from the North and contemplated the South's prospects, the last vestiges of the old way of life on the Agnew plantation disappeared. When December 25 came, Enoch and Letitia waited for the customary throng of blacks to appear at the back porch with shouts of "Christmas gift! Christmas gift!" As master and mistress, they had enjoyed the annual ritual of handing out presents to their people, and they delighted in the merriment that suffused the quarters on this favorite of holidays. But this year the day was different from Christmases past. "The negroes were not as jubilant as customary," Sam observed in his diary that night. "There was fewer cries of Christmas Gift than is common." Instead, the hands came to Enoch demanding their tenth of the proceeds from the sale of the cotton. He gave it to them, and then insisted in turn that they listen while he read aloud pertinent sections of the Black Code. A discussion about next year's contract ensued. "Pa told them," wrote Sam, "that whoever he hired would have to work the whole year and do whatever he told them. The negroes are willing to work in the crop but no more. They . . . went away without making a trade."[53]

One by one, in the days that followed, the blacks packed up and left the plantation. Arch departed on Tuesday the twenty-sixth, after informing the Agnews that he had signed for next year with a widow named Miller who had a farm a few miles north. "If he will work for Mrs. Miller," Sam huffed in his diary, "it is more than he has done for Pa." On Wednesday, a white man named Walker came in a wagon and hauled away the belongings of Big

George and his family, who had agreed to come work for him. "George looks like he was mad and I think he leaves with no very pleasant feelings towards us," Sam wrote, "although he has no cause." On Friday, Wiley announced his intention to go; he would work next year for Frank Young, who lived in the community. Sam had not expected this, for Wiley was closer to the Agnews than were any of the other hands and had seemed more willing to come to terms with Enoch.[54]

By Saturday most of the others were gone, too, or were preparing to leave. All of them informed the Agnews of their destination, but Sam, whose mood grew more sour every day, professed no interest: "I don't care where they go provided they only get away from here." Old Eliza expressed a desire to stay, but Sam dismissed it as "only pretense. I always thought her hypocritical."[55]

No less disturbing than this abrupt exodus of their former slaves was the fact that not a single freedman came to the Agnews seeking work. "I suppose our negroes keep them off," Sam wrote, "either by giving us a bad name or by telling that Pa does not want to hire." He learned that the widow Simmons, whose farm was nearby, "has had 50 applications to hire. She must be popular among the darkies." The Agnews' labor force was now so depleted that the family members had to do almost all the chores themselves. Sam was chopping firewood, Letitia was milking the cows, and she and the girls were doing most of the cooking.[56]

Sunday was the last day of the year. Sam was not scheduled to preach; he planned to go with the rest of the family to the service at Bethany Church. Since they no longer had a stableboy, Sam rounded up the mules that morning and hitched them to the carriage. Before the family set out, Enoch had an argument with some of the hands who had not yet gone. They informed him that they were going to take all the bridles on the place when they left, because they had picked them up after they were abandoned by Yankee cavalry in the battle of June 1864. Enoch got angry: six of those bridles were his, he said, for he had ordered the hands to gather them after getting permission from a Confederate quartermaster. He would discuss the matter further after church.[57]

That night, as he did every New Year's Eve, Sam looked back through his diary and reflected on the events of the past twelve months. It had been a year of dire calamities and momentous changes. Many people had endured great losses, many had suffered, and many had died. But he and his loved ones had been spared the worst, and he felt grateful for God's mercy. If this new world they inhabited was in some respects bleak and inhospitable—well, God had a purpose for all things, and His purpose in destroying the old world would, in the fullness of time, be revealed.[58]

As midnight approached, Sam took up his pen and began his last diary entry for the year. He wrote of the dispute over the bridles, of the muddy roads that had slowed the carriage on the way to church, of the sermon that the Reverend Young had preached from the book of Daniel, of all the other things he had seen and heard that day. Below the last line, in bold print, he wrote: "End of Anno Domini 1865." Then he extinguished the candle and joined Nannie in bed. As he fell asleep, he could hear a soft rain falling.[59]

EPILOGUE

1866 AND BEYOND

SAM AGNEW CONTINUED TO WRITE IN HIS DIARY EVERY DAY UNTIL the end of his long life. His passion for recording everything he saw and heard never slackened, and eventually he filled forty-five volumes with his small script. The reader dogged enough to press on through the thousands of pages written after 1865 is rewarded with a vivid eyewitness account of what happened in one corner of the rural South during the tumultuous decades that saw the rise and fall of radical reconstruction, the populist insurgency of the small farmers, and the birth of Jim Crow.

Sam's personal life is chronicled in those pages, too, of course. It was a life of useful service that brought him deep satisfaction. In 1868, following the death of his friend and mentor the Reverend Young, he accepted a call from the congregation of Bethany Church to become pastor. He served in that capacity for the rest of his days, while continuing to preach frequently at other churches and stations in the vicinity. He devoted his later years not only to his ministry but also to writing works of local history, including an article on the battle of Brice's Crossroads published in *Confederate Veteran* magazine.[1]

While Sam enjoyed many blessings in the years after 1865, he also endured a succession of tragedies. Nannie died of consumption in the summer of 1868, leaving him to care for three-year-old Buddy and a second son, James, who was barely a year old. Buddy died before he turned five, James before he turned nine. Sam grieved profoundly over these losses and had to struggle to accept them as a Christian should. "I try to be resigned," he wrote after Buddy's death, "but it is hard and my heart rebells against this painful affliction." His faith was strong, however. Always he reminded himself that "God knows better what is good than we do," and the rebellion in his heart subsided.[2]

18. White-bearded Sam Agnew (second from right) with his second wife, Rachel, and their children in 1896. Behind them is the plantation Big House, where Sam had lived since the 1850s.

Except for a time in 1867–68 when he taught school in Guntown, Sam continued to live on the family plantation, the greater portion of which he eventually inherited. Labor problems continued to plague the estate. Although Enoch managed to secure field hands for the 1866 season and thereafter, doing so required constant wrangling, for the freedmen continued to resist close supervision. Ultimately much of the plantation was parceled out to sharecroppers, over whom the Agnews exercised no day-to-day control. Hiring kitchen help proved to be as frustrating as recruiting field workers, and the family sometimes found themselves without a cook. Sam's diary in the years after 1865 resounds with complaints. The freed people, he declared, were "unreliable as farm laborers," "unwilling . . . to cook," and had "a predjudice against white people."[3]

The black quest for autonomy in the postwar years disrupted not only Sam's home but also his church. Before the war, the Bethany congregation had included many slaves. Afterward, most of those who stayed in the community continued their association with the church. As late as 1873 there were fifty-six black members, one-third of the total. But in that year came a great rupture, the result of growing dissatisfaction among the

19. Marble grave monument of Sam Agnew

blacks, who resented being denied a say in governing the church while being subject to its authority and discipline. Sam and the Bethany elders wrestled earnestly with this difficulty, treating the blacks with "great forbearance," in Sam's view, and "making allowances for their lack of education and want of judgment." The breach could not be healed, however, and eventually forty-four blacks withdrew from membership, most of them going on to found an African Methodist Episcopal church. The experience perplexed and angered Sam, who saw it as further evidence of irrational hostility on the part of the freedmen toward whites. "Such manifestations," he fumed, "make me feel like having nothing to do with the children of Ham."[4]

For all his railing about the freed people, Sam was not a bitter man in the years after 1865. Nor, despite his tragic losses, was he melancholy. He remarried in 1875, to a much younger woman named Rachel Jane Peoples. Although two of the nine children she eventually bore him died in early childhood, the remaining seven survived him and filled his home with joy to the end of his days. The youngest of these four sons and three daughters was born in 1893, when Sam was almost sixty.[5]

His end came in the summer of 1902, a few months before his sixty-ninth birthday. He died "in the harness," as a historian of his denomination has written, for he was stricken while on his way to preach. He was buried in the Bethany Church cemetery near the resting places of his mother and father. A marble monument almost six feet tall stands at the head of his grave. It is carved in the shape of a pulpit with a Bible lying open on it.[6]

John Robertson spent two years in exile before returning to east Tennessee. His homecoming did not, however, mark the end of his odyssey. Soon he set forth again, on journeys geographical, spiritual, and personal. When at last he put down roots, he was far from where he began in 1865.

He remained in Springfield for close to a year, surviving the Iowa winter and getting sufficient schooling to earn a teaching certificate. In the spring of 1866 he began teaching in the village and at the same time helped organize a Sunday school at the Methodist church, as he had done at Blue Springs the year before. When the school term ended in the summer, he decided to leave Iowa. He wanted to pursue his religious calling and do so in the Southern Methodist church. By wagon and train he traveled to Owen County, Kentucky, where he had some relatives, and there he took a teaching job and resumed studying for the ministry. In 1867 he was licensed to preach in the Southern Methodist church.[7]

Soon after arriving in Kentucky, he went to a drugstore, paid a dollar for a blank account book, and started writing a memoir of his experiences beginning with his enlistment in the Confederate army in 1862. "I have seen many days of sorrow and danger and many of joy and gladness," he wrote on page one, and he intended to recount those days as a record of his moral and spiritual development. By the late summer of 1867 he had filled three volumes.[8]

At that point he was ready to go home. Although Governor Brownlow's unionist regime still ruled Tennessee, the violence against rebels in the eastern section of the state had declined enough that John felt it was safe to return. Other refugees from that region were now going home, too, thankful that the bitter conflict that had set neighbor against neighbor for more than six years was at last subsiding.[9]

Throughout his exile John remained passionately devoted to Tennie, and he headed back to east Tennessee in August 1867 eager to redeem his promise to marry her. He had never wavered in his certainty that "it was our fate to share together the joys and sorrows of this life." Both had affirmed their love in the letters they had exchanged regularly after he left.[10]

What happened between them when he returned to Roane County can never be known. His memoir ends as he is leaving Kentucky, and the records of his life after that are few. It is known that he and Tennie did not marry, and in November 1867 she wed another man, an east Tennessee unionist who had served in the federal army during the war.[11]

John then settled for a time in Greene County, where his parents still lived. He continued to read, think, and argue about theology and doctrine, and before long he abandoned the Methodist church for the Presbyterian, and then the Presbyterian for the Baptist. Around 1868 he enrolled in Shurtleff College, a Baptist school in Illinois. He studied there for several years and then began a long career as a Baptist preacher.[12]

Before leaving Greene County for college, he married a woman four years his senior named Louisa Kitzmiller, from nearby Sullivan County. They had a child in 1869. What became of Louisa and the baby is unknown, for they disappear from the historical record after 1870. It is likely that both died around the time John finished college.[13]

John's first pastorate after graduating from Shurtleff was in Beauregard, Mississippi, where he stayed for a year. While there, he met and married Sazine Tillman, the daughter of a dry goods merchant. He then moved to a church in Kansas, where he spent three years, followed by three years at a church in Missouri. Around 1879 he was called to northwestern Arkansas, where he settled for good, as pastor of Wager's Mill Church in Benton County and, later, of Elm Springs Church, a few miles away in Washington County.[14]

He developed a reputation in his Arkansas community as an avid debater of religion and a skilled defender of the Baptist faith. He was also noted for his extensive collection of books, said to be "the largest library of theological and historical works in the county." Sadly, the whole collection was destroyed, along with his house, when a tornado struck in 1898. Miraculously, he and his family escaped with no injuries worse than bruises.[15]

By that time, ironically enough, Tennie was living less than 150 miles from John, in a small town in western Missouri. Whether they were aware of their proximity is unknown. Surely they at least thought of one another now and then; perhaps she still had the silver dollar he had given her in the summer of 1865 as a token of his love. Her life at this point could not have been easy, for her husband was by then an invalid, suffering from chronic liver and stomach ailments and depression.[16]

John made no mention of Tennie, understandably enough, when he provided information in the late 1880s for a biographical sketch of himself to be published in a local history. What is curious is that he also said not a word about his Confederate military service, his deep engagement with Methodism, his brush with death at the hands of unionists, his exile from east Tennessee, or his first wife and child. The year 1865, and those immediately before and after it, constitute a glaring blank space in the story he told others of himself. He never published his memoir of those years.[17]

Sazine bore John at least seven children. Four were living, as was she, when he died of a stroke in 1909, at the age of sixty-three.[18]

Cornelia McDonald ultimately overcame despair and poverty, thanks to her inner strength and the help of family and friends. Her struggle continued for years after 1865 however. A photograph from 1870 shows her still thin-faced and hollow-eyed, while the census of that year lists the value of her worldly possessions as a mere $150.[19]

She never got much from her husband's estate—a good deal of his property had to be sold for taxes—and so she continued to work to support herself and her family. After 1865 she began taking in Washington College students as boarders and also taught at a girls' school in Lexington. These labors were exhausting, but they brought in enough money to pay for necessities and to enable Harry to enroll in the college. He graduated in 1869 with a degree in civil engineering, quickly secured a good job with a railroad, and thereafter was able to contribute substantially to the family's support. Later Allan was able to finish his education, too, and he in turn helped the family. Eventually all six of her boys earned degrees or at least attended college, and all embarked on careers, most of them in engineering. Nelly was educated at a private academy.[20]

The friends who came to Cornelia's rescue in 1865 continued to lend assistance from time to time. Eventually she learned the source of the mysterious hundred dollars that Ann Pendleton had given her. It was part of a large fund sent to rebel agents in Canada by the Confederate government to finance secret operations against the North. When the war ended, the agents decided to distribute the remaining money to needy widows and orphans of Confederate soldiers. One of the agents was a son-in-law of the Reverend

William Pendleton, and at Pendleton's urging he arranged for Cornelia to get a share. The existence of the fund had to be kept secret after the war, lest the U.S. government confiscate it.[21]

As her financial situation slowly improved, Cornelia resumed an active social life. Among those whose company she enjoyed in the years after 1865 were Robert E. Lee and his family. Cornelia called often on Mrs. Lee, who was confined to a wheelchair, and General Lee returned her calls. A great lover of children, Lee especially enjoyed the company of Nelly and her younger brothers. He helped out the McDonalds on occasion, including writing a letter of recommendation for Harry, whom he called "a very promising young man, of great energy and integrity of character." Lee and the McDonalds also saw each other on Sundays at Grace Episcopal Church, which reopened in 1866 after the federal garrison was withdrawn from Lexington. Ever the dignified gentleman, Lee always pretended not to notice on those occasions when Kenneth or Roy or Donald fell noisily to the floor during the church service, having fallen asleep in the pew. When Lee died in 1870, Cornelia was deeply saddened.[22]

In 1873 Cornelia and her children who were still at home moved to Louisville, Kentucky, where Harry and Allan were pursuing their careers. By then the family was getting along well enough that Cornelia did not have to work and could indulge in her old pastimes, including reading and drawing. She also found a new hobby, china-painting, and became active in church and charity work. In 1875 she compiled a record of her wartime experiences, part diary and part memoir, as a gift to her children. A vivid and frank account of her travails in Winchester and Lexington, it was published in 1934 by her youngest child, Hunter.[23]

Cornelia never remarried. In her later years she lived with Nelly and her husband, a merchant in Henderson, Kentucky. When she died in 1909, at the age of nearly eighty-seven, six of her children were living (Harry had succumbed to pneumonia in 1904), as were twenty-two grandchildren and two great-grandchildren. She was buried next to her husband in Hollywood Cemetery in Richmond, Virginia. Her memory was revered by her surviving sons and daughter, who never forgot how she had suffered and sacrificed for them. "A rare soul was hers," said Nelly, "and one that had few equals."[24]

After arriving in Windsor, Ontario, on Christmas day 1865, Louis Hughes found work as a hotel porter. But the pay was poor and he grew restless again.

Canada was not the land of opportunity he had envisioned. In the spring of 1866 he took a job as a waiter in Detroit. In 1867, still dissatisfied, he shipped out on a Great Lakes steamer. When the sailing season ended, the ship tied up for the winter in Chicago and Lou found work there in a hotel. One of the businessmen who regularly stayed there, Mr. Plankinton of Milwaukee, took a liking to Lou and offered him a job in the hotel he was opening. In September 1868 Lou moved to Milwaukee and took charge of the coatroom at the new Plankinton House.[25]

Matilda, who had remained in Windsor all this time, now joined Lou. The two established a private laundry service for the Plankinton's guests, with Lou collecting the clothes in the course of his hotel duties and Matilda doing the washing. This was such a success that in 1874 Lou quit the Plankinton and went into the laundry business full time with Matilda.[26]

Though never really satisfied with any of his jobs in these years, Lou felt blessed in other ways. In 1867 Matilda presented him with twin babies, "two bright little girls" who brought him great joy and helped ease the painful memory of his first twins. Not long after that, he enrolled in a night school for freedmen in Chicago and began to learn to read and write. During this time, too, he had a spiritual awakening and committed his life to Jesus Christ. He was a founding member and steward of St. Mark's African Methodist Episcopal Church in Milwaukee.[27]

The most remarkable of Lou's post-1865 experiences was finding his long-lost brother, Billy Hughes. It came about through the same kind of chance encounter that had led Matilda to her mother and sister. At the Plankinton one day, a salesman who was one of the regular guests approached Lou and said, "Say, Hughes, have you a brother?" Lou replied that he had two, but had not seen them since he was sold away from his family in Virginia as a boy, some thirty years ago; he had no idea if they were still alive. The man then told Lou that there was a hotel cook in Cleveland who looked just like him. His name was Billy, but that was all the man knew about him. Lou related what little he remembered about his brother Billy—mainly the missing forefinger that Lou had accidentally chopped off one day when the two were playing—and the salesman promised to talk to the cook on his next trip to Cleveland. Lou waited impatiently to see the salesman again. Then one day at work he heard the words, "Hello, Hughes! I have good news for you." The man had been to Cleveland and confirmed that the cook was Lou's brother, missing finger and all. Lou immediately arranged for some time off from work, caught an express train to Cleveland, and had an emotional reunion with the brother he had never expected to see again. There was one sad note: Billy, who also had been separated at a young age from their mother, had returned to the Virginia homeplace after the war seeking her and their other brother, but could discover no trace of either.[28]

In the late 1870s, when he was past the age of forty-five, Lou found his true calling. It happened that a prominent Milwaukee man, Dr. Douglas, was ill and needed private nursing. A friend of Lou's recommended him, and for three months Lou served as Dr. Douglas's night nurse. He also accompanied his patient to a health spa. The experience gave Lou a deep sense of fulfillment and set him on a new path. He realized that this was what he had yearned to do ever since the days when he stood at Boss's side learning the healing potions and visiting sick slaves in their cabins. Now he would become a nurse.[29]

Armed with a letter of recommendation and some newly printed business cards, both courtesy of Dr. Douglas, Lou hung out his shingle and soon gained a reputation in Milwaukee as an excellent private-duty nurse. He pursued this calling for more than two decades. During those years he had the opportunity to travel with many of his patients, going to places as far away as Florida and California.[30]

In 1897, "in compliance with the suggestion of friends," Lou published a memoir of his life as a slave. He probably could not have afforded to do this on his own, and the book is written in a polished style that is clearly not his. It is likely that one of his wealthy patients, captivated by Lou's bedside stories of his years in bondage and his harrowing escape, paid to have those stories transcribed, edited, and published.[31]

To the end of his life, Lou remained bitter about slavery. His memoir is a defiant reply to the romantic legend of plantation life in the Old South that had captured the popular mind of America by the late nineteenth century. In it, he graphically recounts the horrors he witnessed and speaks of "the scars which I still bear upon my person, and . . . the wounds of spirit which will never wholly heal." Nor had he any patience with the popular image of the Confederate States of America as a noble Lost Cause. Fighting to preserve an inhuman institution, he insisted, was hardly noble. Readers of his memoir are reminded that if the Confederacy had won its war for independence, Lou and his loved ones, along with millions of other men and women, would have spent the rest of their lives in harsh servitude.[32]

Though he traveled to the South on a number of occasions in his later years, he apparently never revisited any of the places where he had lived as a slave. Nor did he make any effort to learn what became of those who had held him in bondage. He resided in Milwaukee for the remainder of his days, moving in with one of his daughters and her husband after Matilda's death in 1907. By then he was a well-known figure in Milwaukee, thanks to his extensive business contacts and his published memoir. When he died in 1913, at the age of eighty, every newspaper in the city featured an article about him. He was laid to rest in Forest Home Cemetery next to Matilda.[33]

LIST OF ABBREVIATIONS

CPM	Mrs. Cornelia McDonald, *A Diary with Reminiscences of the War and Refugee Life in the Shenandoah Valley, 1860–1865* (Nashville, 1934)
JCR	John C. Robertson Memoir, McClung Historical Collection, Knox County Public Library, Knoxville, Tennessee
LH	Louis Hughes, *Thirty Years a Slave: From Bondage to Freedom* (Milwaukee, 1897)
SAA	Samuel A. Agnew Diary, Southern Historical Collection, University of North Carolina, Chapel Hill

NOTES

PROLOGUE

1. LH, 5.
2. Ibid., 5–7, 9–12.
3. Ibid., 12–13.
4. Ibid., 14 15, 17–18, 19, 63–64.
5. Ibid., 58, 59–62.
6. Ibid., frontispiece photograph, 78–79, 81.
7. Ibid., 73–74, 86.
8. Ibid., 80–89.
9. Ibid., 93, 94, 111–12.
10. Ibid., 120–22, 136.
11. Ibid., 127–37, 139–46.
12. Ibid., 160–64; McGehee Family Genealogical File, Mississippi Department of Archives and History, Jackson.
13. CPM, xiii-xiv, 1–7.
14. Ibid., 3–4.
15. Ibid., 4, 451–53; Mrs. Flora McDonald Williams, *The Glengarry McDonalds of Virginia* (Louisville, 1911), 331–32.
16. CPM, 5.
17. Ibid., xiii-xiv, 5–6, 340–52; Williams, *Glengarry McDonalds,* 332; James B. Avirett, et al., *The Memoirs of General Turner Ashby and His Compeers* (Baltimore, 1867), 318–31.
18. CPM, xi, 6, 352–53, 413–33; Avirett, *Memoirs,* 331; Virginia Personal Property Tax Books, Frederick County, 1860, Library of Virginia, Richmond.
19. CPM, xiii, 6, 353–54; Avirett, *Memoirs,* 332–33; Eighth Census, 1860, Manuscript Returns of Free Inhabitants, Frederick County, Virginia, p. 257/527, National Archives, Washington; Eighth Census, 1860, Manuscript Returns of Slaves, Frederick County, Virginia, District 4, National Archives, Washington.
20. CPM, 16–38, 356; Avirett, *Memoirs,* 334–48.
21. CPM, 40–176, passim.
22. Ibid., 177–90.
23. Ibid., 197; Avirett, *Memoirs,* 345–46.
24. CPM, 201–37, 277–84; Avirett, *Memoirs,* 348–58.
25. CPM, 234–39.
26. Ibid., 239–45.
27. JCR, 1, 137, 148.
28. *Population of the United States in 1860 . . .* (Washington, 1864), 466; *Agriculture of the United States in 1860 . . .* (Washington, 1864), 132–35, 215, 238; Blanche Henry Clark,

The Tennessee Yeomen, 1840–1860 (Nashville, 1942), chap. 1; Fred Arthur Bailey, *Class and Tennessee's Confederate Generation* (Chapel Hill and London, 1987), chaps. 2, 4.

29. Eighth Census, 1860, Manuscript Returns of Free Inhabitants, Greene County, Tennessee, p. 58/361; Eighth Census, 1860, Manuscript Returns of Productions of Agriculture, Greene County, Tennessee, District 17, National Archives, Washington; J. T. Trowbridge, *The South: A Tour of Its Battle-Fields and Ruined Cities . . .* (Hartford, Conn., 1866), 243; Clark, *Tennessee Yeomen*, chap. 2; Donald L. Winters, *Tennessee Farming, Tennessee Farmers: Antebellum Agriculture in the Upper South* (Knoxville, 1994), chaps. 3, 4.
30. JCR, 149, 156, 157, 236, 293; Bailey, *Class and Tennessee's Confederate Generation*, chap. 3.
31. JCR, 186; Paul H. Bergeron, Stephen V. Ash, and Jeanette Keith, *Tennesseans and Their History* (Knoxville, 1999), 132–40.
32. Noel C. Fisher, *War at Every Door: Partisan Politics and Guerrilla Violence in East Tennessee, 1860–1869* (Chapel Hill and London, 1997), passim; W. Todd Groce, *Mountain Rebels: East Tennessee Confederates and the Civil War* (Knoxville, 1999), passim; Charles Faulkner Bryan Jr., "The Civil War in East Tennessee: A Social, Political, and Economic Study" (Ph.D. diss., University of Tennessee, 1978), passim.
33. JCR, 1–8; Compiled Civil War Service Records, 39th Tennessee Mounted Infantry, National Archives, Washington.
34. JCR, 8, 11–22.
35. Ibid., 22–62; *The War of the Rebellion: A Compilation of the Official Records of the Union and Confederate Armies*, 70 vols. in 128 (Washington, 1880–1901), Series One, 30(2): 639–40.
36. JCR, 16, 63–78.
37. Ibid., 76–80; "List of Persons Taken [*sic*] the Oath," Records of the Provost Marshal, ser. 2764, District of East Tennessee, Records of U.S. Army Continental Commands, RG 393, Pt. 2, No. 173, National Archives, Washington.
38. JCR, 81–110.
39. Ibid., 99, 110–45.
40. Ibid., 1, 8–11, 148.
41. SAA, passim. The forty-five-volume diary spans the years 1851 to 1902.
42. Ibid., 26 January, 26 February, 30 September, 16 October 1864, 6 January, 12, 18 February, 5 September 1865; *The Centennial History of the Associate Reformed Presbyterian Church, 1803–1903* (Charleston, S.C., 1905), 42–44.
43. *Biographical and Historical Memoirs of Mississippi*, 2 vols. (Chicago, 1891), 1:287–88; *Centennial History of the Associate Reformed Presbyterian Church*, 42–44.
44. Eighth Census, 1860, Manuscript Returns of Free Inhabitants, Tippah County, Mississippi, p. 43/691; Tippah County Tax Rolls (Personal), 1861, Mississippi Department of Archives and History, Jackson.
45. SAA, 1860–1865, passim, especially 24 February 1865.
46. Ibid., 1861–1865, passim, especially 13 December 1861.
47. Ibid., 5, 16, 22 January 1865.
48. Rev. Samuel A. Agnew, *Historical Sketch of the Associate Reformed Presbyterian Church of Bethany, Lee County, Miss.* (Louisville, 1881), 12; Andrew Brown, *History of Tippah County, Mississippi: The First Century* (Ripley, Miss., 1976), chaps. 23–26; SAA, 6–15, 23 January, 26 June 1862, 13 December 1865.
49. Brown, *History of Tippah County*, 156–57; O. Davis to William L. Sharkey, 28 June 1865, Provisional Governor William L. Sharkey Letters, Mississippi Department of Archives and History, Jackson; SAA, 6 October, 27–29 November 1863, 21 February, 24 July 1864.
50. SAA, 9–13, 16 June 1864; Samuel A. Agnew, "Battle of Tishomingo Creek," *Confederate Veteran* 8 (1900): 401–403; Margaret Agnew Simpson, "The Battle of Brice's Crossroads," typescript reminiscence in possession of David Frazier of Guntown, Mississippi.
51. Brown, *History of Tippah County*, 150–55.

WINTER: LOUIS HUGHES

1. T. L. Head Jr., "The Salt Works of Clarke County, Alabama," 7, 15, unpublished typescript in Salt Commission File, Quartermaster Department—Civil War and Reconstruction, Public Information Subject Files, Alabama Department of Archives and History, Montgomery; *Clarke County (Alabama) Journal*, 26 January 1865.
2. Head, "Salt Works of Clarke County," 1–2, 12, 14–15; Ella Lonn, *Salt as a Factor in the Confederacy* (New York, 1933), 112–13, 129, 134; LH, 161, 166–67.
3. LH, 161; Malcolm C. McMillan, *The Disintegration of a Confederate State: Three Governors and Alabama's Wartime Home Front, 1861–1865* (Macon, 1986), 95.
4. LH, 164; McGehee Family Genealogical File; Benjamin Woolsey to Sarah McGehee, 8 February 1864, Alabama State Salt Works Letter Book, William R. Perkins Library, Duke University, Durham.
5. Head, "Salt Works of Clarke County," 8, 15–16; N. S. Brooks to E. G. Wagner, 18 December 1863, Benjamin Woolsey to Thomas Watts, 1 March 1864, to Thomas Blewitt, 28 March 1864, Alabama State Salt Works Letter Book; payrolls, February, March 1865, Alabama Salt Commissioner's Quarterly Reports and Abstracts, Alabama Department of Archives and History, Montgomery.
6. Head, "Salt Works of Clarke County," 15–16; Benjamin Woolsey to Thomas Watts, 12 April 1864, payroll, 30 October 1864, and "Abstract of Property Expended," 31 March 1865, Alabama Salt Commissioner's Quarterly Reports; Benjamin Woolsey to Thomas Watts, 1 March 1864, and to Mrs. W. H. Ketchum, 28 March 1864, Alabama Salt Works Letter Book; J. Michael Bunn, "Slavery in the Clarke County Saltworks, 1861–1865," *Clarke County Historical Society Quarterly* 24 (1999): 21.
7. LH, 165–67; Bunn, "Slavery in the Clarke County Saltworks," 22–23; payroll, February 1865, Alabama Salt Commissioner's Quarterly Reports.
8. T. H. Ball, *A Glance into the Great South-East; or, Clarke County, Alabama, and Its Surroundings* (1879; repr., Tuscaloosa, Ala., 1962), 647; N. S. Brooks to Mrs. M. E. Fletcher, 11 November 1863, to Edmund McGehee, 5 December 1863, Benjamin Woolsey to Thomas Blewitt, 5 February 1864, to Thomas Watts, 1 March 1864, Alabama Salt Works Letter Book.
9. Head, "Salt Works of Clarke County," 16; Lonn, *Salt as a Factor*, 61–64; N. S. Brooks to E. G. Wagner, 18 December 1863, Benjamin Woolsey to Thomas Blewitt, 28 March 1864, to Mrs. W. H. Ketchum, 28 March 1864, to Thomas Watts, 1, 12 April 1864, Alabama Salt Works Letter Book; Bunn, "Slavery in the Clarke County Saltworks," 21.
10. Payroll, February 1865, Alabama Salt Commissioner's Quarterly Reports; Benjamin Woolsey to W. H. Ketchum, 26 March 1864, to Mrs. W. H. Ketchum, 28 March 1864, Alabama Salt Works Letter Book; Bunn, "Slavery in the Clarke County Saltworks," 23; John Hope Franklin and Loren Schweninger, *Runaway Slaves: Rebels on the Plantation* (Oxford and New York, 1999), 36–37, 98–99.
11. "Abstract of Monies Paid Out," 31 December 1864, Alabama Salt Commissioner's Quarterly Reports; Franklin and Schweninger, *Runaway Slaves*, 125.
12. Lonn, *Salt as a Factor*, 14–15, 19; Head, "Salt Works of Clarke County," 6; McMillan, *Disintegration of a Confederate State*, 48.
13. Lonn, *Salt as a Factor*, 13–14, 16–18; Head, "Salt Works of Clarke County," 6.
14. Lonn, *Salt as a Factor*, 19–21, 38–39, 87–89, 92, 116–18; Head, "Salt Works of Clarke County," 1–2, 5, 10–11, 12; McMillan, *Disintegration of a Confederate State*, 48–50, 95; Walter L. Fleming, *Civil War and Reconstruction in Alabama* (New York, 1905), 158–59.
15. McMillan, *Disintegration of a Confederate State*, 49; Lonn, *Salt as a Factor*, 21–22, 92, 111–14, 129–36; Head, "Salt Works of Clarke County," 6–10, 14–17; Fleming, *Civil War and Reconstruction in Alabama*, 159; "Statement of Salt Made May 1-June 1, 1864,"

Alabama Salt Commissioner's Quarterly Reports; Benjamin Woolsey to Thomas Watts, 1 March 1864, Alabama Salt Works Letter Book.

16. Head, "Salt Works of Clarke County," 15–16; Lonn, *Salt as a Factor*, 135; N. S. Brooks to Thomas Watts, 4 November 1864, and "Abstract of Supplies Furnished," 31 December 1864, Alabama Salt Commissioner's Quarterly Reports; Bunn, "Slavery in the Clarke County Saltworks," 22.
17. LH, 21–22, 44–45, 67–68, 159.
18. Ibid., 62, 65, 67, 106, 107, 116, 122, 171–72.
19. Head, "Salt Works of Clarke County," 16; *Clarke County Journal*, 26 January, 1 February 1865.
20. *Clarke County Journal*, 26 January, 1, 9 February, 2, 16 March 1865; Head, "Salt Works of Clarke County," 1, 18; Lonn, *Salt as a Factor*, 21–22, 120.
21. LH, 95, 99, 191; Twelfth Census, 1900, Manuscript Returns of Inhabitants, Milwaukee, Wisconsin, ED 194, Sheet 4, National Archives, Washington.
22. LH, 91, 94.
23. Ibid., 91–93.
24. Ibid., 93–94, 95.
25. Ibid., 96–97, 108, 128, 131, 135–36, 145, 174–75, 178.
26. *Clarke County Journal*, 22 December 1864; Mark Mayo Boatner III, *The Civil War Dictionary* (New York, 1959), 559; Head, "Salt Works of Clarke County," 2.
27. Benjamin Woolsey to Thomas Blewitt, 28 March 1864, Alabama Salt Works Letter Book; LH, 167–68; *Clarke County Journal*, 9 March 1865.

WINTER: CORNELIA MCDONALD

1. CPM, 195, 195n, 237n, 265, 265n, photograph facing 193, map facing 324.
2. Ibid., 178–79, 193, 195, 200.
3. Ibid., 27–28, 195n, map facing 324.
4. Oren F. Morton, *A History of Rockbridge County, Virginia* (Staunton, 1920), 1–11; *The Statistics of the Population of the United States. (June 1, 1870)* (Washington, 1872), 282; Charles H. Lynch, *The Civil War Diary 1862–1865 of Charles H. Lynch, 18th Conn. Vols.* (Hartford, 1915), 75; CPM, 190–91, 199.
5. Elizabeth Preston Allan, *The Life and Letters of Margaret Junkin Preston* (Boston and New York, 1903), 341–45.
6. Morton, *History of Rockbridge*, 127–28; Susan P. Lee, *Memoirs of William Nelson Pendleton . . .* (Philadelphia, 1893), 383.
7. CPM, 241–42; Jer. 13:20.
8. CPM, 41, 63, 77, 99, 134–35, 140–41, 163, 189, 196, 224, 242, 413–33; Williams, *Glengarry McDonalds*, 259–87; James Marten, *The Children's Civil War* (Chapel Hill and London, 1998), 103–105.
9. Eighth Census, 1860, Manuscript Returns of Free Inhabitants, Frederick County, Virginia, p. 257/527; Eighth Census, 1860, Manuscript Returns of Slaves, Frederick County, Virginia, District 4; Virginia Personal Property Tax Books, Frederick County, 1860; CPM, 180–88, 190, 205.
10. CPM, 195, 225, 232; Compiled Civil War Service Records, 7th Virginia Cavalry.
11. CPM, 232, 245, 247; Compiled Civil War Service Records, 7th Virginia Cavalry; Lee, *Memoirs*, 392–93; Morton, *History of Rockbridge*, 131; Robert J. Driver, *Lexington and Rockbridge County in the Civil War* (Lynchburg, 1989), 54–55, 97.
12. *Lexington (Virginia) Gazette*, 25 January 1865; "Letters of John Letcher to J. Hierholzer, 1864–1865," *William and Mary Quarterly* 8 (1928): 137; Charles W. Turner, ed., *The Diary of Henry Boswell Jones of Brownsburg (1842–1871)* (Verona, Va., 1979), 87; Ann

Pendleton to William Pendleton, 6 November 1864, 14 March 1865, William N. Pendleton Papers, Southern Historical Collection, University of North Carolina, Chapel Hill; Driver, *Lexington in the Civil War*, 55; CPM, 250.

13. *Agriculture of the United States in 1860*, 158–61; Driver, *Lexington in the Civil War*, 54, 57, 78; Morton, *History of Rockbridge*, 131–32; William Blair, *Virginia's Private War: Feeding Body and Soul in the Confederacy, 1861–1865* (New York and Oxford, 1998), 101, 119.
14. Rockbridge County, Virginia, County Court Minute Book, December 1864, Library of Virginia, Richmond; *Lexington Gazette*, 18 January 1865; Rose Pendleton to William Pendleton, 12 March 1865, Pendleton Papers.
15. Driver, *Lexington in the Civil War*, 78, 84; Morton, *History of Rockbridge*, 133–34; William F. Zornow, "Aid for the Indigent Families of Soldiers in Virginia, 1861–1865," *Virginia Magazine of History and Biography* 69 (1958): 454–58; Blair, *Virginia's Private War*, 70–71, 75–76, 94–95, 119–20; Rockbridge County Court Minute Book, December 1864, January 1865.
16. Lee, *Memoirs*, 391, *Lexington Gazette*, 1 March 1865; George C. Rable, *Civil Wars: Women and the Crisis of Southern Nationalism* (Urbana and Chicago, 1989), 108–11.
17. CPM, 188–89; Mary Elizabeth Massey, *Refugee Life in the Confederacy* (Baton Rouge, 1964), 139–59; Drew Gilpin Faust, *Mothers of Invention: Women of the Slaveholding South in the American Civil War* (Chapel Hill and London, 1996), 40–45.
18. CPM, 188–90, 189n, 192; Williams, *Glengarry McDonalds*, 283–84.
19. CPM, 193, 233, 233n, 235, 244, 266; Ann Pendleton to William Pendleton, 18 October, 8, 30 December 1864, Pendleton Papers; Eighth Census, 1860, Manuscript Returns of Free Inhabitants, Rockbridge County, Virginia, p. 8; Lisa Tolbert, *Constructing Townscapes: Space and Society in Antebellum Tennessee* (Chapel Hill and London, 1999), 130–33, 141–43; Elizabeth Fox-Genovese, *Within the Plantation Household: Black and White Women of the Old South* (Chapel Hill and London, 1988), 225–26.
20. CPM, 195–96, 195n, 235–36; Eighth Census, 1860, Manuscript Returns of Free Inhabitants, Rockbridge County, Virginia, p. 13.
21. CPM, 193, 245, 246.
22. Ibid., 198, 245, 246–47; Massey, *Refugee Life*, 160–64; Rable, *Civil Wars*, 128–31; Faust, *Mothers of Invention*, 80–88; Fox-Genovese, *Within the Plantation Household*, 46.
23. CPM, 246–47.
24. Ibid., 235, 247; Marten, *Children's Civil War*, 170–73.
25. CPM, 199, 201, 236.
26. Ibid., 196n, 199, 209, 224–25, 226, 235, 236n, 245; Williams, *Glengarry McDonalds*, 286n.
27. Virginia Personal Property Tax Books, Frederick County, 1860; CPM, 140n, 200n, 204n, 225, 262.
28. CPM, 234–35, 235n; Williams, *Glengarry McDonalds*, 274, 286.
29. CPM, 197n, 204n, 205, 225, 225n.
30. Ibid., 196, 205, 247.
31. Ibid., 193, 197, 198, 232, 245.
32. Ibid., 193, 265; Faust, *Mothers of Invention*, 47–49, 77–78.
33. CPM, 193, 198n, 207, 237.
34. Ibid., 207; Morton, *History of Rockbridge*, 133; Driver, *Lexington in the Civil War*, 78.
35. Rockbridge County Court Minute Book, December 1863, December 1864.
36. *Agriculture of the United States in 1860*, 244; *Population of the United States in 1860*, 517; Driver, *Lexington in the Civil War*, 82; Blair, *Virginia's Private War*, 121–24; *Lexington Gazette*, 18 January, 1 March 1865; Lynch, *Civil War Diary*, 75; Morton, *History of Rockbridge*, 131; circular from Secretary of the Commonwealth to Virginia county court clerks, 16 November 1864 (Richmond, 1864); Rockbridge County Court Minute Book, December 1864, January, February 1865.

37. "Letters of John Letcher," 137, 138; Rose Pendleton to William Pendleton, 10, 12 March 1865, Pendleton Papers; *War of the Rebellion*, Series One, 46(1): 384; *Lexington Gazette*, 31 March 1865; Blair, *Virginia's Private War*, 108, 119; Mark Grimsley, *The Hard Hand of War: Union Military Policy Toward Southern Civilians, 1861–1865* (Cambridge, Eng., 1995), 167–68, 175, 178.
38. *War of the Rebellion*, Series One, 37(1): 96–98; Grimsley, *Hard Hand of War*, 178–79; Morton, *History of Rockbridge*, 129–30; H. A. Du Pont, *The Campaign of 1864 in the Valley of Virginia and the Expedition to Lynchburg* (New York, 1925), 68–70; Allan, *Life and Letters*, 186–97; Turner, *Diary*, 87; Driver, *Lexington in the Civil War*, 58–78; CPM, 201–208, 316–39.
39. *Lexington Gazette*, 4 January 1865; Driver, *Lexington in the Civil War*, 79, 82, 97, 98.
40. *Lexington Gazette*, 11 January, 22 February 1865; Morton, *History of Rockbridge*, 131.
41. Blair, *Virginia's Private War*, 108–33; Paul D. Escott, *After Secession: Jefferson Davis and the Failure of Confederate Nationalism* (Baton Rouge, 1978), passim; Rable, *Civil Wars*, 78–90, 206–20.
42. Blair, *Virginia's Private War*, 108–33.
43. Escott, *After Secession*, passim.
44. CPM, 238; Albert Burton Moore, *Conscription and Conflict in the Confederacy* (New York, 1924), passim.
45. Lee, *Memoirs*, 383, 387; *Lexington Gazette*, 25 January 1865; CPM, 247.
46. Blair, *Virginia's Private War*, 130–33; *Lexington Gazette*, 25 January 1865; "Letters of John Letcher," 137, 138–39.
47. CPM, 10–15, 18–19, 64, 122–23, 141–42, 144n, 149; Avirett, *Memoirs*, 334; Faust, *Mothers of Invention*, 9–29.
48. CPM, 201, 247–48; Faust, *Mothers of Invention*, 234–47.
49. CPM, 198, 200, 225, 235n, 238–39, 247, photograph facing 414; Marten, *Children's Civil War*, 111–14.
50. CPM, 169, 199, 201; Daniel E. Sutherland, *The Expansion of Everyday Life, 1860–1876* (New York, 1989), 54–55, 63–66; Faust, *Mothers of Invention*, 153–61.
51. CPM, 99, 140n, 247.
52. Ibid., 40n, 199, 241, 244.
53. Ibid., 199, 247.
54. Ibid., 200, 232–33, 245–46; Lee, *Memoirs*, 384, 388, 390–91.
55. Driver, *Lexington in the Civil War*, 84; Turner, *Diary*, 88.
56. *Lexington Gazette*, 1 March 1865.

WINTER: JOHN ROBERTSON

1. *The Tennessee Almanac for the Year of Our Lord 1865* (Nashville); JCR, 147, 148.
2. JCR, 81–82, 145; Eighth Census, 1860, Manuscript Returns of Free Inhabitants, Knox County, Tennessee, p. 73/323; Eighth Census, 1860, Manuscript Returns of Productions of Agriculture, Knox County, Tennessee, District 19.
3. JCR, 137, 148.
4. Ibid., 148. For ease of reading, some of the characters' original spelling has been amended in brackets.
5. Ibid., 145, 149.
6. Ibid., 129, 162; Fisher, *War at Every Door*, chaps. 4, 5; Groce, *Mountain Rebels*, chap. 6; Bryan, "Civil War in East Tennessee," passim.
7. JCR, 149.
8. Ibid.; Eighth Census, 1860, Manuscript Returns of Free Inhabitants, Knox County, Tennessee, pp. 66–67/194–95; Eighth Census, 1860, Manuscript Returns of Productions of Agriculture, Knox County, Tennessee, District 8.

9. JCR, 149.
10. Ibid.
11. Ibid., 10–11, 149–50; Sutherland, *Expansion of Everyday Life*, 83–85.
12. JCR, 136, 150; Christine Leigh Heyrman, *Southern Cross: The Beginnings of the Bible Belt* (Chapel Hill and London, 1997), 33–41; Donald G. Mathews, *Religion in the Old South* (Chicago, 1977), xvi-xvii.
13. JCR, 9–22, 41–49, 54–56, 130–34.
14. Ibid., 150.
15. Ibid.
16. Ibid., 151.
17. John L. Melton, ed., "The Diary of a Drummer," *Michigan History* 43 (1959): 331; JCR, 151.
18. JCR, 151; 2 Kings 19:11–12.
19. JCR, 151–52.
20. Ibid., 152; Heyrman, *Southern Cross*, 34.
21. JCR, 153.
22. Ibid., 71–91; Digby Gordon Seymour, *Divided Loyalties: Fort Sanders and the Civil War in East Tennessee* (2nd ed., Knoxville, 1983), 222–23; Whitelaw Reid, *After the War: A Tour of the Southern States, 1865–1866* (Cincinnati and New York, 1866), 351; Trowbridge, *The South*, 238; Fisher, *War at Every Door*, 121; Louis A. Simmons, *The History of the 84th Reg't. Ill. Vols.* (Macomb, Ill., 1866), 247.
23. Simmons, *History of the 84th*, 246–48; Seymour, *Divided Loyalties*, 108–109, 116–19, 152–55, 158–63, 168–70, 174, 178–81, 206–207, 258.
24. Groce, *Mountain Rebels*, 15; Trowbridge, *The South*, 238; John Y. Simon, ed., *The Papers of Ulysses S. Grant*, 18 vols. (Carbondale and Edwardsville, Ill., 1967–91), 14:65n; Melton, "Diary of a Drummer," 322, 328, 332; JCR, 71–78; *Brownlow's Knoxville Whig and Rebel Ventilator*, 14 December 1864, 11, 25 January 1865.
25. *Brownlow's Knoxville Whig*, 14 December 1864, 25 January 1865; Rhoda Williams to Rufus Williams, 15 November 1864, John and Rhoda Campbell Williams Papers, McClung Historical Collection, Knox County Public Library, Knoxville; Fisher, *War at Every Door*, 147; William C. Harris, "The East Tennessee Relief Movement of 1864–1865," *Tennessee Historical Quarterly* 48 (1989): 86–88, 93; William C. Harris, "East Tennessee's Civil War Refugees and the Impact of the War on Civilians," *Journal of East Tennessee History* 64 (1992): 7–9; James B. Campbell, "East Tennessee During the Federal Occupation, 1863–1865," East Tennessee Historical Society's *Publications* 19 (1947): 70–71; Bryan, "Civil War in East Tennessee," 138–40, 145–46.
26. JCR, 153; *Brownlow's Knoxville Whig*, 7 December 1864.
27. Fisher, *War at Every Door*, 130–39; Groce, *Mountain Rebels*, 123–26.
28. JCR, 81–82, 84, 119, 126–28.
29. *Brownlow's Knoxville Whig*, 14 December 1864; LeRoy P. Graf, Ralph W. Haskins, and Paul H. Bergeron, eds., *The Papers of Andrew Johnson*, 16 vols. (Knoxville, 1967–2000), 7:287, 308–309; Harris, "East Tennessee Relief Movement," 88, 94–95; Harris, "East Tennessee's Civil War Refugees," 10, 12.
30. Harris, "East Tennessee Relief Movement," 86–96; Campbell, "East Tennessee During the Federal Occupation," 71–74; Bryan, "Civil War in East Tennessee," 146–47; *Brownlow's Knoxville Whig*, 7 December 1864.
31. E. Merton Coulter, *William G. Brownlow: Fighting Parson of the Southern Highlands* (1937; repr., Knoxville, 1999), passim, esp. 250–56; Stephen V. Ash, ed., *Secessionists and Other Scoundrels: Selections from* Parson Brownlow's Book (Baton Rouge, 1999), 1–8; Bryan, "Civil War in East Tennessee," 121–23; *Brownlow's Knoxville Whig*, 11 January 1865.

32. Coulter, *William G. Brownlow*, 254–61; *Brownlow's Knoxville Whig*, 25 January 1865; Campbell, "East Tennessee During the Federal Occupation," 75–77; Fisher, *War at Every Door*, 165–67.
33. JCR, 105, 115–17; Bryan, "Civil War in East Tennessee," 128.
34. JCR, 182–83, 188, 354; Reid, *After the War*, 352; Trowbridge, *The South*, 239, 284; Bryan, "Civil War in East Tennessee," 300–302.
35. JCR, 83–84.
36. Coulter, *William G. Brownlow*, 92–109, 289–90; John Cimprich, *Slavery's End in Tennessee, 1861–1865* (University, Ala., 1985), 101–102; Bryan, "Civil War in East Tennessee," 324; JCR, 226, 354.
37. Cimprich, *Slavery's End*, 17, 35–45; Bryan, "Civil War in East Tennessee," 323–24; Trowbridge, *The South*, 239; Ira Berlin et al., eds., *The Destruction of Slavery* (Cambridge, Eng., 1985), 262–68.
38. *War of the Rebellion*, Series One, 49(1): 796; Melton, "Diary of a Drummer," 332, 334; Frederick H. Dyer, *A Compendium of the War of the Rebellion*, 3 vols. (New York and London, 1959), 3:1721.
39. Robert Hamilton to S. S. Josselin, 2 April 1865, Alfred Anderson to W. E. Whiting, 25 April 1865, and Samuel Lowery to M. E. Strieby, 10 May 1865, American Missionary Association, Tennessee Records, Amistad Research Center, Dillard University, New Orleans.
40. *Brownlow's Knoxville Whig*, 11 January 1865.
41. JCR, 153; *Brownlow's Knoxville Whig*, 1 February 1865; Melton, "Diary of a Drummer," 333; *War of the Rebellion*, Series One, 49(1): 13–15, 609–10.
42. JCR, 153; Fisher, *War at Every Door*, 70,79.
43. *Brownlow's Knoxville Whig*, 1 March 1865; JCR, 153.
44. JCR, 153; *Tennessee Almanac 1865*.
45. Eighth Census, 1860, Manuscript Returns of Free Inhabitants, Greene County, Tennessee, p. 84/326; Eighth Census, 1860, Manuscript Returns of Productions of Agriculture, Greene County, Tennessee, District 14; Greene County, Tennessee, Deeds, vol. 34, p. 3, Tennessee State Library and Archives, Nashville; Roane County, Tennessee, Deeds, vol. P-1, p. 305, Tennessee State Library and Archives, Nashville; JCR, 8, 134, 135, 139–40, 145.
46. JCR, 154, 170.
47. Ibid., 154–55.
48. Ibid., 156.
49. Ibid., 157.
50. Graf, Haskins, and Bergeron, *Papers of Andrew Johnson*, 7:441–42; *War of the Rebellion*, Series One, 49(1): 47; *Brownlow's Knoxville Whig*, 11, 25 January 1865; JCR, 162; Fisher, *War at Every Door*, 82, 83–84.
51. JCR, 156, 162.

WINTER: SAMUEL AGNEW

1. SAA, 1 January 1865.
2. Ibid.; *War of the Rebellion*, Series One, 39(1): 100, 196, 204, 212.
3. SAA, 6 October, 27, 28 November, 26 December 1863, 18 February, 10 June, 9, 16 July 1864, 1 January 1865; Agnew, "Battle of Tishomingo Creek," 401–402; Agnew, *Historical Sketch*, 14.
4. SAA, 1 January 1865.
5. Ibid.; Phil. 2:23.
6. SAA, 1 January 1865.
7. Ibid., 9–12 June, 21, 23 July, 14 October 1864, 2, 11 February 1865; Agnew, "Battle of Tishomingo Creek," 401–403.

8. SAA, 19 July, 14, 30 September 1864, 7 February 1865.
9. Ibid., 15, 20, 21 December 1864, 5, 6 January 1865; Brown, *History of Tippah County*, 151–52; John K. Bettersworth, *Confederate Mississippi: The People and Policies of a Cotton State in Wartime* (Baton Rouge, 1943), 153–55.
10. SAA, 24, 26 July, 14 October 1864, 1, 2, 11 February 1865; O. Davis to William L. Sharkey, 28 June 1865, Sharkey Letters; *War of the Rebellion*, Series One, 39(1): 100, 189, 49(2): 791; Brown, *History of Tippah County*, 151–52, 154; Tippah County, Mississippi, Minutes of Police Board, November 1864, Mississippi Department of Archives and History, Jackson; Agnew, *Historical Sketch*, 17; Bettersworth, *Confederate Mississippi*, 86, 124–25.
11. SAA, 18 March, 12 May 1864, 8, 13 January 1865; *War of the Rebellion*, Series One, 49(1): 930–31; Bettersworth, *Confederate Mississippi*, 198–200.
12. SAA, 31 August, 7 December 1864, 22 January, 11, 17 February 1865; Tippah County Minutes of Police Board, December 1864; Brown, *History of Tippah County*, 152–53; *War of the Rebellion*, Series One, 49(1): 950, 1011; Bettersworth, *Confederate Mississippi*, 86–88, 150–51, 174–79.
13. *War of the Rebellion*, Series One, 39(1): 100, 157, 189; Tippah County Minutes of Police Board, September, December 1865; SAA, 6, 9, 13 January, 25 February, 25 November 1865.
14. SAA, 2, 5, 6, 8, 9, 12, 13, 14 January 1865; *War of the Rebellion*, Series One, 45(2): 774–75; Thomas Lawrence Connelly, *Autumn of Glory: The Army of Tennessee, 1862–1865* (Baton Rouge, 1971), 512–14.
15. SAA, 16 June 1864, 3, 5, 6, 12 January 1865; *Memphis Bulletin*, 19 February 1865; *War of the Rebellion*, Series One, 45(2): 775, 783.
16. SAA, 21 November 1863, 26 January, 26 June, 28 September, 8 October 1864, 16, 17, 23, 25, 30 January, 9, 18, 28 February 1865; Moore, *Conscription and Conflict*, 243–46, 305–42.
17. Brown, *History of Tippah County*, 153–54; SAA, 30 November 1864.
18. SAA, 13 February 1865; Moore, *Conscription and Conflict*, 342–49; Bettersworth, *Confederate Mississippi*, 170–72.
19. SAA, 16 February 1865.
20. Tippah County Tax Rolls (Personal), 1861; SAA, 29 November, 7 December 1863, 24 July 1864; Agnew, *Historical Sketch*, 12–14, 20; Tippah County Minutes of Police Board, December 1864; Berlin, *Destruction of Slavery*, 249–62, 300; Bettersworth, *Confederate Mississippi*, 163–65, 167.
21. SAA, 3, 8, 25 December 1863, 28 May, 26 December 1864; Bettersworth, *Confederate Mississippi*, 172–73.
22. SAA, 27 January 1865.
23. Ibid.
24. Ibid., 11, 27 January, 17 February 1865; Eighth Census, 1860, Manuscript Returns of Slaves, Tippah County, Mississippi, Southern Subdivision.
25. SAA, 28 January, 14, 15, 27 February 1865.
26. Ibid., 27, 28 January 1865.
27. Ibid., 18 February 1865.
28. Eighth Census, 1860, Manuscript Returns of Productions of Agriculture, Tippah County, Mississippi, Southern Division; Simpson, "Battle of Brice's Crossroads"; SAA, 21 February 1865.
29. SAA, 11 June 1864, 2 January, 15 February, 8 March 1865; Agnew, "Battle of Tishomingo Creek," 402; *War of the Rebellion*, Series One, 39(1): 173; Eighth Census, 1860, Manuscript Returns of Free Inhabitants, Tippah County, Mississippi, p. 43/691.
30. SAA, 18, 19, 20, 30 January, 18, 20, 24, 25, 27, 28 February 1865; Mary Elizabeth Massey, *Ersatz in the Confederacy: Shortages and Substitutes on the Southern Homefront* (1952; repr., Columbia, S.C., 1993), 120–21.

31. SAA, 14, 15 January, 12, 18, 19, 26 February 1865; Agnew, *Historical Sketch*, 23; *Centennial History*, 493–94.
32. SAA, 8, 15, 21 January, 5, 25, 26 February 1865.
33. Ibid., 6 March, 31 July, 2 October 1864, 12, 29 January, 26 February 1865; Agnew, "Battle of Tishomingo Creek," 401–403; Agnew, *Historical Sketch*, passim, esp. 14–16, 18–19, 23; *Centennial History*, 43, 401–403, 415–17.
34. SAA, January-February 1865, passim, esp. 20 January, 10, 22, 26 February.
35. Ibid., January-February 1865, passim.
36. Ibid., 30 January, 2, 6, 9, 11, 14, 15, 20 February 1865; James M. McPherson, *Battle Cry of Freedom: The Civil War Era* (New York and Oxford, 1988), 822–24.
37. SAA, 9 February 1865.

SPRING: SAMUEL AGNEW

1. SAA, 1, 2, 5 March 1865.
2. Ibid., 1 March 1865.
3. Ibid.
4. Ibid., 1, 2, 3 March 1865.
5. Ibid., 4, 5 March 1865; John 10:9.
6. SAA, 6, 7 March 1865.
7. Ibid., 7 March 1865.
8. Ibid., 7, 8 March, 18 June 1865.
9. Ibid., 8, 9 March 1865.
10. Ibid.; *The Official Atlas of the Civil War* (New York and London, 1958), plate 73–3; *War of the Rebellion*, Series One, 39(1): 188.
11. SAA, 9, 10 March 1865.
12. Ibid., 10 March 1865.
13. Ibid., 10, 11, 12 March 1865; *War of the Rebellion*, Series One, 49(1): 75–84; Brown, *History of Tippah County*, 150–51.
14. SAA, 11, 12, 15 March, 21 April 1865.
15. Ibid., 13, 14, 17, 24, 29 March, 1, 3 April 1865.
16. Ibid., 12, 13 March 1865; *War of the Rebellion*, Series One, 49(1): 78, 84; Brown, *History of Tippah County*, 152; William C. Harris, *Presidential Reconstruction in Mississippi* (Baton Rouge, 1967), 8; Bettersworth, *Confederate Mississippi*, 144–45.
17. SAA, 13, 14, 28 March, 3 April 1865.
18. Ibid., 13 March, 12, 13 April 1865; Tippah County Minutes of Police Board, December 1865.
19. SAA, 10, 19, 26 March, 7 May 1865.
20. Ibid., 15, 17, 18 March, 1, 2, 8, 11, 13 April 1865; Moore, *Conscription and Conflict*, 336–39, 350–52; Bettersworth, *Confederate Mississippi*, 202–205, 261–63.
21. SAA, 16 April, 3 May 1865.
22. Ibid., 11, 13 April 1865.
23. Ibid., 4, 17, 19 April 1865.
24. Ibid., 20, 21, 22, 23, 24 April 1865.
25. Ibid., 5, 6, 9 May 1865; *War of the Rebellion*, Series One, 49(2): 619–20, 752, 830–31; Harris, *Presidential Reconstruction in Mississippi*, 16.
26. SAA, 25 April, 8, 10, 11, 12, 13, 15, 17, 18, 19, 22, 24 May 1865; *Centennial History*, 403; Eighth Census, 1860, Manuscript Returns of Free Inhabitants, Oktibbeha County, p. 11.
27. SAA, 8, 10 May 1865.
28. Ibid., 12 May 1865.
29. Ibid., 5, 8, 9, 13, 15, 22, 24 May 1865.

30. Ibid., 7, 14, 27, 30 May 1865; *War of the Rebellion*, Series One, 49(2): 751, 874, 906.
31. SAA, 11 April, 1 May 1865.
32. Ibid., 8, 24, 25 May 1865.
33. Ibid., 28 March, 15, 27, 29 May, 1 June 1865.
34. Ibid., 24, 25, 29 May 1865; James L. Roark, *Masters Without Slaves: Southern Planters in the Civil War and Reconstruction* (New York, 1977), 111, 120, 138, 159–60; Vernon L. Wharton, *The Negro in Mississippi, 1865–1890* (Chapel Hill, 1947), 48–49.
35. SAA, 6, 9, 18, 24, 25, 27, 30 May 1865; Harris, *Presidential Reconstruction in Mississippi*, 3, 16–17, 35; Bettersworth, *Confederate Mississippi*, 59; Tippah County Minutes of Police Board, December 1864, May 1865; Brown, *History of Tippah County*, 151.
36. SAA, 27 May 1865.
37. Ibid., 20 January, 6 August 1864, 22 January, 9, 10, 15, 16, 17, 19, 20, 24 May 1865.
38. Ibid., 21, 22 April, 5, 6, 18, 22, 26, 30, 31 May 1865.

SPRING: JOHN ROBERTSON

1. J. B. Killebrew and J. M. Safford, *Introduction to the Resources of Tennessee* (Nashville, 1874), 597–601; *Agriculture of the United States in 1860*, 136–39; Jack Shelley and Jere Hall, *Valley of Challenge and Change: The History of Roane County, Tennessee, 1860–1900* (Kingston, Tenn., 1986), 1.
2. JCR, 152, 156, 180.
3. Ibid., 157.
4. Ibid., 100–106, 148, 152, 180.
5. Ibid., 158–59.
6. Ibid.
7. Ibid., 162; Eighth Census, 1860, Manuscript Returns of Free Inhabitants, Greene County, Tennessee, p. 84/326; Roane County Deeds, vol. P-1, p. 305.
8. *Brownlow's Knoxville Whig*, 22 March 1865; Bryan, "Civil War in East Tennessee," passim; Fisher, *War at Every Door*, 63, 86, 87–89.
9. *Brownlow's Knoxville Whig*, 25 January, 1 February, 8 March 1865; Graf, Haskins, and Bergeron, *Papers of Andrew Johnson*, 7:4, 441; *War of the Rebellion*, Series One, 49(1): 13–15, 73, 74, 609–10; Shelley and Hall, *Valley of Challenge and Change*, 9; Fisher, *War at Every Door*, 80, 82, 83–84, 153.
10. *Official Records of the Union and Confederate Navies in the War of the Rebellion*, 30 vols. (Washington, 1894–1922), Series One, 27: 87–89; Graf, Haskins, and Bergeron, *Papers of Andrew Johnson*, 7:500; *Brownlow's Knoxville Whig*, 8 March 1865.
11. *Brownlow's Knoxville Whig*, 8 March 1865; *Official Records of the Union and Confederate Navies*, Series One, 11: 795, 27: 87–89; Graf, Haskins, and Bergeron, *Papers of Andrew Johnson*, 7:500.
12. *Official Records of the Union and Confederate Navies*, Series One, 27: 88–89; Graf, Haskins, and Bergeron, *Papers of Andrew Johnson*, 7:500; *Brownlow's Knoxville Whig*, 8 March 1865.
13. *Official Records of the Union and Confederate Navies*, Series One, 27: 86–89; Graf, Haskins, and Bergeron, *Papers of Andrew Johnson*, 7:500.
14. *Official Records of the Union and Confederate Navies*, Series One, 27: 88–89.
15. Ibid., 86–89 (reprinting article from *Chattanooga Gazette*, 2 March 1865); Graf, Haskins, and Bergeron, *Papers of Andrew Johnson*, 7:442, 500; *Brownlow's Knoxville Whig*, 1 February, 8 March 1865; Groce, *Mountain Rebels*, 123–26, 128–31; Fisher, *War at Every Door*, 130–53, 155; Grimsley, *Hard Hand of War*, passim; Stephen V. Ash, *When the Yankees Came: Conflict and Chaos in the Occupied South, 1861–1865* (Chapel Hill and London, 1995), chap. 2.
16. JCR, 12, 79–80, 105, 115–17, 126–28.

17. Ibid., 97–99, 156, 163, 166; Ellen K. Rothman, *Hands and Hearts: A History of Courtship in America* (New York, 1984), 102–14; Sutherland, *Expansion of Everyday Life*, 117.
18. JCR, 134–35, 138, 411.
19. Ibid., 134–35.
20. Ibid., 99, 135–36, 141–44, 154–56, 158; Compiled Civil War Service Records, 43rd Tennessee Infantry (Lt. John W. Robertson); Seventh Census, 1850, Manuscript Returns of Free Inhabitants, Roane County, Tennessee, p. 335, National Archives, Washington; Eighth Census, 1860, Manuscript Returns of Free Inhabitants, Roane County, Tennessee, p. 162/182; Ninth Census, 1870, Manuscript Returns of Inhabitants, Roane County, Tennessee, p. 419, National Archives, Washington; Eighth Census, 1860, Manuscript Returns of Productions of Agriculture, Roane County, Tennessee, District 8; Roane County, Tennessee, County Court Minutes, Book S, pp. 43–44, 57, Tennessee State Library and Archives, Nashville.
21. JCR, 139, 158, 165, 194.
22. Ibid., 53, 136, 155, 159, 163.
23. Ibid., 154, 156, 159, 161, 164.
24. *Brownlow's Knoxville Whig*, 3, 10, 17 May 1865; Graf, Haskins, and Bergeron, *Papers of Andrew Johnson*, 8:78; *War of the Rebellion*, Series One, 49(2): 437; Fisher, *War at Every Door*, 154–56.
25. *Brownlow's Knoxville Whig*, 3 May 1865; William Joseph Fowler, "History of Roane County, Tennessee, 1860–1870" (M.A. thesis, University of Tennessee, 1964), 39–40, 105–107; Shelley and Hall, *Valley of Challenge and Change*, 6, 10; Fisher, *War at Every Door*, 156–57; Bailey, *Class and Tennessee's Confederate Generation*, 106–10.
26. Fowler, "History of Roane County," 11–12, 38–39, 108–109; Shelley and Hall, *Valley of Challenge and Change*, 6, 10–11; Fisher, *War at Every Door*, 156; Groce, *Mountain Rebels*, 128, 131; Richard Nelson Current, *Lincoln's Loyalists: Union Soldiers from the Confederacy* (Boston, 1992), 58–60, 214–15.
27. Coulter, *William G. Brownlow*, 261, 263–64, 267–68; Robert H. White and Stephen V. Ash, eds., *Messages of the Governors of Tennessee*, 10 vols. to date (Nashville, 1952-), 5:394–95, 397–401; Fisher, *War at Every Door*, 165–67; Graf, Haskins, and Bergeron, *Papers of Andrew Johnson*, 8:251.
28. Coulter, *William G. Brownlow*, 262–65, 270–73; *Brownlow's Knoxville Whig*, 17 May 1865; White and Ash, *Messages of the Governors of Tennessee*, 5:395, 439–40; Graf, Haskins, and Bergeron, *Papers of Andrew Johnson*, 8:251.
29. *Brownlow's Knoxville Whig*, 17 May 1865; Graf, Haskins, and Bergeron, *Papers of Andrew Johnson*, 7:4; Shelley and Hall, *Valley of Challenge and Change*, 11; Fisher, *War at Every Door*, 159–63; Groce, *Mountain Rebels*, 135–40.
30. Session minutes, March 1865, Cedar Fork Baptist Church, Philadelphia, Loudon (formerly Roane) County, Records, Tennessee State Library and Archives, Nashville. See also session minutes, October 1865, Shiloh Primitive Baptist Church, Kingston, Roane County, Records, Tennessee State Library and Archives, Nashville.
31. Graf, Haskins, and Bergeron, *Papers of Andrew Johnson*, 8:155, 250; Fisher, *War at Every Door*, 157–59, 163–64; Groce, *Mountain Rebels*, 131–32, 133–35, 147–49; Bailey, *Class and Tennessee's Confederate Generation*, 116–18.
32. JCR 162; Fisher, *War at Every Door*, 157; Bailey, *Class and Tennessee's Confederate Generation*, 117.
33. JCR, 160.
34. Ibid., 155, 162.
35. Ibid., 158, 164.
36. Ibid., 159, 163.

SPRING: CORNELIA MCDONALD

1. CPM, 200–201, 200n; Williams, *Glengarry McDonalds*, 286.
2. CPM, 197n, 204n, 205, 225, 235n, 254–55.
3. Ibid., 254; Compiled Civil War Service Records, 7th Virginia Cavalry.
4. CPM, 250. Edward, age thirty-two in 1865, was one of nine children born to Angus McDonald by his first wife, who died in 1843. See CPM, appendix G.
5. Ibid., 250–51, 251n.
6. Ibid., 225–26, 251; Massey, *Ersatz in the Confederacy*, 106–107.
7. CPM, 251.
8. *Lexington Gazette*, 4 January, 22 February, 31 March 1865; Lee, *Memoirs*, 392; CPM, 250.
9. *Lexington Gazette*, 31 March 1865; CPM, 250.
10. CPM, 248–50, 255; Lee, *Memoirs*, 386–92; J. Tracy Power, *Lee's Miserables: Life in the Army of Northern Virginia from the Wilderness to Appomattox* (Chapel Hill and London, 1998), 217–70, 307–15.
11. Blair, *Virginia's Private War*, 130–31, 150; Faust, *Mothers of Invention*, 238–44; *Lexington Gazette*, 31 March 1865; CPM, 248, 255.
12. CPM, 252; "Maj. E. H. McDonald," *Confederate Veteran* 20 (1912): 530; Driver, *Lexington in the Civil War*, 98.
13. CPM, 252–53; Williams, *Glengarry McDonalds*, 265.
14. CPM, 21, 52–53, 147–48, 252, 253; Williams, *Glengarry McDonalds*, 259–65, 276–77; Marten, *Children's Civil War*, 158–67.
15. CPM, 253.
16. Ibid., 259; Power, *Lee's Miserables*, 272–77.
17. CPM, 252, 259; Williams, *Glengarry McDonalds*, 265; Power, *Lee's Miserables*, 276–77.
18. CPM, 259; Power, *Lee's Miserables*, 278–85; Lee, *Memoirs*, 406.
19. CPM, 258–59; *Lexington Gazette*, 13 April 1865; D. Gardiner Tyler, "Diary for 1865," *Tyler's Quarterly Historical and Genealogical Magazine* 30 (1949): 252; Lee, *Memoirs*, 407; Allan, *Life and Letters*, 207.
20. CPM, 259.
21. Ibid., 259–60, 259n; "Maj. E. H. McDonald," 530; Williams, *Glengarry McDonalds*, 172–73.
22. CPM, 260; *Lexington Gazette*, 13, 20, 27 April 1865; Tyler, "Diary for 1865," 253–54; F. N. Boney, "Virginia," in W. Buck Yearns, ed., *The Confederate Governors* (Athens, Ga., 1985), 230–31; "Letters of John Letcher," 139.
23. *Lexington Gazette*, 13, 20 April 1865; CPM, 257.
24. *Lexington Gazette*, 13 April 1865.
25. Ibid., 13, 20 April, 4, 11 May 1865.
26. Ibid., 4 May 1865; Lee, *Memoirs*, 410; Rockbridge County Court Minute Book, 1, 2 May 1865.
27. Rockbridge County Court Minute Book, 1, 2 May 1865; *Lexington Gazette*, 13 April 1865; Lee, *Memoirs*, 410.
28. Lee, *Memoirs*, 410; Driver, *Lexington in the Civil War*, 99–100.
29. Blair, *Virginia's Private War*, 150; "Letters of John Letcher," 139; *Lexington Gazette*, 27 April 1865.
30. CPM, 257–58; Allan, *Life and Letters*, 207–208.
31. CPM, 247–48, 256–59; Rable, *Civil Wars*, 222–24.
32. CPM, 17–19, 50, 63, 117–18, 120, 122, 134, 138, 153–54, 248, 260.
33. Ibid., 259, 261; William Pendleton to J. G. Paxton, 5 May 1865, Pendleton Papers; *Lexington Gazette*, 11 May 1865.

34. CPM, 258–59; Lee, *Memoirs*, 408n.
35. Lee, *Memoirs*, 408–10, 411, 412; Driver, *Lexington in the Civil War*, 99; CPM, 264.
36. CPM, 257, 259, 505–507.
37. Ibid., 50, 50n, 59–60, 60–61, 76, 82, 83, 117–18, 132, 135–36, 139–40, 140n, 165–66, 261; Williams, *Glengarry McDonalds*, 271, 280.
38. CPM, 261, 264.
39. Ibid., 261.

SPRING: LOUIS HUGHES

1. *War of the Rebellion*, Series One, 49(1): 99, 117, 123, 49(2): 1232; Boatner, *Civil War Dictionary*, 68, 559, 780–81; LH, 167–68; *Clarke County Journal*, 6, 13 April, 25 May 1865; Head, "Salt Works of Clarke County," 17.
2. LH, 167–68, 169.
3. Ibid., 168–69; Head, "Salt Works of Clarke County," 17.
4. LH, 168–69.
5. Ibid., 168, 169.
6. George Rogers Taylor and Irene D. Neu, *The American Railroad Network, 1861–1890* (Cambridge, Mass., 1956), map III; *Official Atlas of the Civil War*, plates 148, 154, 155; John W. Kyle, "Reconstruction in Panola County," Mississippi Historical Society *Publications* 13 (1913): 12.
7. Everard Green Baker Diary, 23 April 1865, Southern Historical Collection, University of North Carolina, Chapel Hill; Kyle, "Reconstruction in Panola County," 10; George P. Rawick, ed., *The American Slave: A Composite Autobiography*, 41 vols. (Westport, Conn., 1972–1979), 11(2): 252; *Agriculture of the United States in 1860*, 85.
8. LH, 122, 139, 150, 169, 181.
9. Ibid., 169.
10. Ibid., 150, 169, 170, 182, 183; McGehee Family Genealogical File; petition of John S. McGehee, 278-M-1864, Letters Received by the Confederate Secretary of War, 1861–1865, M-437, National Archives, Washington; "History of Panola County, Compiled from Reminiscences of Oldest Citizens," unpublished typescript, Mississippi Department of Archives and History, Jackson.
11. Eighth Census, 1860, Manuscript Returns of Slaves, Panola County, Mississippi, p. 32; Eighth Census, 1860, Manuscript Returns of Productions of Agriculture, Panola County, Mississippi, Spring Pool post office, p. 15; *Agriculture of the United States in 1860*, 206, 232; LH, 150, 152, 175.
12. LH, 136, 151–53, 156, 160; Panola County Tax Rolls (Personal), 1864, Mississippi Department of Archives and History, Jackson; F. B. Irby et al. to William Sharkey, 17 July 1865, Sharkey Letters; Rawick, *American Slave*, 9(2): 225–26, 10(1): 60, 8(Suppl., Series One): 1300; Kyle, "Reconstruction in Panola County," 81.
13. LH, 137–38; Bettersworth, *Confederate Mississippi*, 85.
14. Panola County Tax Rolls (Personal), 1861, 1864; John S. McGehee file, Amnesty Papers (Case Files of Applications from Former Confederates for Presidential Pardons, 1865–1867), RG 94, M-1003, National Archives, Washington; petition of John S. McGehee, 278-M-1864, Letters Received by Confederate Secretary of War; Bettersworth, *Confederate Mississippi*, 86. See also receipts for provisions purchased from John S. McGehee, 1862–64, by Confederate quartermaster and commissary officers, in Confederate Papers Relating to Citizens or Business Firms, M-346, National Archives, Washington.
15. Petition of John S. McGehee, 278-M-1864, Letters Received by Confederate Secretary of War; McGehee Family Genealogical File; LH, 117, 148–49, 157, 164.

16. Petition of John S. McGehee, 278-M-1864, Letters Received by Confederate Secretary of War; John S. McGehee file, Amnesty Papers; LH, 156–58.
17. "History of Panola County."
18. LH, 69, 94, 151–52, 155–56, 171.
19. Ibid., 70, 100–101.
20. Ibid., 15, 25–26, 37, 41–42, 62, 63, 136, 153, 155.
21. Panola County Tax Rolls (Personal), 1864; Eighth Census, 1860, Manuscript Returns of Slaves, Panola County, Mississippi, p. 32; petition of John S. McGehee, 278-M-1864, Letters Received by Confederate Secretary of War; LH, 37, 40, 43–44, 173, 174; Panola County Apprentice Bonds and Indentures, 1865–66, pp. 180–205, Mississippi Department of Archives and History, Jackson.
22. LH, 38–39.
23. Ibid., 26–28, 33–34, 35, 39; Baker Diary, 4 February–31 May 1865, passim; John Solomon Otto, *Southern Agriculture During the Civil War Era, 1860–1880* (Westport, Conn., 1994), 13; Sam B. Hilliard, *Hog Meat and Hoecake: Food Supply in the Old South, 1840–1860* (Carbondale, Ill., 1972), 152–53; Sutherland, *Expansion of Everyday Life*, 141–42, 146–47.
24. *Tennessee Almanac 1865*.
25. LH, 173.
26. Panola County Genealogical and Historical Society, *History of Panola County, Mississippi* (n.p., 1987), 119–20; Panola Historical and Genealogical Society, *Cemeteries of Panola County, Mississippi* (n.p., 1994), 125.
27. Panola County Genealogical and Historical Society, *History of Panola County*, 119–20; Rawick, *American Slave*, 11(2): 252.
28. LH, 53–54, 90–91, 147, 174; Albert J. Raboteau, *Slave Religion: The "Invisible Institution" in the Antebellum South* (New York, 1978), passim.
29. Baker Diary, 23 April–31 May 1865, passim.
30. LH, 16–17, 43–44, 96, 169; Fox-Genovese, *Within the Plantation Household*, 148.
31. Eighth Census, 1860, Manuscript Returns of Free Inhabitants, Shelby County, Tennessee, District 14, p. 134; McGehee Family Genealogical File.
32. McGehee Family Genealogical File; Florence Warfield Sillers, et al., comps., *History of Bolivar County, Mississippi* (Jackson, Miss., 1948), 473; LH, 13, 169–70.
33. LH, 18, 19, 39, 40–41, 70–74, 80, 86, 89.
34. Ibid., 94–99.
35. Ibid., 13, 18, 21–22, 42, 46, 50–51, 64, 68, 95, 101–102, 188–89.
36. Ibid., 19–21, 22–25, 45–46, 55–58, 97, 99, 112–13, 189–90.
37. Ibid., 89–90.
38. Ibid., 111–14, 121, 139, 146–47, 168, 172.
39. Ibid., 127–37; Berlin, *Destruction of Slavery*, 300.
40. LH, 46, 139–46; Bettersworth, *Confederate Mississippi*, 160–63.
41. *Population of the United States in 1860*, 270; *Agriculture of the United States in 1860*, 232; Kyle, "Reconstruction in Panola County," 15–16, 16–17, 19, 83; Rawick, *American Slave*, 10(2): 76, 11(2): 255, 7(Suppl., Series One): 628; Benjamin Bedford to Captain Merriweather, 9 June 1863, Benjamin W. Bedford Letterbook, 1853–1867, Tennessee State Library and Archives, Nashville.
42. LH, 154.
43. Ibid., 154–55.
44. Ibid., 139; Rawick, *American Slave*, 11(2): 254, 7(Suppl., Series One): 628–29, 8(Suppl., Series One): 1257; *Memphis Bulletin*, 14 March 1865; Benjamin Bedford to Captain Merriweather, 9 June 1863, Bedford Letterbook.
45. LH, 149–50.

46. Ibid., 150–51.
47. Ibid., 151; Leon F. Litwack, *Been in the Storm So Long: The Aftermath of Slavery* (New York, 1979), 172–74.
48. Ash, *When the Yankees Came*, chap. 5.
49. Benjamin Bedford to E. M. Georges, 11 December 1864, to Thomas Hudson, 20 April 1865, and to H. W. Wall, 10 May 1866, Bedford Letterbook; petition of John S. McGehee, 278-M-1864, Letters Received by Confederate Secretary of War; Rawick, *American Slave*, 10(1): 60, 11(2): 253, 8(Suppl., Series One): 1257; Kyle, "Reconstruction in Panola County," 43, 55.
50. Baker Diary, 10, 31 May 1865; *Memphis Bulletin*, 20 May 1865; General Orders No. 57, 27 May 1865, reprinted in *Weekly Panola (Mississippi) Star*, 8 July 1865; Rawick, *American Slave*, 11(2): 254.
51. LH, 172–74, 180, 181–82, 183–84; Wharton, *Negro in Mississippi*, 47–48; Circular, 24 July 1865, reprinted in *Weekly Panola Star*, 29 July 1865; Compiled Civil War Service Records, Captain Jackson's Company, Tennessee cavalry (Confederate); Roark, *Masters Without Slaves*, 103–104; Litwack, *Been in the Storm So Long*, 179–84.
52. LH, 172–73.
53. Ibid., 169, 172–73.

SUMMER: LOUIS HUGHES

1. Baker Diary, 8, 15, 23 June 1865; *Weekly Panola Star*, 1, 8 July 1865.
2. LH, 172–73; *Weekly Panola Star*, 1, 22, 29 July 1865; Kyle, "Reconstruction in Panola County," 55–56; Wharton, *Negro in Mississippi*, 47–48.
3. General Order No. 3, 1 August 1865, Orders and Circulars, Records of the Assistant Commissioner for the State of Mississippi, Bureau of Refugees, Freedmen, and Abandoned Land, 1865–1869, M-826, National Archives, Washington; Wharton, *Negro in Mississippi*, 48; Litwack, *Been in the Storm So Long*, 183.
4. LH, 173–74.
5. Ibid.
6. LH, 155–56, 174; *Tennessee Almanac 1865*.
7. LH, 174–75.
8. Ibid.
9. Ibid., 167–68, 175.
10. Ibid., 175; *Official Atlas of the Civil War*, plate 154; *Tennessee Almanac 1865*.
11. *Tennessee Almanac 1865;* LH, 175, 177; *Weekly Panola Star*, 1 July 1865; *Memphis Bulletin*, 28 June 1865.
12. LH, 175; *Official Atlas of the Civil War*, plate 154; *Weekly Panola Star*, 1 July 1865; *Memphis Bulletin*, 27 June 1865.
13. LH, 175–76; William Hackley to wife, 26 June 1865, William R. Hackley Letters, Special Collections, University of Tennessee, Knoxville; *Memphis Argus*, 27 June 1865.
14. LH, 176; *Memphis Argus*, 23 July 1865.
15. LH, 109, 176; Reid, *After the War*, 291–92; J. E. Hilary Skinner, *After the Storm; or, Jonathan and His Neighbours in 1865–6*, 2 vols. (London, 1866), 2: 11; Trowbridge, *The South*, 333; Jack D. L. Holmes, "The Underlying Causes of the Memphis Race Riot of 1866," *Tennessee Historical Quarterly* 17 (1958): 206; William Hackley to wife, 6 March 1864, 4, 11 June 1865, Hackley Letters.
16. LH, 59–67, 176.
17. Ibid., 176; *Memphis Argus*, 30 June 1865; *Memphis Bulletin*, 29, 30 June 1865; Ernest W. Hooper, "Memphis, Tennessee: Federal Occupation and Reconstruction, 1862–1870"

(Ph.D. diss., University of North Carolina, 1957), 192; Holmes, "Memphis Race Riot," 198–99.

18. LH, 176–77; Compiled Civil War Service Records, 27th Ohio Infantry.
19. *Memphis Bulletin*, 29 June 1865.
20. Compiled Civil War Service Records, 27th Ohio Infantry and 63rd United States Colored Infantry; Dyer, *Compendium of the War*, 3: 1509; T. A. Walker to Samuel Thomas, 17 June 1865, Letters Received, Records of the Assistant Commissioner for Mississippi; Ira Berlin et al., eds., *The Black Military Experience* (Cambridge, Eng., 1982), 719–20; Bobby Lee Lovett, "Memphis Riots: White Reaction to Blacks in Memphis, May 1865-July 1866," *Tennessee Historical Quarterly* 38 (1979): 10.
21. LH, 177.
22. Ibid., 177–78.
23. Ibid., 177, 178.
24. Ibid., 178; *Memphis Argus*, 2 July 1865.
25. LH, 178.
26. Ibid.
27. Ibid., 178–79.
28. Ibid., 179.
29. Ibid., 179–81.
30. Ibid., 181.
31. Ibid.
32. Ibid., 154, 181, 183–84; Compiled Civil War Service Records, 25th Mississippi Infantry, 1st Battalion Mississippi Sharp Shooters, 1st and 4th Consolidated Missouri Infantry (Confederate), and Captain Jackson's Company, Tennessee cavalry (Confederate); petition of John S. McGehee, 278-M-1864, Letters Received by Confederate Secretary of War; Civil War Centennial Commission, *Tennesseans in the Civil War: A Military History of Confederate and Union Units with Available Rosters of Personnel*, 2 vols. (Nashville, 1964), 1:16–17.
33. LH, 181, 183–84.
34. Ibid., 181.
35. Ibid., 181–82, 183.
36. Ibid., 182, 184.
37. Ibid., 182.
38. Ibid., 182–83, 185, 186.
39. Ibid., 183, 185, 198.
40. *Tennessee Almanac 1865;* LH, 184, 186.
41. LH, 184–85.
42. Ibid., 185–86; *Tennessee Almanac 1865.*
43. LH, 186–87.
44. Ibid., 187; Charles Brown to G. W. McKeag, 4 July 1865, Letters Sent, Records of Post and Defenses of Memphis, ser. 2837, Records of U. S. Army Continental Commands, Pt. 2, No. 181, RG 393, National Archives, Washington.
45. LH, 187, 188, 191.
46. Ibid., 116, 191, 194.
47. Ibid., 108–109; *Memphis Argus*, 18 July, 9 August 1865; Trowbridge, *The South*, 333, 334–35.
48. *Memphis Argus*, 7, 28 July 1865; Skinner, *After the Storm*, 1: 296–97; Trowbridge, *The South*, 334–35.
49. "Statement of Some of the Facts . . . ," n.d. (c. 18 August 1865), Letters Sent by the Office of the Superintendent, Memphis District, vol. 133, Selected Records of the Tennessee Field Office, Bureau of Refugees, Freedmen, and Abandoned Land, 1865–1872,

T-142, National Archives, Washington; Lovett, "Memphis Riots," 9–10, 13; Cimprich, *Slavery's End*, 46–47, 49–50, 55, 109–13; Hooper, "Memphis, Tennessee," 138–42, 149; Joseph H. Parks, "Memphis under Military Rule, 1862 to 1865," East Tennessee Historical Society's *Publications* 14 (1942): 40.

50. *Memphis Bulletin*, 28 June 1865; B. H. Campbell to J. G. Kappner, 31 July 1865, Letters Sent, Records of Post and Defenses of Memphis; T. E. Bliss to Dear Brethren, 23 August 1865, American Missionary Association, Tennessee Records; Berlin, *Black Military Experience*, 719; Lovett, "Memphis Riots," 13; Cimprich, *Slavery's End*, 47; Holmes, "Memphis Race Riot," 203–204; Hooper, "Memphis, Tennessee," 152.
51. *Memphis Argus*, 18, 21 July, 12 August 1865; Davis Tillson to W. T. Clarke, 10 July 1865, Letters Sent by the Office of the Superintendent, Memphis District, vol. 133, Selected Records of the Tennessee Field Office; Holmes, "Memphis Race Riot," 198–99, 204–205, 215–17; Lovett, "Memphis Riots," 10–14.
52. Reid, *After the War*, 291–92; T. E. Bliss to Dear Brethren, 23 August 1865, American Missionary Association, Tennessee Records; William Hackley to wife, 28 May, 4 June 1865, Hackley Letters; Lovett, "Memphis Riots," 10–14; Charles Brown to George Clark, 10 June 1865, and to commander of 156th Illinois Infantry, 8 July 1865, Letters Sent, Records of Post and Defenses of Memphis.
53. Cimprich, *Slavery's End*, 54–55, 77–79; Alrutheus Ambush Taylor, *The Negro in Tennessee, 1865–1880* (1941; repr., Spartanburg, S.C., 1975), 168–70, 205–207, 216–17; Holmes, "Memphis Race Riot," 214–15; Lovett, "Memphis Riots," 11, 13; Edward Wasmuth Diary, 13 April 1865, Southern Historical Collection, University of North Carolina, Chapel Hill.
54. Davis Tillson to Clinton Fisk, 6 July 1865, to W. T. Clarke, 10, 21 July 1865, and to Memphis mayor and aldermen, 21 July 1865, Letters Sent by the Office of the Superintendent, Memphis District, vol. 133, Selected Records of the Tennessee Field Office; *Memphis Argus*, 27, 28 July 1865; Holmes, "Memphis Race Riot," 208–209; Hooper, "Memphis, Tennessee," 143–45.
55. Cimprich, *Slavery's End*, 78–79; C. Stuart McGehee, "E. O. Tade, Freedmen's Education, and the Failure of Reconstruction in Tennessee," *Tennessee Historical Quarterly* 43 (1984): 376–78; Ewing O. Tade to Dear Brethren, 1 August 1865, American Missionary Association, Tennessee Records.
56. Davis Tillson to W. T. Clarke, 10, 21 July, 18 August 1865, and to General Morgan, 26 August 1865, and W. W. Deane to Major Smith, 12 August 1865, Letters Sent by the Office of the Superintendent, Memphis District, vol. 133, Selected Records of the Tennessee Field Office; *Memphis Argus*, 14, 23 July, 1 August 1865; Hooper, "Memphis, Tennessee," 142–43, 149, 152, 155; Lovett, "Memphis Riots," 15–16.
57. LH, 191.
58. Ibid., 91–94, 191–92.
59. Ibid., 183, 187–88.
60. Ibid., 192.
61. Ibid., 192–93.

SUMMER: SAMUEL AGNEW

1. SAA, 4, 17, 21 March, 3, 11, 20, 27, 29 April, 5, 15, 26, 30, 31 May, 1 June 1865; Massey, *Ersatz in the Confederacy*, 121.
2. SAA, 31 May–28 June 1865, passim.
3. Ibid., 1, 8, 16, 20 June, 3 July 1865.
4. Ibid., June 1865, passim, esp. 5, 10, 17 June.

5. O. Davis to William Sharkey, 28 June 1865, Sharkey Letters; *War of the Rebellion*, Series One, 49(2): 1015, 1025; SAA, 11 June 1865.
6. SAA, 11 May, 2, 6, 14, 19, 22, 26 June, 25 November 1865; *War of the Rebellion*, Series One, 49(2): 850–51, 1015; William Hackley to wife, 28 May 1865, Hackley Letters; Otto, *Southern Agriculture*, 51–53.
7. SAA, 7 June 1865; Dan T. Carter, *When the War Was Over: The Failure of Self-Reconstruction in the South* (Baton Rouge and London, 1985), 24–25; Eighth Census, 1860, Manuscript Returns of Free Inhabitants, Tippah County, Mississippi, p. 43/691.
8. Harris, *Presidential Reconstruction in Mississippi*, 42–43, 58; Carter, *When the War Was Over*, 28; SAA, 2, 3, 7, 10, 12, 13, 19, 22, 23 June 1865.
9. SAA, 22 May, 3, 6, 7, 10 June, 30 August 1865.
10. Ibid., 28 March, 6 April, 2, 5, 6, 12, 22 June 1865; Harris, *Presidential Reconstruction in Mississippi*, 79–82.
11. SAA, 3, 9, 12, 22, 25 June 1865; report of Thomas Smith, 3 November 1865, Letters Received, Records of the Assistant Commissioner for Mississippi; Wharton, *Negro in Mississippi*, 58–59; Harris, *Presidential Reconstruction in Mississippi*, 88–89.
12. SAA, 9 June 1865.
13. Ibid.
14. Ibid., 31 March, 4, 21, 25, 26, 29, 30 June, 5 July 1865; *Biographical and Historical Memoirs of Mississippi*, 1: 288.
15. SAA, 14, 21, 28 May, 4, 11 June, 2 July 1865.
16. Ibid., 22 April, 18 June 1865.
17. Ibid., 19, 23, 24 June, 6, 8, 12 July, 14 August 1865; Eighth Census, 1860, Manuscript Returns of Free Inhabitants, Tishomingo County, Mississippi, Carrollville post office, p. 6.
18. SAA, 4, 5, 9, 14 July 1865; Pontotoc County officials to William Sharkey, 17 July 1865, Sharkey Letters; Harris, *Presidential Reconstruction in Mississippi*, 34–35, 68–70.
19. Tippah County Minutes of Police Board, July, August 1865.
20. Kyle, "Reconstruction in Panola County," 56; Harris, *Presidential Reconstruction in Mississippi*, 44; SAA, 15, 16, 17, 18, 26, 27 July 1865.
21. SAA, 7 August 1865.
22. Ibid., 7, 8, 11, 18, 26, 29 August 1865; Harris, *Presidential Reconstruction in Mississippi*, 51–57.
23. SAA, 4, 6, 7, 11, 27 July 1865.
24. Ibid., 17, 18, 28, 29 July 1865; Simpson, "Battle of Brice's Crossroads"; Otto, *Southern Agriculture*, 51.
25. SAA, 28, 29 July 1865.
26. Ibid., 24, 28 July, 4, 11, 21, 22, 30 August 1865.
27. Ibid., 11, 23 June, 4, 5, 6 July, 13 August 1865.
28. Ibid., 4, 5, 19 July 1865.
29. Brown, *History of Tippah County*, 152; SAA, 22, 25 June, 12, 15 July, 6, 30 August 1865; John Watson to William Sharkey, 11 July 1865, Sharkey Letters.
30. SAA, 18, 24, 25, 28 July, 1 August 1865; Carter, *When the War Was Over*, 147–50, 153–56, 164–65.
31. SAA, 3, 22 June, 18, 24, 28, 30 July, 4, 5, 15 August 1865; report of Thomas Smith, 3 November 1865, Letters Received, Records of the Assistant Commissioner for Mississippi; *War of the Rebellion*, Series One, 49(2): 1024; Wharton, *Negro in Mississippi*, 51–52; Carter, *When the War Was Over*, 157–60; Litwack, *Been in the Storm So Long*, chap. 6.
32. SAA, 21 June, 20, 25 July 1865; report of R. S. Donaldson, 4 October 1865, and report of Thomas Smith, 3 November 1865, Letters Received, Records of the Assistant Commissioner for Mississippi; General Order No. 3, 1 August 1865, Orders and Circulars,

Records of the Assistant Commissioner for Mississippi; Wharton, *Negro in Mississippi*, 47–49, 74–76; Harris, *Presidential Reconstruction in Mississippi*, 82–89.

33. General Order No. 3, 1 August 1865, Orders and Circulars, Records of the Assistant Commissioner for Mississippi; *War of the Rebellion*, Series One, 49(2): 1024–25; Wharton, *Negro in Mississippi*, 74–76; Harris, *Presidential Reconstruction in Mississippi*, 93–97; Carter, *When the War Was Over*, 179–83; SAA, 25 July 1865.
34. SAA, 31 July 1865.
35. Ibid., 1, 2 August 1865; O. Davis to William Sharkey, 28 June 1865, Sharkey Letters.
36. SAA, 28 June, 28 July 1865; report of R. S. Donaldson, 4 October 1865, Letters Received, Records of the Assistant Commissioner for Mississippi; Roark, *Masters Without Slaves*, 135–39, 143.
37. SAA, 2 August 1865.
38. Ibid., 30 July, 1, 3, 4, 12, 14, 17, 20, 26 August 1865.
39. Ibid., 9 August, 17 October 1865; John Murray to J. Watson, 23 September 1865, Margaret E. Blackwell Papers, Southern Historical Collection, University of North Carolina, Chapel Hill; Wharton, *Negro in Mississippi*, 58–59; Roark, *Masters Without Slaves*, 141–43; Carter, *When the War Was Over*, 206–11; Litwack, *Been in the Storm So Long*, chaps. 7, 8.
40. SAA, 29 June, 7 July, 6, 8, 9, 10, 24, 25, 28 August 1865; Agnew, *Historical Sketch*, 10.
41. SAA, 13, 22 June, 7, 14 July, 6, 8 August 1865; *Biographical and Historical Memoirs of Mississippi*, 1:288.
42. SAA, 25, 26 May, 1, 8, 10, 11, 17, 24, 29 July 1865; Sutherland, *Expansion of Everyday Life*, 147–48.
43. SAA, 19, 20, 28, 29 August 1865; Academy Baptist Church, Tippah County, Mississippi, Minutes, August 1865, Mississippi Department of Archives and History, Jackson; Hilliard, *Hog Meat and Hoecake*, 153.
44. SAA, 27 August 1865; Acts 16:30–31; Isa. 33:14.
45. SAA, 27 August–1 September 1865.

SUMMER: CORNELIA MCDONALD

1. CPM, 263–64, map facing 324.
2. Ibid., 261, 263–64.
3. Ibid., 261, 264, 267.
4. Ibid., 261–62.
5. Ibid., 262.
6. Rose Pendleton to Dear Friend, 10 June 1865, Pendleton Papers; Cecil Clay to General Curtis, 22 July 1865, and to Newton Bunker, 10 August 1865, Letters Sent, ser. 749, Records of Sub-district of Staunton, Virginia, Records of U.S. Army Continental Commands, Pt. 3, RG 393, National Archives, Washington; Cecil Clay to General Curtis, 4 August 1865, Telegrams Sent, ser. 750, ibid.; Allan, *Life and Letters*, 208; Blair, *Virginia's Private War*, 137.
7. Lee, *Memoirs*, 411, 415; Cecil Clay to Newton Bunker, 28 July 1865, Letters Sent, ser. 749, Records of Sub-district of Staunton.
8. Lee, *Memoirs*, 409, 414; Rose Pendleton to Dear Friend, 5 June 1865, Pendleton Papers.
9. CPM, 262; Lee, *Memoirs*, 422; Allan, *Life and Letters*, 208; Blair, *Virginia's Private War*, 134–36, 139.
10. CPM, 43, 45–48, 50, 58–59, 60, 62–63, 75, 167–68; Faust, *Mothers of Invention*, 200.
11. Cecil Clay to E. W. Smith, 28 August 1865, and to George Hicks, 30 September 1865, 14 October 1865, Letters Sent, ser. 749, Records of Sub-district of Staunton.

12. Cecil Clay to Lieutenant Colonel Smith, 18 September 1865, and to Newton Bunker, 10 August 1865, ibid.; *Lexington Gazette*, 23 August 1865; Driver, *Lexington in the Civil War*, 100; Blair, *Virginia's Private War*, 137–39.
13. *Lexington Gazette*, 2 August 1865.
14. Lee, *Memoirs*, 413–16, 419–21.
15. William Pendleton to Colonel Stuart, 10 July 1865, Pendleton Papers.
16. William Pendleton to commander of federal troops in Lexington, 14 July 1865, ibid.; Lee, *Memoirs*, 423.
17. Ann Pendleton to daughter, 18 July 1865, Pendleton Papers.
18. Lee, *Memoirs*, 422; Ann Pendleton to daughter, 18 July 1865, and William Pendleton to Dear General, 28 July 1865, Pendleton Papers.
19. Ann Pendleton to daughter, 18 July 1865, William Pendleton to lieutenant colonel commanding federal troops in Lexington, 16 July 1865, and William Pendleton to Dear General, 28 July 1865, Pendleton Papers; Lee, *Memoirs*, 422–23.
20. Ann Pendleton to daughter, 18 July 1865, Mary Pendleton to unknown correspondent, 24 July 1865, and William Pendleton to Dear General, 28 July 1865, Pendleton Papers; Lee, *Memoirs*, 421, 424n.
21. Lee, *Memoirs*, 412, 422; William Pendleton to Dear General, 28 July 1865, Pendleton Papers.
22. General Orders No. 1, 1 August 1865, Pendleton Papers; Lee, *Memoirs*, 423–24.
23. Lee, *Memoirs*, 422, 423; Robert Redmond to Captain McMurry, 7 November 1865, Letters Sent, ser. 749, Records of Sub-district of Staunton.
24. CPM, 264, 265.
25. Ibid., 239; Drew Gilpin Faust, "The Civil War Soldier and the Art of Dying," *Journal of Southern History* 67 (2001): 3–38.
26. CPM, 5–6, 183–84, 277, 289, 352; Compiled Civil War Service Records, 7th Virginia Cavalry; *Report of Col. A. W. McDonald, Relative to His Mission to England*, document xxxix, *Virginia General Assembly Documents* (Richmond, 1861), 5; Avirett, *Memoirs*, 331, 345–46, 349; Williams, *Glengarry McDonalds*, 263, 269.
27. CPM, 34–37, 197–98, 277, 340–47, 356; Avirett, *Memoirs*, 318–46; Compiled Civil War Service Records, 7th Virginia Cavalry; Haskell M. Monroe Jr., James T. McIntosh, and Lynda Lasswell Crist, eds., *The Papers of Jefferson Davis*, 10 vols. to date (Baton Rouge and London, 1971-), 7: 365.
28. CPM, 201–203, 210, 212, 277–78; Avirett, *Memoirs*, 346.
29. CPM, 210, 278.
30. Ibid., 209–11, 278.
31. Ibid., 211, 278; Cecil D. Eby Jr., ed., *A Virginia Yankee in the Civil War: The Diaries of David Hunter Strother* (Chapel Hill, 1961), 260–61.
32. CPM, 212–24, 226–32, 233–34, 236–37, 278–84, 289–91; Compiled Civil War Service Records, 7th Virginia Cavalry; *Richmond Whig*, 3 December 1864; Avirett, *Memoirs*, 337–38, 356–59; *Lexington Gazette*, 7 December 1864; Williams, *Glengarry McDonalds*, 96–98, 155–57, 264–65.
33. CPM, 209–10, 211–12.
34. Ibid., 83, 106, 184, 188, 209, 232, 265, 266–67.
35. Ibid., 264, 266, 267, 271.
36. Ibid., 195n, 265.
37. Ibid., 265, 265n.
38. Ibid., 265–66.
39. Ibid.
40. Ibid., 268.

41. Ibid., 266–67.
42. Ibid., 267.
43. Ibid., 267–68.
44. Ibid., 268.
45. Ibid.

SUMMER: JOHN ROBERTSON

1. Melton, "Diary of a Drummer," 345; JCR, 130, 162.
2. JCR, 162; *Tennessee Almanac 1865;* F. D. Srygley, *Seventy Years in Dixie* (Nashville, 1891), 162–63; Sutherland, *Expansion of Everyday Life*, 141–42.
3. JCR, 158; Roane County Deeds, vol. P-1, p. 305.
4. JCR, 162; Srygley, *Seventy Years in Dixie*, 166–70; Bailey, *Class and Tennessee's Confederate Generation*, 27; Winters, *Tennessee Farming*, 120, 157; Eighth Census, 1860, Manuscript Returns of Productions of Agriculture, Greene County, Tennessee, District 17.
5. JCR, 162–63.
6. Ibid., 163; Lewis C. Gray, *History of Agriculture in the Southern United States to 1860*, 2 vols. (Washington, 1933), 2:818.
7. JCR, 160, 167.
8. Ibid., 167.
9. Graf, Haskins, and Bergeron, *Papers of Andrew Johnson*, 9: 10–11, 69, 215–16; Trowbridge, *The South*, 239–40; Bailey, *Class and Tennessee's Confederate Generation*, 116–18; Fisher, *War at Every Door*, 156–65; Groce, *Mountain Rebels*, 131–35, 147–51.
10. Fisher, *War at Every Door*, 167; Coulter, *William G. Brownlow*, 268–80.
11. Coulter, *William G. Brownlow*, 268–69; Groce, *Mountain Rebels*, 136; White and Ash, *Messages of the Governors of Tennessee*, 5: 436–38, 442–48.
12. JCR, 97.
13. Coulter, *William G. Brownlow*, 294–96; Campbell, "East Tennessee During the Federal Occupation," 78.
14. Coulter, *William G. Brownlow*, 296–301; Fisher, *War at Every Door*, 85–86; Campbell, "East Tennessee During the Federal Occupation," 78–80; *Brownlow's Knoxville Whig*, 24, 31 May, 14 June 1865; *Journal of the Twenty-Second Session of the Holston Annual Conference of the Methodist Episcopal Church . . . Athens, Tennessee, June 1–5, 1865* (Knoxville, n.d.), 15–21.
15. JCR, 159, 163–64.
16. Ibid., 164–65.
17. Ibid.
18. Ibid., 165.
19. Ibid., 165–66; Roane County Deeds, vol. P-1, p. 305.
20. JCR, 166.
21. Ibid.
22. Ibid.
23. Ibid., 41–49, 99, 167, 179; Eighth Census, 1860, Manuscript Returns of Free Inhabitants, Greene County, Tennessee, p. 58/361.
24. JCR, 97–99, 113, 162; Bailey, *Class and Tennessee's Confederate Generation*, 46–49; Sutherland, *Expansion of Everyday Life*, 97–98.
25. JCR, 167–68.
26. Ibid., 168; Bailey, *Class and Tennessee's Confederate Generation*, 47–48; Sutherland, *Expansion of Everyday Life*, 98–102.
27. JCR, 168.
28. Ibid.

29. Ibid., 10–22.
30. Ibid., 168.
31. Ibid.
32. Ibid., 168–69.
33. Ibid., 169.
34. Ibid.
35. Ibid.
36. Ibid., 169–70.
37. Ibid., 170.
38. Ibid., 170–71.
39. Ibid., 171.
40. Ibid.
41. Ibid., 171–72.
42. Ibid.
43. Ibid., 172.
44. Ibid.
45. Ibid.
46. Ibid.
47. Ibid., 172, 173, 178, 194.
48. Ibid., 172–73.

FALL: JOHN ROBERTSON

1. JCR, 173.
2. Ibid.; Graf, Haskins, and Bergeron, *Papers of Andrew Johnson*, 9:41, 69, 215–16; Shelley and Hall, *Valley of Challenge and Change*, 10–11.
3. JCR, 173, 238.
4. Ibid., 92, 181.
5. Ibid., 1, 99, 173, 178.
6. Ibid., 174, 178.
7. Ibid., 178.
8. Ibid., 179.
9. Ibid., 179–80; Eighth Census, 1860, Manuscript Returns of Free Inhabitants, Greene County, Tennessee, p. 58/361.
10. JCR, 180–81.
11. Ibid., 181, 184; Robert C. Black III, *The Railroads of the Confederacy* (Chapel Hill, 1952), 18, 21, 23; William H. Clark, *Railroads and Rivers: The Story of Inland Transportation* (Boston, 1939), 134–35; Sarah H. Gordon, *Passage to Union: How the Railroads Transformed American Life, 1829–1929* (Chicago, 1996), 79, 80.
12. JCR, 139–40, 182.
13. Ibid., 182, 183; Gordon, *Passage to Union*, 79, 80–82; *Tennessee Almanac 1865*.
14. JCR, 182.
15. Ibid.; *Official Atlas of the Civil War*, plate 149; *Brownlow's Knoxville Whig*, 6 September 1865; Trowbridge, *The South*, 248–54; McGehee, "E. O. Tade," 376–77; James A. Hoobler, *Cities Under the Gun: Images of Occupied Nashville and Chattanooga* (Nashville, 1986), 115–206.
16. JCR, 182; *Brownlow's Knoxville Whig*, 6 September 1865.
17. JCR, 182.
18. Ibid., 182–83, 184; *Brownlow's Knoxville Whig*, 13 September 1865.
19. JCR, 183; *Official Atlas of the Civil War*, plate 149; Melton, "Diary of a Drummer," 321–22.

20. JCR, 183–85; Trowbridge, *The South*, 270; *Official Atlas of the Civil War*, plate 149; Melton, "Diary of a Drummer," 322.
21. JCR, 185; Trowbridge, *The South*, 273; Stephen V. Ash, *Middle Tennessee Society Transformed, 1860–1870: War and Peace in the Upper South* (Baton Rouge and London, 1988), passim, esp. chaps. 1, 5.
22. JCR, 185; Trowbridge, *The South*, 273, 275, 279; *Official Atlas of the Civil War*, plate 112.
23. JCR, 185–86; Trowbridge, *The South*, 276–78.
24. JCR, 186; *Brownlow's Knoxville Whig*, 6 September 1865; *Nashville Dispatch*, 20, 21 September 1865; Gordon, *Passage to Union*, 99–100.
25. JCR, 186; Hoobler, *Cities Under the Gun*, 17–112; Walter T. Durham, *Nashville, the Occupied City: The First Seventeen Months—February 16, 1862 to June 30, 1863* (Nashville, 1985), passim, esp. 184–85; Walter T. Durham, *Reluctant Partners: Nashville and the Union, July 1, 1863 to June 30, 1865* (Nashville, 1987), passim, esp. 114, 296–97; *Nashville Dispatch*, 20 September 1865; *Nashville Daily Press and Times*, 19 September 1865; Trowbridge, *The South*, 287.
26. JCR, 186–87; Trowbridge, *The South*, 281; Hoobler, *Cities Under the Gun*, 29–40.
27. JCR, 187; *Nashville Dispatch*, 21 September 1865; Gordon, *Passage to Union*, 88–89; *Nashville Daily Press and Times*, 19 September 1865.
28. JCR, 187–88; *Tennessee Almanac 1865*.
29. JCR, 188–89; Gordon, *Passage to Union*, 84–85, 97.
30. JCR, 189.
31. Ibid.
32. Ibid., 189–90.
33. Ibid., 190.
34. Ibid.
35. Ibid., 191.
36. Ibid., 191–92; *Tennessee Almanac 1865*.
37. JCR, 193.
38. Ibid., 193–99.
39. Ibid., 199.
40. Ibid., 200–202.
41. Ibid., 202–203, 209, 233, 237.
42. Ibid., 203–208, 210–22.
43. Ibid., 209, 234–36.
44. Ibid., 202, 204, 298.
45. Ibid., 201, 291.
46. Ibid., 292–93.
47. Ibid., 291–92.
48. Ibid., 294.
49. Ibid., 130, 132–34, 294.
50. Ibid., 203, 233, 237.
51. Ibid., 237.
52. Ibid., 194, 298.
53. Ibid., 239.

FALL: CORNELIA MCDONALD

1. Special Order No. 1, 9 September 1865, Letters Sent and Orders Issued, ser. 4044, Records of Assistant Sub-assistant Commissioner, Lexington, Virginia, Bureau of Refugees, Freedmen, and Abandoned Land, RG 105, National Archives, Washington.

2. Compiled Civil War Service Records, 58th Pennsylvania Infantry; pension record of Christopher J. Tubbs, 58th Pennsylvania Infantry, Civil War Pension Files, RG 15, National Archives, Washington; Dyer, *Compendium of the War*, 3:1594.
3. C. Jerome Tubbs to W. Storer How, 30 October 1865, Letters Sent and Orders Issued, ser. 4044, Records of Assistant Sub-assistant Commissioner, Lexington.
4. Special Order No. 2, 9 September 1865, ibid.; CPM, 262.
5. Robert Redmond to Captain McMurry, 7 November 1865, Letters Sent, ser. 749, Records of Sub-district of Staunton; CPM, 262.
6. CPM, 262–63.
7. Ibid., 263; Compiled Civil War Service Records, 58th Pennsylvania Infantry.
8. Cases 22, 87, and 89, Letters Sent and Orders Issued, ser. 4044, Records of Assistant Sub-assistant Commissioner, Lexington. See also cases 24, 65, 72, and 112, ibid.
9. Cases 10, 32, and 50, and C. Jerome Tubbs to W. S. How, 30 November 1865, ibid.; Rockbridge County Court Minute Book, October 1865.
10. Cases 20 and 43, Letters Sent and Orders Issued, ser. 4044, Records of Assistant Sub-assistant Commissioner, Lexington. See also cases 14, 18, 21, and 45, ibid.
11. Cases 15 and 19, ibid. See also case 70 and Circular, 18 September 1865, ibid.
12. Cecil Clay to George Hicks, 30 September, 14, 24 October 1865, and Robert Redmond to Captain McMurry, 7 November 1865, Letters Sent, ser. 749, Records of Sub-district of Staunton.
13. Ann Pendleton to daughter, 9 October 1865, Pendleton Papers; Robert Redmond to Captain McMurry, 7 November 1865, Letters Sent, ser. 749, Records of Sub-district of Staunton; Lee, *Memoirs*, 424, 424n.
14. Charles Bracelen Flood, *Lee: The Last Years* (Boston and New York, 1998), 89–95; CPM, 268–69.
15. Douglas Southall Freeman, *R. E. Lee: A Biography*, 4 vols. (New York, 1934–35), 4: 222–23; Flood, *Lee: The Last Years*, 78–79, 115; Lee, *Memoirs*, 426; Driver, *Lexington in the Civil War*, 72.
16. Freeman, *R. E. Lee*, 4:188–215, 221–22; Flood, *Lee: The Last Years*, 79–80.
17. Freeman, *R. E. Lee*, 4:216; Flood, *Lee: The Last Years*, 83.
18. Freeman, *R. E. Lee*, 4:215–18, 226–27; Flood, *Lee: The Last Years*, 81–84, 88–93; *Lexington Gazette*, 20 September 1865.
19. CPM, 269; Freeman, *R. E. Lee*, 4:227–29, 230; Flood, *Lee: The Last Years*, 94–95, 96.
20. Freeman, *R. E. Lee*, 4:229–30; Flood, *Lee: The Last Years*, 98–99, 105.
21. Freeman, *R. E. Lee*, 4:218, 219–21; Flood, *Lee: The Last Years*, 87–88, 93, 98–99, 102, 110. For a somewhat different interpretation of Lee's postwar political sentiments, see Michael Fellman, "Robert E. Lee, Postwar Southern Nationalist," *Civil War History* 46 (2000): 185–204.
22. Freeman, *R. E. Lee*, 4:233, 246; Flood, *Lee: The Last Years*, 94, 103, 112–13; Driver, *Lexington in the Civil War*, 72; Allan, *Life and Letters*, 212; *Lexington Gazette*, 25 October 1865; Lee, *Memoirs*, 426–27.
23. CPM, 150n, 233, 269; Driver, *Lexington in the Civil War*, 101.
24. CPM, 267, 268, 269–70.
25. Ibid., 270.
26. Ibid., 221, 270, map facing 324; *Lexington Gazette*, 27 September, 11 October 1865; Driver, *Lexington in the Civil War*, 66.
27. CPM, 233, 244, 270; Lee, *Memoirs*, 368–73; *Lexington Gazette*, 26 October 1864; Driver, *Lexington in the Civil War*, 82.
28. CPM, 270; Lee, *Memoirs*, 423.
29. CPM, 270.

30. Ibid.
31. Ibid., 270–71.
32. Ibid., 265, 270–71.
33. Ibid., 259n, 271, 271n; Lee, *Memoirs*, 427; Ann Pendleton to daughter, 9 October 1865, Pendleton Papers; Williams, *Glengarry McDonalds*, 275, 287.
34. CPM, 269; *Lexington Gazette*, 6 December 1865; Freeman, *R. E. Lee*, 4:241–42.
35. Ann Pendleton to daughter, 5 December 1865, Pendleton Papers; Cecil Clay to Joseph Johnson, 1 December 1865, to Henry Robinson, 15 December 1865, and to William Pendleton, 17 December 1865, Letters Sent, ser. 749, Records of Sub-district of Staunton.
36. "Report of Freedmen's Schools in Operation," December 1865, and monthly report, December 1865, Letters Sent and Orders Issued, ser. 4044, Records of Assistant Sub-assistant Commissioner, Lexington; *Lexington Gazette*, 20 December 1865; Freeman, *R. E. Lee*, 4:345–46.
37. *Lexington Gazette*, 20 December 1865; note written by Mary Pendleton in Ann Pendleton to daughter, 12 December 1865, Pendleton Papers; Litwack, *Been in the Storm So Long*, 485–87.
38. "Report of Freedmen's Schools in Operation," December 1865, Letters Sent and Orders Issued, ser. 4044, Records of Assistant Sub-assistant Commissioner, Lexington; Flood, *Lee: The Last Years*, 98; Freeman, *R. E. Lee*, 4:354–55; Robert C. Morris, *Reading, 'Riting, and Reconstruction: The Education of Freedmen in the South, 1861–1870* (Chicago and London, 1981), 230–31.
39. CPM, 44–45, 90–91, 267, 268, 269, 271.

FALL: LOUIS HUGHES

1. LH, 92–93, 96–97, 192–94.
2. Ibid., 195; *Cincinnati Daily Commercial*, 7 September 1865; *Cincinnati Daily Enquirer*, 15 September 1865; *Cincinnati Daily Gazette*, 5 September 1865.
3. *Statistics of the Population (1870)*, 231; *Cincinnati Daily Commercial*, 14, 18, 28 August 1865; Sutherland, *Expansion of Everyday Life*, 178; Oscar E. Anderson Jr., ed., "Harvey W. Wiley Spends the Christmas Holidays in the Miami Valley, 1865–1866," *Historical and Philosophical Society of Ohio Bulletin* 12 (1954): 213; *Cincinnati Daily Enquirer*, 20 September, 11 October 1865; *Cincinnati Daily Gazette*, 11, 14, 15 September, 7, 9, 19 October 1865; Joe William Trotter Jr., *River Jordan: African American Urban Life in the Ohio Valley* (Lexington, Ky., 1998), 11.
4. *Cincinnati Daily Commercial*, 21 August, 21 September 1865; *Cincinnati Daily Enquirer*, 26 August, 7, 14 September 1865; Sutherland, *Expansion of Everyday Life*, 216–18.
5. Steven J. Ross, *Workers on the Edge: Work, Leisure, and Politics in Industrializing Cincinnati, 1788–1890* (New York, 1985), 215; *Cincinnati Daily Enquirer*, 31 August 1865.
6. Ross, *Workers on the Edge*, 72; Trotter, *River Jordan*, 17, 19.
7. Trotter, *River Jordan*, 20–21; Ross, *Workers on the Edge*, 196.
8. *Cincinnati Daily Commercial*, 19 August, 11, 15 September 1865; *Cincinnati Daily Enquirer*, 25 August, 17 October 1865; *Cincinnati Daily Gazette*, 11 September, 4 October 1865.
9. *Cincinnati Daily Enquirer*, 15, 20 September, 11 October 1865; *Cincinnati Daily Gazette*, 10, 13 October 1865; *Cincinnati Daily Commercial*, 31 August, 16 September 1865; Trotter, *River Jordan*, 31.
10. *Cincinnati Daily Gazette*, 1, 13 September 1865; Henry A. Ford and Kate B. Ford, comps., *History of Cincinnati, Ohio, with Illustrations and Biographical Sketches* (Cleveland, 1881), 106; Ross, *Workers on the Edge*, 194–95; Trotter, *River Jordan*, 11, 14; *Cincinnati Daily Enquirer*, 16, 17, 22, 24 August 1865.

11. Trotter, *River Jordan*, 11–14; Ford and Ford, *History of Cincinnati*, 106, 107, 109–10; Ross, *Workers on the Edge*, 195; *Cincinnati Daily Enquirer*, 22 August 1865.
12. *Cincinnati Daily Enquirer*, 14, 15, 17, 22, 23, 28, 31 August, 12, 15, 23 September, 3, 17 October 1865.
13. *Cincinnati Daily Gazette*, 1 September 1865.
14. *Cincinnati Daily Commercial*, 16, 25 September 1865.
15. Ross, *Workers on the Edge*, 193, 195–97; *Cincinnati Daily Commercial*, 23 August, 13 September 1865; *Cincinnati Daily Gazette*, 13 October 1865.
16. Ross, *Workers on the Edge*, 193, 199, 206–207; Trotter, *River Jordan*, 17–19; Sutherland, *Expansion of Everyday Life*, 159; Eric Foner, *Reconstruction: America's Unfinished Revolution, 1863–1877* (New York, 1988), 460, 475–78.
17. *Cincinnati Daily Gazette*, 7, 8, 11, 22 September, 2 October 1865; *Cincinnati Daily Commercial*, 21 August 1865; Ross, *Workers on the Edge*, 195–97, 198–201; Foner, *Reconstruction*, 477–79.
18. Ross, *Workers on the Edge*, 198–99, 211–13; Trotter, *River Jordan*, 18, 19–20, 22–23; Foner, *Reconstruction*, 479–80.
19. Ross, *Workers on the Edge*, 72, 195; Trotter, *River Jordan*, 24–37, 41–42, 55–56; Foner, *Reconstruction*, 471–72; *Cincinnati Daily Enquirer*, 14, 21, 22, 23 August, 8 September, 11 October 1865; *Cincinnati Daily Commercial*, 4, 16 September 1865.
20. *Cincinnati Daily Enquirer*, 11 October 1865; Trotter, *River Jordan*, 47–48; *Cincinnati Daily Commercial*, 14 August 1865; *Cincinnati Daily Gazette*, 27 September, 16 October 1865.
21. *Cincinnati Daily Commercial*, 8, 9 September 1865; *Cincinnati Daily Gazette*, 9 September 1865; Litwack, *Been in the Storm So Long*, 77.
22. LH, 195.
23. Ibid.; Ford and Ford, *History of Cincinnati*, 104.
24. *Statistics of the Population (1870)*, 228; *Hamilton (Ohio) True Telegraph*, 19 October 1865.
25. LH, 195.
26. *Hamilton True Telegraph*, 19, 26 October, 2, 9, 30 November, 7 December 1865.
27. *Statistics of the Population (1870)*, 228; *Hamilton True Telegraph*, 5, 12, 19, 26 October, 16 November 1865.
28. LH, 80, 100–106, 195; Robin W. Winks, *The Blacks in Canada: A History* (Montreal and Kingston, 1997), chap. 8.
29. Winks, *Blacks in Canada*, 231–32; LH, 195.
30. *Hamilton True Telegraph*, 23 November, 14, 21 December 1865.
31. LH, 195; *Hamilton True Telegraph*, 21 December 1865.

FALL: SAMUEL AGNEW

1. SAA, 1, 2, 3 September 1865.
2. Ibid., 4, 5, 6, 16 September 1865.
3. Ibid., 9 September 1865.
4. Ibid., 9–15 September 1865.
5. Ibid., 10, 12, 13, 14, 19 September 1865.
6. Ibid., 8, 11 September 1865; Agnew, *Historical Sketch*, 10, 32.
7. SAA, 16, 17, 27, 28, 29 September, 1 October 1865.
8. Ibid., 1 October 1865.
9. Ibid., 20 September, 1–5 October 1865.
10. Ibid., 1, 2 October 1865.
11. Ibid., 1, 3, 8, 15, 19, 25 September 1865; Harris, *Presidential Reconstruction in Mississippi*, 104–109.

12. SAA, 5, 6, 9, 11, 14, 30 October, 3 November 1865; Harris, *Presidential Reconstruction in Mississippi*, 106, 116.
13. SAA, 17 November 1865; Harris, *Presidential Reconstruction in Mississippi*, 106, 109–16; Roark, *Masters Without Slaves*, 182–83.
14. SAA, 4–6 July, 25 August 1864, 4 October 1865.
15. Ibid., 10 October 1865.
16. Ibid., 11 October 1865.
17. Ibid., 25 June 1864, 10 February, 12 October 1865; Agnew, "Battle of Tishomingo Creek," 402–403.
18. SAA, 12 October 1865.
19. Ibid.
20. Ibid., 12 June 1864, 12, 13 October 1865.
21. Ibid., 20, 29 September, 17 October 1865; Otto, *Southern Agriculture*, 30–32, 54–55; Eighth Census, 1860, Manuscript Returns of Productions of Agriculture, Tippah County, Mississippi, Southern Division.
22. SAA, 17 October 1865; Gray, *History of Agriculture*, 2:702.
23. SAA, 18, 19, 25, 31 October 1865.
24. Ibid., 20, 27 August, 1 September, 21 October, 30 December 1865; Gray, *History of Agriculture*, 2:814–15; Hilliard, *Hog Meat and Hoecake*, 154.
25. SAA, 9, 11 November, 2, 5, 6 December 1865; Otto, *Southern Agriculture*, 55–56.
26. SAA, 4, 11, 27, 28 November 1865; Carter, *When the War Was Over*, 207–208; Roark, *Masters Without Slaves*, 141–42.
27. SAA, 3 November, 8, 9, 15 December 1865.
28. Ibid., 29 May, 30 October, 8, 11, 25, 28 November, 5, 6, 15 December 1865.
29. Ibid., 19, 21, 25 September, 11 October, 2, 17, 19 November, 4, 20 December 1865; Wharton, *Negro in Mississippi*, 58–59; Harris, *Presidential Reconstruction in Mississippi*, 70–71, 89, 97; John Watson to Benjamin Humphreys, 29 November 1865, Governor Benjamin G. Humphreys Correspondence, Mississippi Department of Archives and History, Jackson; Berlin, *Black Military Experience*, 747–49; Carter, *When the War Was Over*, 197–98.
30. SAA, 11 October, 3, 4, 5 November 1865; Joel Berry to F. Wolfe, 1 November 1865, Joel H. Berry Letter, Mississippi Department of Archives and History, Jackson; report of Thomas Smith, 3 November 1865, and report of R. S. Donaldson, 6 November 1865, Letters Received, Records of the Assistant Commissioner for Mississippi; Harris, *Presidential Reconstruction in Mississippi*, 89–90.
31. SAA, 3, 14 November 1865; Harris, *Presidential Reconstruction in Mississippi*, 89–91; Wharton, *Negro in Mississippi*, 218; Carter, *When the War Was Over*, 194; Trowbridge, *The South*, 342.
32. SAA, 3 November 1865; Carter, *When the War Was Over*, 191–92, 195–97.
33. SAA, 21, 22, 24 November 1865.
34. Ibid., 21, 22, 24 November, 2 December 1865.
35. Ibid., 24 November 1865.
36. Ibid., 24, 26, 28 November 1865.
37. Ibid., 26 November 1865.
38. Harris, *Presidential Reconstruction in Mississippi*, 104 and passim.
39. SAA, 3 November 1865; Harris, *Presidential Reconstruction in Mississippi*, 117–18, 121–23; Carter, *When the War Was Over*, 215–26, 231; Roark, *Masters Without Slaves*, 182–85; Foner, *Reconstruction*, 176–84, 239–40.
40. Harris, *Presidential Reconstruction in Mississippi*, 99, 121–40; Wharton, *Negro in Mississippi*, 84–89.

41. SAA, 20, 29, 30, 31 October, 14, 16, 30 November 1865; Harris, *Presidential Reconstruction in Mississippi*, 87–89, 92, 96, 99–100, 129–30, 131, 147; Wharton, *Negro in Mississippi*, 58–59, 117.
42. SAA, 18 October, 2, 4, 11 November, 6, 8, 13, 15 December 1865.
43. Ibid., 9, 24, 30 October, 6, 12, 21, 29 November, 6, 9, 14, 19, 20, 22, 24, 27, 29 December 1865; Ash, *When the Yankees Came*, 178–80, 234–35.
44. SAA, 10, 22 October, 15, 20, 22, 23 November, 14 December 1865; *Tennessee Almanac 1865*.
45. SAA, 24 November 1865.
46. Ibid., 11 October, 8, 16, 17, 19, 21, 23, 24, 27 November 1865; Gray, *History of Agriculture*, 2:703–705.
47. SAA, 20 October, 2, 13, 14, 27, 28 November, 4, 6 December 1865.
48. Ibid., 8, 13, 14, 16 December 1865.
49. Ibid., 21, 22 December 1865.
50. Ibid., 3 November, 5–8, 15, 27 December 1865.
51. Ibid., 19 December 1865; Foner, *Reconstruction*, 228–47.
52. Harris, *Presidential Reconstruction in Mississippi*, 140, 141, 152; Carter, *When the War Was Over*, 191–202, 217, 226–31; Foner, *Reconstruction*, 216–27.
53. SAA, 25 December 1863, 26 December 1864, 22, 25 December 1865; Roark, *Masters Without Slaves*, 143–47, 196–203.
54. SAA, 19, 26–29 December 1865.
55. Ibid., 26–31 December 1865.
56. Ibid., 7, 9, 14, 15, 16, 19, 21, 26, 29, 30 December 1865.
57. Ibid., 31 December 1865.
58. Ibid.; Ray A. King, *A History of the Associate Reformed Presbyterian Church* (Charlotte, 1966), 44, 99, 112.
59. SAA, 31 December 1865.

EPILOGUE

1. *Biographical and Historical Memoirs of Mississippi*, 1: 288; *Centennial History*, 42–44, 416; Agnew, "Battle of Tishomingo Creek," 401–403.
2. SAA, 22, 24 July 1868, 5, 6 November 1869, 21 April 1870, 23 April 1876; Ninth Census, 1870, Manuscript Returns of Inhabitants, Tippah County, Mississippi, p. 267.
3. SAA, 1866–1902, passim, esp. 27 January, 1, 24 February, 19 April, 7 May 1866, 2 March 1867, 1 January, 1 October 1869, 27 April 1874, 29 January, 3 February 1875; Ninth Census, 1870, Manuscript Returns of Productions of Agriculture, Tippah County, Mississippi, Township 6, Range 5, National Archives, Washington; Tenth Census, 1880, Manuscript Returns of Productions of Agriculture, Union County, Mississippi, Township 6, Range 5, National Archives, Washington; Tenth Census, 1880, Manuscript Returns of Inhabitants, Union County, Mississippi, p. 11/314, National Archives, Washington.
4. Agnew, *Historical Sketch*, 9, 11, 14, 20–21, 24, 25; SAA, 4 January, 2 March, 30 December 1873, 2 August 1874.
5. *Biographical and Historical Memoirs of Mississippi*, 1:288; "Rev. Samuel Andrew Agnew," unpublished typescript in Brice's Crossroads Museum and Visitors Center, Baldwyn, Mississippi; Twelfth Census, 1900, Manuscript Returns of Inhabitants, Union County, Mississippi, ED 128, Sheet 13.
6. *Centennial History*, 44; *Ripley (Mississippi) Southern Sentinel*, 24 July 1902.
7. JCR, 240–418.
8. Ibid., unnumbered initial page, 1, 417.

9. Ibid., 418; Fisher, *War at Every Door,* 154, 164.
10. JCR, 166, 178, 194, 276–77, 314–16, 392–93, 404, 412–13, 418.
11. Patsy Pierce, comp., *Marriage Records, Roane County, Tennessee, 1856–1880* (n.p., 1987), 68; pension record of George W. Wester, 3rd Tennessee Cavalry (U.S.), Civil War Pension Files.
12. *History of Benton, Washington, Carroll, Madison, Crawford, Franklin, and Sebastian Counties, Arkansas* (Chicago, 1889), 1011–12; *Catalogue of the Officers, Trustees and Students of Shurtleff College, for the Year 1870–71* (Alton, Ill., 1871; copy in Illinois State Historical Library, Springfield).
13. Shelia Steele Hunt, transcriber, *Sullivan County, Tennessee, Marriage Records, 1863–1893* (Kingsport, Tenn., 1997), 140; Ninth Census, 1870, Manuscript Returns of Inhabitants, Madison County, Illinois, Upper Alton post office, family 140.
14. *History of Benton,* 1011–12; Eighth Census, 1860, Manuscript Returns of Free Inhabitants, Copiah County, Mississippi, pp. 60–61; Ninth Census, 1870, Manuscript Returns of Inhabitants, Copiah County, Mississippi, p. 113; Tenth Census, 1880, Manuscript Returns of Inhabitants, Benton County, Arkansas, p. 367.
15. *History of Benton,* 1011–12; Barbara Pickering Easley and Verla Pickering McAnelly, eds., *Obituaries of Washington County, Arkansas,* 4 vols. (Bowie, Md., 1996–98), 2:159, 4:90–91.
16. Pension record of George W. Wester, 3rd Tennessee Cavalry (U. S.), Civil War Pension Files.
17. *History of Benton,* 1011–12.
18. Ibid.; Easley and McAnelly, *Obituaries of Washington County,* 4:90–91.
19. CPM, 271, photograph facing 414; Ninth Census, 1870, Manuscript Returns of Inhabitants, Rockbridge County, Virginia, p. 21/468.
20. CPM, 264n, 271, 271n, 414–28; Williams, *Glengarry McDonalds,* 265–68, 275, 286–88.
21. CPM, 270–71, 270n.
22. Ibid., photograph facing 271, 272–75; Lee, *Memoirs,* 428; Hunter McDonald, "General Lee After Appomattox," *Tennessee Historical Magazine* 9 (1925): 94–95.
23. CPM, ix, 7–8, 271n, 404; Williams, *Glengarry McDonalds,* 287.
24. CPM, 9, 413–33.
25. LH, 195–99.
26. Ibid., 197, 199–200, 205–206; *Milwaukee City Directory,* annual editions (Milwaukee, 1869–79).
27. LH, 197–98, 205; Twelfth Census, 1900, Manuscript Returns of Inhabitants, Milwaukee, Wisconsin, ED 194, Sheet 4; *Milwaukee Sentinel,* 20 January 1913.
28. LH, 196–97, 201–204.
29. Ibid., 206, 208.
30. Ibid., 208–209; *Milwaukee City Directory,* annual editions (Milwaukee, 1880–84); *Wright's Directory of Milwaukee,* annual editions (Milwaukee, 1885–92, 1900–01).
31. LH, 3.
32. Ibid., 3, 79, 119, 189–90, 209–10.
33. Ibid., 206–208, 209; Interment Records, Hughes family plot, Forest Home Cemetery, Milwaukee; Thirteenth Census, 1910, Manuscript Returns of Inhabitants, Milwaukee, Wisconsin, ED 233, Sheet 11, National Archives, Washington; *Milwaukee Journal,* 20 January 1913; *Milwaukee Sentinel,* 20 January 1913; *Milwaukee Free Press,* 20 January 1913.

BIBLIOGRAPHY

MANUSCRIPTS

Academy Baptist Church, Tippah County, Mississippi, Minutes. Mississippi Department of Archives and History, Jackson.

Agnew, Samuel A., Diary. Southern Historical Collection, University of North Carolina, Chapel Hill.

Alabama Salt Commissioner's Quarterly Reports and Abstracts. Alabama Department of Archives and History, Montgomery.

Alabama State Salt Works Letter Book. William R. Perkins Library, Duke University, Durham.

American Missionary Association, Tennessee Records. Amistad Research Center, Dillard University, New Orleans.

Amnesty Papers (Case Files of Applications from Former Confederates for Presidential Pardons, 1865–1867). RG 94, M-1003, National Archives, Washington.

Baker, Everard Green, Diary. Southern Historical Collection, University of North Carolina, Chapel Hill.

Bedford, Benjamin W., Letterbook, 1853–1867. Tennessee State Library and Archives, Nashville.

Berry, Joel H., Letter. Mississippi Department of Archives and History, Jackson.

Blackwell, Margaret E., Papers. Southern Historical Collection, University of North Carolina, Chapel Hill.

Cedar Fork Baptist Church, Philadelphia, Loudon (formerly Roane) County, Records. Tennessee State Library and Archives, Nashville.

Civil War Pension Files. RG 15, National Archives, Washington.

Compiled Civil War Service Records. National Archives, Washington.

Confederate Papers Relating to Citizens or Business Firms. M-346, National Archives, Washington.

Eighth Census, 1860, Manuscript Returns of Free Inhabitants. National Archives, Washington.

Eighth Census, 1860, Manuscript Returns of Productions of Agriculture. National Archives, Washington.

Eighth Census, 1860, Manuscript Returns of Slaves. National Archives, Washington.

Greene County, Tennessee, Deeds. Tennessee State Library and Archives, Nashville.

Hackley, William R., Letters. Special Collections, University of Tennessee, Knoxville.

Head, T. L., Jr., "The Salt Works of Clarke County, Alabama." Unpublished typescript, Salt Commission File, Quartermaster Department—Civil War and Reconstruction, Public Information Subject Files, Alabama Department of Archives and History, Montgomery.

"History of Panola County, Compiled from Reminiscences of Oldest Citizens." Unpublished typescript, Mississippi Department of Archives and History, Jackson.

Humphreys, Governor Benjamin G., Correspondence. Mississippi Department of Archives and History, Jackson.

Interment Records. Forest Home Cemetery, Milwaukee.
Letters Received by the Confederate Secretary of War, 1861–1865. M-437, National Archives, Washington.
McGehee Family Genealogical File. Mississippi Department of Archives and History, Jackson.
Ninth Census, 1870, Manuscript Returns of Inhabitants. National Archives, Washington.
Ninth Census, 1870, Manuscript Returns of Productions of Agriculture. National Archives, Washington.
Panola County Apprentice Bonds and Indentures, 1865–66. Mississippi Department of Archives and History, Jackson.
Panola County Tax Rolls (Personal). Mississippi Department of Archives and History, Jackson.
Pendleton, William N., Papers. Southern Historical Collection, University of North Carolina, Chapel Hill.
Records of Assistant Sub-assistant Commissioner, Lexington, Virginia, Bureau of Refugees, Freedmen, and Abandoned Land. RG 105, National Archives, Washington.
Records of Post and Defenses of Memphis, ser. 2837, Records of U. S. Army Continental Commands, Pt. 2, No. 181. RG 393, National Archives, Washington.
Records of Sub-district of Staunton, Virginia, Records of U. S. Army Continental Commands, Pt. 3. RG 393, National Archives, Washington.
Records of the Assistant Commissioner for the State of Mississippi, Bureau of Refugees, Freedmen, and Abandoned Land, 1865–1869. M-826, National Archives, Washington.
Records of the Provost Marshal, ser. 2764, District of East Tennessee, Records of U. S. Army Continental Commands, Pt. 2, No. 173. RG 393, National Archives, Washington.
"Rev. Samuel Andrew Agnew." Unpublished typescript, Brice's Crossroads Museum and Visitors Center, Baldwyn, Mississippi.
Roane County, Tennessee, County Court Minutes. Tennessee State Library and Archives, Nashville.
Roane County, Tennessee, Deeds. Tennessee State Library and Archives, Nashville.
Robertson, John C., Memoir. McClung Historical Collection, Knox County Public Library, Knoxville.
Rockbridge County, Virginia, County Court Minute Book. Library of Virginia, Richmond.
Selected Records of the Tennessee Field Office, Bureau of Refugees, Freedmen, and Abandoned Land, 1865–1872. T-142, National Archives, Washington.
Seventh Census, 1850, Manuscript Returns of Free Inhabitants. National Archives, Washington.
Sharkey, Provisional Governor William L., Letters. Mississippi Department of Archives and History, Jackson.
Shiloh Primitive Baptist Church, Kingston, Roane County, Records. Tennessee State Library and Archives, Nashville.
Simpson, Margaret Agnew, "The Battle of Brice's Crossroads." Typescript reminiscence in possession of David Frazier, Guntown, Mississippi.
Tenth Census, 1880, Manuscript Returns of Inhabitants. National Archives, Washington.
Tenth Census, 1880, Manuscript Returns of Productions of Agriculture. National Archives, Washington.
Thirteenth Census, 1910, Manuscript Returns of Inhabitants. National Archives, Washington.
Tippah County, Mississippi, Minutes of Police Board. Mississippi Department of Archives and History, Jackson.
Tippah County Tax Rolls (Personal). Mississippi Department of Archives and History, Jackson.
Twelfth Census, 1900, Manuscript Returns of Inhabitants. National Archives, Washington.
Virginia Personal Property Tax Books. Library of Virginia, Richmond.
Wasmuth, Edward, Diary. Southern Historical Collection, University of North Carolina, Chapel Hill.

Williams, John and Rhoda Campbell, Papers. McClung Historical Collection, Knox County Public Library, Knoxville.

NEWSPAPERS

Brownlow's Knoxville Whig and Rebel Ventilator
Cincinnati Daily Commercial
Cincinnati Daily Enquirer
Cincinnati Daily Gazette
Clarke County (Alabama) Journal
Hamilton (Ohio) True Telegraph
Lexington (Virginia) Gazette
Memphis Argus
Memphis Bulletin
Milwaukee Free Press
Milwaukee Journal
Milwaukee Sentinel
Nashville Daily Press and Times
Nashville Dispatch
Richmond Whig
Ripley (Mississippi) Southern Sentinel
Weekly Panola (Mississippi) Star

PUBLISHED SOURCES

Agnew, Rev. Samuel A. *Historical Sketch of the Associate Reformed Presbyterian Church of Bethany, Lee County, Miss.* Louisville, 1881.

———. "Battle of Tishomingo Creek." *Confederate Veteran* 8 (1900): 401–403.

Agriculture of the United States in 1860; Compiled from the Original Returns of the Eighth Census. Washington, 1864.

Allan, Elizabeth Preston. *The Life and Letters of Margaret Junkin Preston.* Boston and New York, 1903.

Anderson, Oscar E., Jr., ed. "Harvey W. Wiley Spends the Christmas Holidays in the Miami Valley, 1865–1866." *Historical and Philosophical Society of Ohio Bulletin* 12 (1954): 209–17.

Ash, Stephen V. *Middle Tennessee Society Transformed, 1860–1870: War and Peace in the Upper South.* Baton Rouge and London, 1988.

———. *When the Yankees Came: Conflict and Chaos in the Occupied South, 1861–1865.* Chapel Hill and London, 1995.

———, ed. *Secessionists and Other Scoundrels: Selections from* Parson Brownlow's Book. Baton Rouge, 1999.

Avirett, James B., et al. *The Memoirs of General Turner Ashby and His Compeers.* Baltimore, 1867.

Bailey, Fred Arthur. *Class and Tennessee's Confederate Generation.* Chapel Hill and London, 1987.

Ball, T. H. *A Glance into the Great South-East; or, Clarke County, Alabama, and Its Surroundings.* N.p., 1879; repr., Tuscaloosa, Ala., 1962.

Bergeron, Paul H., Stephen V. Ash, and Jeanette Keith. *Tennesseans and Their History.* Knoxville, 1999.

Berlin, Ira, et al., eds. *The Black Military Experience.* Cambridge, Eng., 1982.

———. *The Destruction of Slavery.* Cambridge, Eng., 1985.

Bettersworth, John K. *Confederate Mississippi: The People and Policies of a Cotton State in Wartime.* Baton Rouge, 1943.

Biographical and Historical Memoirs of Mississippi, Embracing an Authentic and Comprehensive Account of the Chief Events in the History of the State, and a Record of the Lives of Many of the Most Worthy and Illustrious Families and Individuals. 2 vols. Chicago, 1891.

Black, Robert C., III. *The Railroads of the Confederacy.* Chapel Hill, 1952.

Blair, William. *Virginia's Private War: Feeding Body and Soul in the Confederacy, 1861–1865.* New York and Oxford, 1998.

Boatner, Mark Mayo, III. *The Civil War Dictionary.* New York, 1959.

Boney, F. N. "Virginia." In W. Buck Yearns, ed., *The Confederate Governors.* Athens, Ga., 1985.

Brown, Andrew. *History of Tippah County, Mississippi: The First Century.* Ripley, Miss., 1976.

Bryan, Charles Faulkner, Jr. "The Civil War in East Tennessee: A Social, Political, and Economic Study." Ph.D. diss., University of Tennessee, Knoxville, 1978.

Bunn, J. Michael. "Slavery in the Clarke County Saltworks, 1861–1865." *Clarke County Historical Society Quarterly* 24 (1999): 20–23.

Campbell, James B. "East Tennessee During the Federal Occupation, 1863–1865." East Tennessee Historical Society's *Publications* 19 (1947): 64–80.

Carter, Dan T. *When the War Was Over: The Failure of Self-Reconstruction in the South.* Baton Rouge and London, 1985.

Catalogue of the Officers, Trustees and Students of Shurtleff College, for the Year 1870-'71. Alton, Ill., 1871.

The Centennial History of the Associate Reformed Presbyterian Church, 1803–1903. Charleston, S. C., 1905.

Cimprich, John. *Slavery's End in Tennessee, 1861–1865.* University, Ala., 1985.

Circular from Secretary of the Commonwealth to Virginia county court clerks, 16 November 1864. Richmond, 1864.

Civil War Centennial Commission. *Tennesseans in the Civil War: A Military History of Confederate and Union Units with Available Rosters of Personnel.* 2 vols. Nashville, 1964.

Clark, Blanche Henry. *The Tennessee Yeomen, 1840–1860.* Nashville, 1942.

Clark, William H. *Railroads and Rivers: The Story of Inland Transportation.* Boston, 1939.

Connelly, Thomas Lawrence. *Autumn of Glory: The Army of Tennessee, 1862–1865.* Baton Rouge, 1971.

Coulter, E. Merton. *William G. Brownlow: Fighting Parson of the Southern Highlands.* Chapel Hill, 1937; repr., Knoxville, 1999.

Current, Richard Nelson. *Lincoln's Loyalists: Union Soldiers from the Confederacy.* Boston, 1992.

Driver, Robert J. *Lexington and Rockbridge County in the Civil War.* Lynchburg, Va., 1989.

Du Pont, H. A. *The Campaign of 1864 in the Valley of Virginia and the Expedition to Lynchburg.* New York, 1925.

Durham, Walter T. *Nashville, the Occupied City: The First Seventeen Months—February 16, 1862 to June 30, 1863.* Nashville, 1985.

———. *Reluctant Partners: Nashville and the Union, July 1, 1863 to June 30, 1865.* Nashville, 1987.

Dyer, Frederick H. *A Compendium of the War of the Rebellion.* 3 vols. New York and London, 1959.

Easley, Barbara Pickering, and Verla Pickering McAnelly, eds. *Obituaries of Washington County, Arkansas.* 4 vols. Bowie, Md., 1996–98.

Eby, Cecil D., Jr., ed. *A Virginia Yankee in the Civil War: The Diaries of David Hunter Strother.* Chapel Hill, 1961.

Escott, Paul D. *After Secession: Jefferson Davis and the Failure of Confederate Nationalism.* Baton Rouge, 1978.

Faust, Drew Gilpin. *Mothers of Invention: Women of the Slaveholding South in the American Civil War.* Chapel Hill and London, 1996.

———. "The Civil War Soldier and the Art of Dying." *Journal of Southern History* 67 (2001): 3–38.

Fellman, Michael. "Robert E. Lee, Postwar Southern Nationalist." *Civil War History* 46 (2000): 185–204.

Fisher, Noel C. *War at Every Door: Partisan Politics and Guerrilla Violence in East Tennessee, 1860–1869.* Chapel Hill and London, 1997.

Fleming, Walter L. *Civil War and Reconstruction in Alabama.* New York, 1905.

Flood, Charles Bracelen. *Lee: The Last Years.* Boston and New York, 1998.

Foner, Eric. *Reconstruction: America's Unfinished Revolution, 1863–1877.* New York, 1988.

Ford, Henry A., and Kate B. Ford, comps. *History of Cincinnati, Ohio, with Illustrations and Biographical Sketches.* Cleveland, 1881.

Fowler, William Joseph. "History of Roane County, Tennessee, 1860–1870." M. A. thesis, University of Tennessee, 1964.

Fox-Genovese, Elizabeth. *Within the Plantation Household: Black and White Women of the Old South.* Chapel Hill and London, 1988.

Franklin, John Hope, and Loren Schweninger. *Runaway Slaves: Rebels on the Plantation.* Oxford and New York, 1999.

Freeman, Douglas Southall. *R. E. Lee: A Biography.* 4 vols. New York, 1934–35.

Gordon, Sarah H. *Passage to Union: How the Railroads Transformed American Life, 1829–1929.* Chicago, 1996.

Graf, LeRoy P., Ralph W. Haskins, and Paul H. Bergeron, eds. *The Papers of Andrew Johnson.* 16 vols. Knoxville, 1967–2000.

Gray, Lewis C. *History of Agriculture in the Southern United States to 1860.* 2 vols. Washington, 1933.

Grimsley, Mark. *The Hard Hand of War: Union Military Policy Toward Southern Civilians, 1861–1865.* Cambridge, Eng., 1995.

Groce, W. Todd. *Mountain Rebels: East Tennessee Confederates and the Civil War.* Knoxville, 1999.

Harris, William C. *Presidential Reconstruction in Mississippi.* Baton Rouge, 1967.

———. "The East Tennessee Relief Movement of 1864–1865." *Tennessee Historical Quarterly* 48 (1989): 86–96.

———. "East Tennessee's Civil War Refugees and the Impact of the War on Civilians." *Journal of East Tennessee History* 64 (1992): 3–19.

Heyrman, Christine Leigh. *Southern Cross: The Beginnings of the Bible Belt.* Chapel Hill and London, 1997.

Hilliard, Sam B. *Hog Meat and Hoecake: Food Supply in the Old South, 1840–1860.* Carbondale, Ill., 1972.

History of Benton, Washington, Carroll, Madison, Crawford, Franklin, and Sebastian Counties, Arkansas. Chicago, 1889.

Holmes, Jack D. L. "The Underlying Causes of the Memphis Race Riot of 1866." *Tennessee Historical Quarterly* 17 (1958): 195–221.

Hoobler, James A. *Cities Under the Gun: Images of Occupied Nashville and Chattanooga.* Nashville, 1986.

Hooper, Ernest W. "Memphis, Tennessee: Federal Occupation and Reconstruction, 1862–1870." Ph.D. diss., University of North Carolina, 1957.

Hughes, Louis. *Thirty Years a Slave: From Bondage to Freedom.* Milwaukee, 1897.

Hunt, Shelia Steele, transcriber. *Sullivan County, Tennessee, Marriage Records, 1863–1893.* Kingsport, Tenn., 1997.

Journal of the Twenty-Second Session of the Holston Annual Conference of the Methodist Episcopal Church, Being Assembled in the M. E. Church at Athens, Tennessee, June 1- 5, 1865. Knoxville, n.d.

Killebrew, J. B., and J. M. Safford. *Introduction to the Resources of Tennessee.* Nashville, 1874.

King, Ray A. *A History of the Associate Reformed Presbyterian Church.* Charlotte, 1966.

Kyle, John W. "Reconstruction in Panola County." Mississippi Historical Society *Publications* 13 (1913): 9–98.

Lee, Susan P. *Memoirs of William Nelson Pendleton, D. D., Rector of Latimer Parish, Lexington, Virginia; Brigadier-General C. S. A.; Chief of Artillery, Army of Northern Virginia.* Philadelphia, 1893.

"Letters of John Letcher to J. Hierholzer, 1864–1865." *William and Mary Quarterly* 8 (1928): 137–40.

Litwack, Leon F. *Been in the Storm So Long: The Aftermath of Slavery.* New York, 1979.

Lonn, Ella. *Salt as a Factor in the Confederacy.* New York, 1933.

Lovett, Bobby Lee. "Memphis Riots: White Reaction to Blacks in Memphis, May 1865-July 1866." *Tennessee Historical Quarterly* 38 (1979): 9–33.

Lynch, Charles H. *The Civil War Diary 1862–1865 of Charles H. Lynch, 18th Conn. Vol's.* Hartford, Conn., 1915.

McDonald, Hunter. "General Lee After Appomattox." *Tennessee Historical Magazine* 9 (1925): 87–101.

McDonald, Mrs. Cornelia. *A Diary with Reminiscences of the War and Refugee Life in the Shenandoah Valley, 1860–1865.* Nashville, 1934.

McGehee, C. Stuart. "E. O. Tade, Freedmen's Education, and the Failure of Reconstruction in Tennessee." *Tennessee Historical Quarterly* 43 (1984): 376–89.

McMillan, Malcolm C. *The Disintegration of a Confederate State: Three Governors and Alabama's Wartime Home Front, 1861–1865.* Macon, Ga., 1986.

McPherson, James M. *Battle Cry of Freedom: The Civil War Era.* New York and Oxford, 1988.

"Maj. E. H. McDonald." *Confederate Veteran* 20 (1912): 530.

Marten, James. *The Children's Civil War.* Chapel Hill and London, 1998.

Massey, Mary Elizabeth. *Refugee Life in the Confederacy.* Baton Rouge, 1964.

———. *Ersatz in the Confederacy: Shortages and Substitutes on the Southern Homefront.* Columbia, S. C., 1952; repr., Columbia, S.C., 1993.

Mathews, Donald G. *Religion in the Old South.* Chicago, 1977.

Melton, John L., ed. "The Diary of a Drummer." *Michigan History* 43 (1959): 315–48.

Milwaukee City Directory. Annual editions. Milwaukee, 1869–84.

Monroe, Haskell M., Jr., James T. McIntosh, and Lynda Lasswell Crist, eds. *The Papers of Jefferson Davis.* 10 vols. to date. Baton Rouge and London, 1971-.

Moore, Albert Burton. *Conscription and Conflict in the Confederacy.* New York, 1924.

Morris, Robert C. *Reading, 'Riting, and Reconstruction: The Education of Freedmen in the South, 1861–1870.* Chicago and London, 1981.

Morton, Oren F. *A History of Rockbridge County, Virginia.* Staunton, Va., 1920.

The Official Atlas of the Civil War. New York and London, 1958.

Official Records of the Union and Confederate Navies in the War of the Rebellion. 30 vols. Washington, 1894–1922.

Otto, John Solomon. *Southern Agriculture During the Civil War Era, 1860–1880.* Westport, Conn., 1994.

Panola County Genealogical and Historical Society. *History of Panola County, Mississippi.* N.p., 1987.

Panola Historical and Genealogical Society. *Cemeteries of Panola County, Mississippi.* N.p, 1994.

Parks, Joseph H. "Memphis Under Military Rule, 1862 to 1865." East Tennessee Historical Society's *Publications* 14 (1942): 31–58.

Pierce, Patsy, comp. *Marriage Records, Roane County, Tennessee, 1856–1880.* N.p., 1987.

Population of the United States in 1860; Compiled from the Original Returns of the Eighth Census. Washington, 1864.

Power, J. Tracy. *Lee's Miserables: Life in the Army of Northern Virginia from the Wilderness to Appomattox.* Chapel Hill and London, 1998.

Rable, George C. *Civil Wars: Women and the Crisis of Southern Nationalism.* Urbana and Chicago, 1989.

Raboteau, Albert J. *Slave Religion: The "Invisible Institution" in the Antebellum South.* New York, 1978.

Rawick, George P., ed. *The American Slave: A Composite Autobiography.* 41 vols. Westport, Conn., 1972–79.

Reid, Whitelaw. *After the War: A Tour of the Southern States, 1865–1866.* Cincinnati and New York, 1866.

Report of Col. A. W. McDonald, Relative to his Mission to England. Document xxxix, *Virginia General Assembly Documents.* Richmond, 1861.

Roark, James L. *Masters Without Slaves: Southern Planters in the Civil War and Reconstruction.* New York, 1977.

Ross, Steven J. *Workers on the Edge: Work, Leisure, and Politics in Industrializing Cincinnati, 1788–1890.* New York, 1985.

Rothman, Ellen K. *Hands and Hearts: A History of Courtship in America.* New York, 1984.

Seymour, Digby Gordon. *Divided Loyalties: Fort Sanders and the Civil War in East Tennessee.* 2nd ed. Knoxville, 1983.

Shelley, Jack, and Jere Hall. *Valley of Challenge and Change: The History of Roane County, Tennessee, 1860–1900.* Kingston, Tenn., 1986.

Sillers, Florence Warfield, et al., comps. *History of Bolivar County, Mississippi.* Jackson, Miss., 1948.

Simmons, Louis A. *The History of the 84th Reg't. Ill. Vols.* Macomb, Ill., 1866.

Simon, John Y., ed. *The Papers of Ulysses S. Grant.* 18 vols. Carbondale and Edwardsville, Ill., 1967–91.

Skinner, J. E. Hilary. *After the Storm; or, Jonathan and His Neighbours in 1865–6.* 2 vols. London, 1866.

Srygley, F. D. *Seventy Years in Dixie.* Nashville, 1891.

The Statistics of the Population of the United States; Compiled from the Original Returns of the Ninth Census (June 1, 1870) . . . Washington, 1872.

Sutherland, Daniel E. *The Expansion of Everyday Life, 1860–1876.* New York, 1989.

Taylor, Alrutheus Ambush. *The Negro in Tennessee, 1865–1880.* Washington, 1941; repr., Spartanburg, S.C., 1975.

Taylor, George Rogers, and Irene D. Neu. *The American Railroad Network, 1861–1890.* Cambridge, Mass., 1956.

The Tennessee Almanac for the Year of Our Lord 1865. Nashville, n.d.

Tolbert, Lisa. *Constructing Townscapes: Space and Society in Antebellum Tennessee.* Chapel Hill and London, 1999.

Trotter, Joe William, Jr. *River Jordan: African American Urban Life in the Ohio Valley.* Lexington, Ky., 1998.

Trowbridge, J. T. *The South: A Tour of Its Battle-Fields and Ruined Cities, a Journey Through the Desolated States, and Talks with the People.* Hartford, Conn., 1866.

Turner, Charles W., ed. *The Diary of Henry Boswell Jones of Brownsburg (1842–1871).* Verona, Va., 1979.

Tyler, D. Gardiner. "Diary for 1865." *Tyler's Quarterly Historical and Genealogical Magazine* 30 (1949): 251–55.

The War of the Rebellion: A Compilation of the Official Records of the Union and Confederate Armies. 70 vols. in 128. Washington, 1880–1901.

Wharton, Vernon L. *The Negro in Mississippi, 1865–1890.* Chapel Hill, 1947.

White, Robert H., and Stephen V. Ash, eds., *Messages of the Governors of Tennessee.* 10 vols. to date. Nashville, 1952-.

Williams, Mrs. Flora McDonald. *The Glengarry McDonalds of Virginia.* Louisville, 1911.

Winks, Robin W. *The Blacks in Canada: A History.* Montreal and Kingston, 1997.

Winters, Donald L. *Tennessee Farming, Tennessee Farmers: Antebellum Agriculture in the Upper South.* Knoxville, 1994.

Wright's Directory of Milwaukee. Annual editions. Milwaukee, 1885–92, 1900–1901.

Zornow, William F. "Aid for the Indigent Families of Soldiers in Virginia, 1861–1865." *Virginia Magazine of History and Biography* 69 (1958): 454–58.

INDEX